Museum of Anthropology, University of Michigan (AP 90)

Physical Attractiveness and the Theory of Sexual Selection

Results from Five Populations

by
Doug Jones

with a foreword by Donald Symons

Ann Arbor
1996

For David and Jennette
And for Barbara
"Você mora no meu coração, e não paga aluguel."

© 1996 by the Regents of the University of Michigan
The Museum of Anthropology
All rights reserved

Printed in the United States of America
ISBN 0-915703-40-8

Cover design by Katherine Clahassey.

The University of Michigan Museum of Anthropology currently publishes three monograph series: Anthropological Papers, Memoirs, and Technical Reports. We have over seventy titles in print. For a complete catalog, write to Museum of Anthropology Publications, 4009 Museums Bldg., Ann Arbor, MI 48109-1079.

Library of Congress Cataloging-in-Publication Data

Jones, Doug, 1959–
    Physical attractiveness and the theory of sexual selection :
results from five populations / by Doug Jones ; with a foreword by
Donald Symons.
      p. cm. — (Anthropological papers ; no. 90)
    Includes bibliographical references.
    ISBN 0-915703-40-8 (pbk. alk. paper)
    1. Sex role—Cross-cultural studies. 2. Sex differences—Cross-
cultural studies. 3. Sexual attraction—Cross-cultural studies.
4. Mate selection—Cross-cultural studies. 5. Body, Human—Social
aspects—Cross-cultural studies. I. Title. II. Series:
Anthropological papers (University of Michigan. Museum of
Anthropology) ; no. 90
GN2.M5 no.9
[GN62.85]
305.3—dc20   96-12603

The paper used in this publication meets the requirements of the ANSI Standard Z39.48-1984 (Permanence of Paper)

Contents

List of tables, *vii*
List of figures, *vii*
Foreword, *Donald Symons*, *viii*
Preface, *xii*
Acknowledgments, *xiv*

CHAPTER 1. PHYSICAL ATTRACTIVENESS: EVOLUTION, PSYCHOLOGY AND ANTHROPOLOGY, *1*

The rise and fall of physical attractiveness, *1*
Evolution and human behavior today, *2*
    Reproductive competition, *3*
    Domain specificity, *5*
    The weight of the past, *7*
    Genes and culture, *8*
Psychological perspectives on attractiveness, *9*
Anthropological perspectives on attractiveness, *13*
    Cross-cultural differences in standards of attractiveness, *13*
    Cross-cultural differences in the importance of attractiveness, *14*
    Sex differences in the importance of attractiveness, *16*

CHAPTER 2. THE THEORY OF SEXUAL SELECTION, *19*

Natural selection and sexual selection, *19*
Mate choice, *20*
    The operational sex ratio, *21*
    Competition, coercion and choice, *22*
    Monogamy and mate quality, *22*
Mate preference, *22*
    Mate value and the ultimate bases of physical attraction, *22*
    Direct benefits: good phenotypes, *23*
    Indirect benefits: good genes, *25*
    Sensory bias, *32*
    Learning, imitation and the proximate bases of physical attraction, *35*
Sexual selection and macroevolution, *38*
Sexual selection and human evolution, *40*
    Signal selection and human differentiation, *40*
    Sexual selection and physical attractiveness: a preview of hypotheses, *42*

CHAPTER 3. FIVE POPULATIONS, *45*

Sites and itinerary, *45*
    Brazilians, *45*
    US Americans, *47*
    Russians, *48*
    Ache, *48*
    Hiwi, *49*

Itinerary, *49*
Research methods, *50*
    Photography, anthropometry, and questionnaires, *50*
    Rating pictures, *54*
    Scanning faces, *55*
Results and discussion: comparing standards of attractiveness, *56*
    Within groups, *56*
    Between groups, *59*

CHAPTER 4. AGE, MATE VALUE AND ATTRACTIVENESS, *65*

Age, fecundity and mate value: theory, *65*
    Menopause and marriage, *65*
    Short-term and long-term mate value, *67*
Age and attractiveness: evidence, *76*
Age and attractiveness: nature, nurture and mechanisms, *79*
    Age and attractiveness: beyond fecundity?, *80*
    Possible mechanisms, *81*

CHAPTER 5. SIGNS OF AGE AND FECUNDITY, *83*

Facial proportions, *83*
    Facial proportions, age and sex, *83*
    Facial proportions and attractiveness, *86*
    Eyes, noses, lips: age predictors as attractiveness predictors, *87*
    Students and models, *90*
    Cardioidal strain and facial attractiveness, *92*
    Summary of results, and discussion, *93*
Skin and hair color, *96*
    Color symbolism, *96*
    Lightness, femininity and fecundity, *97*
    How important is color?, *97*
Body shape, *98*
    The waist to hip ratio, *98*
    Breasts, buttocks and thighs, *99*
Conclusion: sexual selection and human proportions, *103*

CHAPTER 6. SYMMETRY, AVERAGENESS AND HEALTH, *107*

Fluctuating asymmetry, *107*
The attraction of averageness: health, age and information processing, *111*
Summing up: neoteny, asymmetry, averageness, *119*

CHAPTER 7. RACE, SOCIAL STATUS AND ATTRACTIVENESS, *121*

Psychological mechanisms, social consequences, *121*
    Average features, somatic distance and the somatic norm image, *122*
    Supernormal features, *125*
    Social status, *128*
Beauty in the world system, *130*
Beleza tropical: race and somatic prejudice in Brazil, *132*
    Race in Brazil, *132*
    Racial classification and perceptions of attractiveness, *136*

CHAPTER 8. CONCLUSION, *145*

BIBLIOGRAPHY, *147*

PLATES, *167*

Tables

3.1. List of facial landmarks, *57*
3.2. Agreement in standards of facial attractiveness within groups, *58*
3.3. Descriptive statistics for Ache subgroups, *59*
3.4. Agreement in standards of facial attractiveness across populations, *60–61*
4.1. Age and short-term mate value (female), *68*
4.2. Age and short-term mate value (male), *69*
4.3. Age and long-term mate value (female), *72*
4.4. Age and long-term mate value (male), *73*
4.5. Age and facial attractiveness, *79*
5.1. Age predictors for Ache faces, *88*
5.2. Facial proportions and ratings of attractiveness, *89*
5.3. Indices of facial neoteny and ratings of attractiveness, *91*
5.4. Facial proportions of students and models, *92*
6.1. Fluctuating asymmetry and physical attractiveness, *110*
6.2. Non-average facial proportions and attractiveness, *114*
6.3. Correlations between different indices of facial proportions, *118*
6.4. Summing up: comparison of different indices of facial proportions, *118*
7.1. Brazilian racial categories, *138–139*

Figures

3.1 Facial landmarks, *56*
4.1 Age and short-term mate value (female), *70*
4.2 Age and short-term mate value (male), *70*
4.3 Age and long-term mate value (female), *74*
4.4 Age and long-term mate value (male), *74*
5.1 The effects of positive and negative cardioidal strain on a 5 × 5 grid and a face, *85*
5.2 Cardioidal strain and ratings of attractiveness, *94*
5.3 Preferences of Brazilian, US and Russian males and females regarding female breasts, buttocks and thighs, *101*
7.1 Mean ratings of attractiveness given to three ethnic subdivisions of the US photographic samples, *124*
7.2 Race, averageness and social status, *129*
7.3 Brazilian racial categories and multidimensional scaling, *140*
7.4 Attractiveness and the *negra/branca* axis, *141*

Plates

Sample of facial photographs used in this study: Brazilians, *169-170*
Sample of facial photographs used in this study: US Americans, *171-172*
Sample of facial photographs used in this study: Ache, *173-174*

vii

Foreword

Donald Symons, University of California

"My fourth Cosmetic Discovery occurred at 18 . . . I awoke to a realization that would take a long time to play out, but in essence Cosmetic Discovery #4 was this: if you're a young, blue-ribbon egg-bearer, there's *nothing* you can't get away with.

Nobody who hasn't been there has *any* idea, and even those who have won't really understand until after the stampede [of sperm-bearers] has passed because there's so much dust in the air."
—*supermodel Lauren Hutton, 1995*

Beauty is said to be "only skin deep" and "in the eye of the beholder." The former implies that beauty is an unreliable index of other, presumably more important, personal qualities and, therefore, that the perception of beauty is nonutilitarian. The latter usually implies that the determinants of beauty are largely or completely arbitrary, capricious, whimsical, idiosyncratic. Darwin's view of life, as embodied in his theory of evolution by selection, should lead us to view both of these epigrams with deep skepticism. An organism, including a human being, is an integrated bundle of adaptations. An adaptation is a mechanism shaped by selection over evolutionary time to solve some recurrent adaptive problem and thereby promote the survival of the genes that directed its construction. One recurrent adaptive problem that our ancestors faced was mate choice. Potential mates necessarily varied in mate value—that is, in the degree to which they would promote the reproductive success of the individuals who mated with them—just as potential food varied in food value and potential habitats varied in habitat value. Because information about mate value was reliably available in specific, observable bodily features, selection can be expected to have produced adaptations—psychological mechanisms—to extract and process this information, so that in ancestral populations physical attractiveness can be expected to have varied, on average, directly with mate value. Psychological mechanisms that led to largely or completely nonutilitarian, arbitrary, capricious, whimsical, idiosyncratic mate choices could not have been produced by selection.

An alternative connotation of the epigram "beauty is in the eye of the beholder," however, is right on the target: beauty is not imminent in nature; it exists only in minds. If a tree falls in the forest and there is no one to hear it the air vibrates but there is no sound. Sound exists only in minds. Similarly, dung is inherently neither attractive nor unattractive. It just is. As Leda Cosmides has noted, dung is more attractive to dung flies because for their ancestors it was an ideal place to find a date, to mate, and to settle down and raise a family. Dung is unattractive to human beings, however, because for their ancestors it was an ideal place to catch a disease. Beauty exists in the adaptations of the beholder.

Because selection could not have produced psychological mechanisms that led, on balance, to nonutilitarian or arbitrary mate choices, the determinants of human physical attractiveness cannot be completely or largely "culturally constructed." To see why this is so, imagine an ancestral human population in which individuals acquired their standards of physical attractiveness in much the same way that they acquired the words in their language: from one another. In human language the relationships between sounds and meanings are arbitrary, and for good adaptive reasons. The function of language is communication within a local group of native speakers, hence it makes no functional difference whether a certain sort of large mammal is called a horse or a caballo. All that matters is that everyone in the group understand and use the same word. (The psychological machinery underpinning this system of language acquisition must be orders of magnitude simpler, cheaper, and more flexible than a system in which the relations between sounds and meanings are specified innately.) A by-product of this system of language acquisition is that languages drift with the passage of time, so that ancestor and descendant languages eventually become mutually unintelligible. This was not a problem in the nonliterate human populations in which language evolved, as individuals needed to communicate only with the living, not with their long dead ancestors. But what if the perception of physical attractiveness was completely or largely underpinned by a psychological mechanism that instantiated a rule such as: "Look around and see what physical characteristics others people are attracted to, then be attracted to those same characteristics"? The determinants of physical attractiveness would drift capriciously with the passage of time, just as languages do, and the relationship between attractiveness and mate value would be as arbitrary as that between sound and meaning. For example, in some populations, men would perceive wrinkles as attractive, in others as unattractive, and in most as having no systematic effect whatever on attractiveness. In such circumstances, any genetic mutation that caused its bearers to detect and prefer, even slightly, a reliable cue of high mate value in the other sex (such as smooth female skin) would have a strong selective advantage, hence any system in which the criteria of physical attractiveness were completely or largely "culturally constructed" would be replaced by one in which attractiveness varied directly with observable cues of mate value.

To what extent imitation plays a role in the development of standards of attractiveness and to what extent standards of attractiveness undergo "cultural drift" are open questions. Some Darwinians, including Doug Jones (and Charles Darwin himself), have proposed that imitation/copying and cultural drift may play significant roles, whereas others, including me, are dubious. All Darwinians, however, probably would agree that (a) human beings are virtually certain to have psychological mechanisms for detecting external cues of mate value that are independent of other people's preferences, and (b) these mechanisms account for a large proportion of variance in attractiveness and are resistant to "cultural" modification.

Psychological mechanisms designed by selection to extract and process information about mate value inevitably will be ill-designed to extract and process information in other domains. The adaptations underpinning our esthetic perceptions and feelings about members of the other sex, for example, would be utterly dysfunctional if used to assess landscapes, because the criteria that determine mate value have nothing in common with those that determine habitat value. Darwin's view of life implies that different, specialized psychological mechanisms underpin our esthetic perceptions and feelings in different domains, hence the search for *general* esthetic principles is doomed.

Even within the domain of mate choice, many different psychological adaptations can be expected to contribute to the perception of physical attractiveness because in ancestral human populations a variety of observable physical qualities (body shape and size, skin texture, facial form, and so forth) reliably indexed different aspects of mate value, and a psychological mechanism designed to assess one of these qualities almost certainly would be ill-designed to assess any other. For example, female body shape and facial form must be assessed by different psychological mechanisms (selection would not necessarily favor females with hour-glass faces merely because it favors females with hourglass figures).

As selection is the only known evolutionary process capable of producing and maintaining complex adaptations, one might suppose that Darwin's view of life has informed research on human physical attractiveness at least for the last century or so. Surprisingly, this has not been the case: only within the last decade have a handful of researchers begun to test hypotheses explicitly based on the assumptions that many specialized psychological mechanisms underpin our perceptions of physical attractiveness and that these mechanisms have the specific forms that they do because these forms promoted reproductively functional behavior in the environments and conditions in which our ancestors evolved. Doug Jones's research program, however, is the only one in which a uniform methodology has been systematically applied across samples that include preliterate peoples with little exposure to industrialized societies and their cultural products. This is important, first, because judgments of physical attractiveness among such peoples have not been significantly influenced by the mass media or other external agents that might promote cross-cultural uniformity, and, second, because in many respects the environments and conditions of such peoples approximate those in which the psychological machinery of physical attraction evolved (that is, the environments and conditions in which this machinery was designed to develop and function).

Recently, a number of students of physical attractiveness, employing very different methodologies, have shown that women with short lower faces are perceived, on average, as more attractive than women with average or long lower faces. Jones replicated this finding in each of his samples. A number of hypotheses (which are not necessarily mutually exclusive) have been proposed to account for this apparent human universal: a relatively short lower face may index high estrogen levels, a favorable estrogen/testosterone ratio, or nulliparity. Jones argues herein that this facial conformation may be perceived as attractive because it constitutes a supernormal cue of youth (see epigraph above).

Jones's analysis of the evidence for cross-cultural variation in standards of physical attractiveness is uncommonly insightful. He notes that the existence among human beings of species-typical psychological mechanisms of physical attraction does *not* imply the existence of cross-cultural uniformity in attractiveness judgments. For one thing, many of these mechanisms are designed to be calibrated by local phenotypes, which vary substantially from place to place. Jones also argues persuasively that certain differences between the United States and Brazil in standards of physical attractiveness can be understood only in light of the differing histories of race relations in these two countries. *Physical Attractiveness and the Theory of Sexual Selection* is a sophisticated, subtle, and original work, firmly grounded in the empirical literature on the role of sexual selection in shaping mate choice mechanisms. It will influence not only students of physical attractiveness who already are evolution minded, but also those researchers who have not heretofore appreciated the power of adaptationism to guide research, to inspire hypotheses, to integrate findings, and, in Darwin's words, to provide a stable foundation to argue from.

Preface

"Except for some arbitrary beauty-contest conventions about 'ideal' female dimensions, we know less about attractive stimuli for man than we do about those for fish."

quoted in Berscheid and Walster (1974)

This book brings together evolutionary theory—specifically the theory of sexual selection—and psychology and anthropology in a cross-cultural investigation of standards of physical attractiveness in humans. The research reported in this study was carried out from 1989 to 1994 in five populations: Brazilians, United States Americans, Russians, Ache Indians of Paraguay, and Hiwi Indians of Venezuela. Kim Hill, now of the Department of Anthropology at the University of New Mexico, helped with data collection among the Ache and collected all the data for the Hiwi.

The first two chapters present theory and a review of the literature. Chapter 1 defends the application of evolutionary theory to human behavior and reviews some findings from psychology and anthropology concerning standards of physical attractiveness and their relation to mate choice. Chapter 2 presents relevant aspects of the modern theory of sexual selection as it has been developed for nonhuman organisms, and concludes with some hypotheses about variants and invariants of attractiveness in our species.

The third chapter introduces the five populations studied, and reviews methods of data collection. It concludes by presenting data showing significant agreement in standards of attractiveness within and between societies.

The fourth, fifth and sixth chapters consider possible adaptations for assessing the fecundity and health of potential mates. Chapter 4 develops models of short-term and long-term "mate value" which suggest that natural selection may produce adaptations for detecting age-related changes in fecundity, and presents evidence of changes in attractiveness with age. Chapter 5 considers attractiveness in relation to specific cues associated with age and fecundity, including facial proportions, skin and hair color, and body shape. Chapter 6 considers some characters that may be markers of health and developmental stability, including facial "averageness" and symmetry, and presents data regarding the importance of some of these characters in comparison with those in Chapter 5.

Owing to the operation of natural selection over hundreds of millennia, humans are likely to have species-typical adaptations which regulate the development of standards of physical attractiveness. But these standards are also influenced by particularities of cultural history and social structure. Chapter 7 is concerned with how the principles discussed in earlier chapters, together with historical circumstances, can produce "racial somatic prejudice" in multiethnic societies. The chapter presents data suggesting that Brazilian esthetic responses to racial differences are influenced both by species-typical principles of physical attraction and by the Brazilian system of racial stratification.

The major findings of the study are summarized in Chapter 8.

Throughout this work I indicate statistical significance levels as follows:

+	$p < .1$	marginally significant
*	$p < .05$	significant
**	$p < .01$	significant

Doug Jones
January, 1996

Acknowledgments

The research presented in this book would have been impossible without the assistance of many people. In particular, Professors Kim Hill and Conrad Kottak were both very generous in assisting me in work at their own field sites in Paraguay and Brazil. Kim Hill gave many useful theoretical suggestions, helped with research planning, and took time off from his own fieldwork to introduce me to the Ache of Paraguay and to help with data collection in three Ache communities. He also collected data for this study from the Hiwi of Venezuela. Conrad Kottak provided an introduction to the residents of the village of Arembepe in Brazil, where he has worked since the 1960s, and suggested several important lines of inquiry.

In Paraguay, two Ache, Martin Achipurangi and Carlos Beijiwagi, and a missionary, Bjarne Forsterwald, were of great assistance under difficult conditions.

In Bahia, Brazil, Professors Julio Braga, Carlos Alberto Caroso and Maria Hilda Paraiso, all of the Federal University of Bahia, offered a great deal of useful advice, and help in setting up a station for photography and interviews. Gutemberg Pires was of great help in "Campo Alto."

In Moscow, Barbara Walker helped in setting up interviews with Russians. She also gave support and useful advice at every stage.

David Buss, Kim Hill, Conrad Kottak and John Mitani all provided thorough and painstaking criticism of multiple drafts of this thesis, and helped to make it a better organized and more carefully thought out work than I could ever have produced on my own. Sally Horvath provided careful copy editing.

Professor Roberto Frisancho of the University of Michigan, three anonymous reviewers of a paper published in the journal *Human Nature*, and three anonymous reviewers of a paper published in *Current Anthropology* also had valuable suggestions.

Research for this study was supported by NSF Doctoral Dissertation Research Improvement Grant BNS-9006394, and by grants from the University of Michigan Department of Anthropology, and University of Michigan Evolution and Human Behavior Program. The Department of Anthropology at Cornell University provided access to library and computer facilities.

CHAPTER 1

Physical Attractiveness
Evolution, Psychology and Anthropology

THE RISE AND FALL OF PHYSICAL ATTRACTIVENESS

When Charles Darwin presented the theory of natural selection in *On the Origin of Species,* he was circumspect about the possible human implications, limiting himself to the observation that "In the distant future . . . psychology will be based on a new foundation, that of the necessary acquirement of each mental power and capacity by gradation. Light will be thrown on the origin of man and his history" (Darwin 1967[1859]:488). Thirteen years later, in *The Descent of Man and Selection in Relation to Sex* (1981[1871]), he was more forthright, arguing in the first half of this book "that man is the modified descendant of some pre-existing form" (p. 9).

Only the first half of his book, however, is given over to making the case for the animal origins of our species. The second half is devoted to a subject that would prove nearly as contentious, the theory of sexual selection. Darwin put these two topics together in a single volume because he was convinced that sexual selection, in the form of sexual rivalry and mate choice, had played a leading role in the origin of the human species and the differentiation of human races. Because Darwin believed that mate choice on the basis of physical appearance was an important cause of human morphological evolution, he gave considerable attention to available evidence about standards of physical attractiveness in different human populations.

In the fifty or so years after the appearance of Darwin's book, other scholars took up the topic of physical attractiveness in relation to the theory of sexual selection. Ellis (1926) and Westermarck (1921) carried Darwin's argument a step further: while Darwin had been concerned only with the possible evolutionary *consequences* of standards of physical attractiveness, they attempted to understand the evolutionary *causes* of these standards. Both argued that signs of fertility, health and vigor are almost universals of attractiveness; both considered that factors specific to populations also played a part. Their work was part of a larger effort, begun by Darwin himself, and carried on by William James (1980[1890]) and others, to understand human psychology in the light of natural selection.

This early evolutionary psychology petered out in the 1920s and 1930s. The decline of Darwinism in Anglo-American social theory partly reflected political and moral concerns. In the eyes of many social scientists, the abuse of biology to rationalize American segregation, European colonialism and Nazi genocide discredited virtually all attempts to explore the biological bases of human behavior. The revulsion against doctrines of racial supremacy contributed to the rise of behaviorism in psychology and cultural determinism in anthropology (Degler 1991). The rise of psychoanalysis also contributed to the decline of evolutionary psychology. Freudianism began as a variant of evolutionary psychology, and Freud saw individual psychological maturation as a recapitulation of the evolution of the species. But Freud had virtually no understanding of the *mechanisms* of evolutionary change, and his followers showed little interest in the evolutionary dimension of psychoanalytic theory. As a result, those scholars who felt that mainstream social science paid too little attention to human nature and human sexuality, and turned to Freud in consequence, received little encouragement to ground their thinking in Darwin's theories of natural selection and sexual selection (Sulloway 1979).

Even within evolutionary biology, there was little interest in social behavior and in sexual selection until the 1970s, for reasons discussed more fully in Chapter 2. Thus the topic of physical attractiveness in relation to the theory of sexual selection, which Darwin gave a central role in his account of human evolution, has been neglected until recently, and research on human attractiveness has been largely divorced from the theory of sexual selection. The review of the literature in the first two chapters of this book reflects this divorce between the study of human behavior and evolutionary theory. Chapter 1 focuses on human behavior, with an overview of attempts to revive the earlier project of an evolutionary psychology and a review of major findings from psychology and anthropology. Chapter 2 focuses on the theory of sexual selection as it has developed within evolutionary biology. The conclusion to Chapter 2, and the rest of this book, are an attempt to reunite the study of human physical attractiveness and the theory of sexual selection.

EVOLUTION AND HUMAN BEHAVIOR TODAY

How, or even whether, to use the theory of natural selection in explaining human behavior is still a hotly debated topic, and any work proposing to use sexual selection theory to investigate and explain standards of physical attractiveness in human populations needs to consider some of the larger issues. The approach followed in this book is known as evolutionary psychology (or Darwinian psychology). Evolutionary psychologists regard the human mind, like the human body, as a complex system of mechanisms shaped by natural selection to solve recurrent adaptive problems. This section will introduce several principles that distinguish this approach to human behavior from other approaches. These principles include an emphasis on reproductive competition, the principle of domain specificity in psychology, a concern for the evolutionary past, and models of gene-culture coevolution. The discussion of these topics will also provide the opportunity to introduce material that will be relevant in later chapters. For example, in this chapter, I will illustrate the principle of "domain specificity" by discussing the evidence that human beings have adaptive specializations for recognizing faces; in Chapter 6, I return to this topic when discussing the possibility that mechanisms for recognizing faces overlap with mechanisms for assessing facial attractiveness.

Reproductive Competition

> Sexual love . . . next to the love of life . . . shows itself as the strongest and most active of motives, and constantly lays claim to half the powers and thoughts of the younger portion of mankind. It is the ultimate goal of almost all human effort. It exerts an unfavorable influence on the most important affairs, interrupts every hour the most serious occupations, and sometimes confuses for a while even the greatest minds. It does not hesitate to intrude with its trash, interfering with the negotiations of statesmen and the investigations of the learned. . . . It devises daily the most entangled and the worst actions, destroys the most valuable relationships, breaks the strongest bonds, demands the sacrifice sometimes of life or health, sometimes of wealth, rank and happiness. Indeed, it destroys the conscience of the otherwise honest, makes traitors of the once loyal. . . . One is forced to cry: Why all this noise? Why the strain, turmoil, worry and effort? . . . Why should such a trifle play so important a part, and constantly introduce disturbance and confusion into the well-regulated life of man? But to the earnest investigator the spirit of truth gradually reveals the answer: it is no trifle that is in question here; on the contrary, the importance of the matter is quite proportionate to the seriousness and ardor of the effort. The ultimate aim of all love affairs . . . is actually more important than all other aims in human life, and is therefore quite worthy of the profound seriousness with which everyone pursues it. What is decided by it is nothing less than the *composition of the next generation*. . . . This is the key to the problem. [Schopenhauer 1911 (1844): 608–9, tr. by author, italics in the original]

One of the great obstacles to a theoretical understanding of physical attraction is its seeming impracticality, a quality reflected in the Brazilian saying "*Beleza não põe na mesa*" ("Good looks don't put anything on the table"). Arthur Schopenhauer wrestled with the impracticality of sexual attraction more than a decade before the publication of *On the Origin of Species* in an appendix ("The Metaphysics of Sexual Love") to *The World as Will and Representation*. He argued that human sexuality could only be explained if it was considered to be directed not toward the survival and well-being of the individual, but toward reproduction. Equipped with the idea that much human behavior is unconsciously directed toward reproduction, and with a knowledge of basic human physiology, Schopenhauer developed an account of human sexuality, including males' greater desire for sexual variety and the connection between physical attractiveness and age- and health-related changes in reproductive value, which closely parallels the modern adaptationist account.

Schopenhauer's explanation of *why* biological reproduction is so important to humans was frankly metaphysical—he believed that species have essences, and that the will to live is part of the essential nature of each species. The modern account of reproductive design proceeds differently, appealing to selection rather than essences to explain the composition of populations, and making the individual (or perhaps the gene)—not the species—the "unit of selection." As a result of natural selection, the phenotypes of organisms are adapted to perpetuate the genes that produce those phenotypes. Organisms are designed not only for making a living, but for genetic reproduction. As Dawkins (1987:v) puts it, "we are survival machines . . . blindly programmed to preserve the selfish molecules known as genes." While there is no guarantee that organisms will do what they are adapted to do, looking for reproductive adaptations and their by-products is one of the most powerful tools at the disposal of biologists.

Darwinism is not only reproduction-minded, but competition-minded. Darwin hit on the idea of natural selection while "reading for amusement Malthus on population" (1956), and commentators ever since have noted the similarities between evolutionary theory and economic theory. The economic, cost-benefit paradigm shared by modern evolutionary theory and modern economics posits that *scarcity* is an inescapable fact of life, and *competition* over scarce resources the great engine of adaptive change. There is a major dividing line in the human sciences between this view of life and theories according to which social change is driven by *inequality, domination* and *resistance* to domination. In these theories, symmetric contests take second place to asymmetric, unequal contests. Thus in many modern social science theories of gender, systems of gender hierarchy are the starting point, and sex differences in behavior are interpreted as the product of systems of sexual domination and resistance (Ortner and Whitehead 1981; Collier 1987). By contrast, in modern evolutionary theories of sex differences, reproductive competition is the starting point, and gender hierarchies are merely one possible outcome of competition over mating opportunities.

It is a central premise of this work that understanding human sexuality means recognizing that the human psyche is adapted not merely for individual survival and well-being but for reproductive competition, and that physical sexual attraction is partly the expression of adaptations for mate choice. While there is room for argument about specific proposed adaptations, there is no real alternative to adaptationism in the study of living things and their behavior. Only theories that invoke the *differential reproduction* of variants as a consequence of *selection* can account for the origin of complex adaptive systems, and such theories imply that the most complex adaptive system known, the human mind, consists of a set of adaptations for reproductive competition.

Domain Specificity

"Domain specificity"—or "mental modularity"—is the theory that the human mind consists of a number of specialized information processing mechanisms, rather than a single general purpose learning/reasoning/symbol-processing mechanism. A number of lines of argument and evidence from linguistics, developmental psychology, cognitive psychology, cognitive anthropology, and neuroscience support the existence of specialized cognitive systems. There are both ontogenetic and evolutionary arguments for domain specificity.

William James remarked that the human capacity for intelligent adaptation to a wide range of environments is evidence not that human instincts are few, but that they are many and complex (James 1980[1890]:491). Chomsky (1980), considering the particular case of human syntax acquisition, argues that no child—and no thinking creature—exposed to the limited linguistic stimuli which a child typically experiences, could figure out the grammar of a language unless she started out with some innate "hypothesis" or template of grammar. Basic principles of mechanics make it clear that no organism could have a general purpose locomotor system, equally efficient at moving on the ground and in the trees, underwater and in the air. By the same token, the advocates of domain specificity in cognitive psychology claim that treating the process of learning explicitly (as in "learnability theory" in linguistics), instead of leaving it in a black box, shows that an organism must start out with a whole array of specialized cognitive systems if it is learn to produce any kind of intelligent behavior.

Even where specialized innate mechanisms of information processing are not *logically* necessary for intelligent behavior in the face of limited information from the environment, they may still be expected on evolutionary grounds, if they cut down on the costs of trial and error learning, or reduce the chances of exploitation by conspecifics. In Chapter 2, I summarize the now generally accepted view that an organism will have multiple specialized learning mechanisms adapted to its ancestral ecological niche and social system. The same evolutionary arguments apply to cognitive abilities as apply to learning.

Among the innate specialized perceptual/cognitive mechanisms that have been proposed and defended to date are adaptations for processing and producing phonology and syntax (Chomsky 1980; Pinker 1994), visual imagery (Kosslyn 1980), musical tone and rhythm (Jackendoff and Lerdahl 1983), evaluations of landscape (Orians 1992), taxonomies of living things (Atran 1990), principles of hygiene (Rozin 1987), facial expression of emotion (Ekman 1984), "theories of mind" (theories about the beliefs and desires of other actors) (Baron-Cohen et al. 1993), and kin and ethnic classifications (Hirschfeld

1993). Available evidence supports some of these proposals more strongly than others: the case for innate specializations for acquiring grammar is now very strong; the case for species-typical emotional responses to landscapes is still more tentative. I will review evidence for one particular cognitive specialization, face recognition.

It is fairly simple to devise model nervous systems that are good at detecting paired eyelike stimuli (Braitenberg 1984). Simple face detectors are common in the animal world. More sophisticated is the capacity to recognize individual faces, which appears among birds and mammals. There is considerable evidence that birds and mammals have brain regions specifically given over to face recognition. The neurological evidence in humans is not as strong, since experimental possibilities are more limited. Nonetheless, there are many clinical cases of individuals with neurological deficits which impair face recognition (facial agnosia, or prosopagnosia). Often these impairments in face recognition are accompanied by other visual recognition deficits—a case in point being the title character of Oliver Sacks popular collection of neurological case histories, *The Man Who Mistook His Wife for a Hat* (1985). But there are also some clear-cut cases of selective impairment of face recognition alone. Interestingly, individuals incapable of recognizing individual faces are still generally capable of reading facial expressions of emotion (Carey 1979).

Neurological localization alone is not proof of innateness. Probably stronger evidence comes from studies of infants. Goren (1975) shows that newborn infants pay less attention to representations of scrambled faces, with facial features in the wrong positions, than they do to unscrambled representations.

While evidence suggests that humans are born with a template of how faces look, this template is probably modified by experience. Several lines of evidence suggest that individuals form a representation of average or prototypical facial features in the local population, and use this average in recognizing individual faces. Several researchers (Bruce 1988; Benson and Perrett 1992) have used computer graphics software to produce facial caricatures—pictures of faces which exaggerate the features that distinguish the face being caricatured from the average face. They demonstrate that caricatures of public figures are more readily recognized than noncaricatured pictures. They argue that people do not remember faces by memorizing all the features of every remembered face. Instead, people mentally average the faces they see around them to form an image of a composite or prototypical face, and remember an individual face by remembering only those features which differ between that face and the average face. Consistent with this line of reasoning, research shows that unusual faces are easier to remember than faces with proportions close to average (Light et al. 1981).

More evidence along these lines comes from studies of cross-racial face recognition, reviewed in Brigham (1986). There is a large literature on this topic, in part because of the practical importance of knowing how reliably witnesses can identify criminal suspects of another race. On the "facial prototype" theory of face recognition one might expect that cross-race face recognition would be unreliable. An individual with extensive experience of European faces and limited experience of East Asian faces will have a strong prototype of the former, but not the latter. If this individual attempts to remember an East Asian face by comparing it with a prototypical European face, she will end up recording the "racial" features that distinguish that face from a European face, more than the individual features that distinguish that face from other East Asian faces. She will find that East Asian faces all look alike to her. Individuals commonly do worse at cross-racial than own-racial face recognition. There is little or no evidence that racial prejudice affects performance in cross-racial face recognition. The evidence is stronger (although not overwhelming) that cross-racial *experience* leads to more accurate cross-racial face recognition. As far as I have been able to discover, none of the work on cross-racial face recognition has studied anthropologists or others whose professions put them in close contact with somatically distinctive populations for long periods of time, but my informal conversations with some half dozen anthropologists suggest that cross-racial face recognition abilities improve over the course of fieldwork, typically on a time scale of months, rather than weeks or years.

Face recognition is a classic case of evolutionarily adaptive domain-specific information processing. At the same time, it probably shows how an innate perceptual template can be modified by experience. Finally, as I will argue in Chapter 6, mechanisms of face recognition probably overlap with mechanisms of face evaluation.

The Weight of the Past

Organisms, as George Williams notes, are historical documents. "Every organism shows features that are functionally arbitrary or even maladaptive" as a result of adaptation to past circumstances (Williams 1992:72). These historical legacies result both from local (as opposed to global) optimization, and from evolutionary time lags. Local optimization means that natural selection cannot take one step back in order to take two steps forward. Organisms with different evolutionary histories may be trapped at different local adaptive optima even if they face similar current problems. Time lags mean that organisms may not attain even local optima when environments change rapidly. John Endler's massive review of natural selection in the wild suggests that such time lags are common in wild populations, which are often changing rapidly in response to directional selection (Endler 1986). This means that evolution-minded research needs to consider the evolutionary past as well as current adaptive problems. For example, an evolution-minded account of physical attractiveness in industrial societies will keep in mind that human beings are likely to have psychological machinery for detecting malnutrition and parasitic infestation in potential mates, even if these conditions are rare in the society studied. Practitioners of evolutionary psychology will have to pay far more attention to the anthropology of band and tribal societies than psychologists have traditionally done, because the human psyche, like the human frame, must bear the stamp of a tribal way of life.

Genes and Culture

Human abilities to learn and reason have been shaped by natural selection. Most complex human behaviors vary across populations as a result of the interaction of these abilities with environmental—especially cultural—contingencies. Culture exists because of constraints on each individual's capacity to form mental representations of the world, constraints which deserve attention alongside more "material" constraints like limited nutrients and mating opportunities. One sort of constraint results from limitations on the availability of information, another from limitations on the ability to process available information.

1) *Limits on information.* Chapter 2 presents a discussion of some of the causes and consequences of dependence on imitation as opposed to individual learning in humans and other animals. The model of informational cascades discussed there is only one of a whole family of models of gene-culture coevolution, or dual inheritance theory, developed by Boyd and Richerson (1985), Cavalli-Sforza and Feldman (1981), Durham (1991), Lumsden and Wilson (1981) and Pulliam and Dunford (1980). In the area of cultural transmission of standards of physical attractiveness, Lumsden and Wilson (1981) and Lowe and Lowe (1982) show how cultural transmission of standards of fashion can produce regular oscillations in clothing styles similar to those observed in Europe over the past two centuries (Richardson and Kroeber 1940).

2) *Limits on information processing.* Human reasoning seems to depend on schemas, or mental models, more than on logical deduction. Rather than come up with new schemas for each new cognitive problem, people frequently borrow and modify pre-existing schemas from other domains (Lakoff and Johnson 1980). As a result, human cognition is shot through with metaphor and symbolism—indeed, we might define symbolism as putting representations to uses other than those to which they were originally adapted. Symbolic anthropologists have been fairly successful in showing how representations adapted for one sphere of life are coopted (or *exapted,* to use Gould and Vrba's [1982] terminology) for use in another, so that common (homologous) themes run through disparate domains. For example, symbolic anthropologists are often able to show that shared color symbolism runs through body ornaments, house decorations, funeral rites, and puberty ceremonies (Turner 1967). I will have more to say about color symbolism and physical attractiveness in Chapters 5 and 7.

All this can be seen as a special case of the phenomenon of "sensory bias" discussed in Chapter 2, and common to all organisms with sensory systems. West-Eberhard (1991) notes how often in the course of sexual selection, signals originally adapted for another purpose (soliciting parental care, attracting attention) have been "exapted" to attract mates. Thanks to the evolutionary history of populations and the experiences of individuals, not only sensory systems, but more abstract, "cognitive" representational systems may have biases built into them that allow representations adapted for one domain to "spill over" and affect representation in other domains.

The evolutionary approach to physical attractiveness thus does not imply that standards of beauty are always adaptive or entirely "hard-wired." In humans as in other animals the development of standards of attractiveness is likely to involve a range of processes, from innate templates to imprinting to imitation and other forms of social learning. The final section of Chapter 2 advances some more specific proposals.

PSYCHOLOGICAL PERSPECTIVES

Almost twenty years ago, in a review of the existing psychological literature on physical attractiveness, Berscheid and Walster noted that "most social scientists have shown a studied professional disinterest in . . . how our physical appearance influence[s] our relationship with others" (1974:158). The situation has changed dramatically since then. A recent glance at the PsychInfo database revealed more than a thousand journal articles and other publications on the topic, most apparently published in the last ten years. This literature has been surveyed at book length by Bull and Rumsey (1988), Hatfield and Sprecher (1986), Jackson (1992) and Patzer (1985). I present a very brief review here.

Agreement in standards of attractiveness. There is strong and consistent agreement in standards of physical attractiveness across raters. Iliffe (1960) and Udry (1965) printed photographs of a dozen female faces in newspapers in England and the United States, and asked readers to send in their ratings. They found strong agreement between raters across ages and regions. Studies since then have consistently found strong agreement across raters in standards of physical attractiveness, with correlations typically around .5 or higher (Berscheid and Walster 1974). Agreement in standards of physical attractiveness holds across sexes, sexual orientations and ages: men agree with women about which men's and which women's faces are most attractive, as do heterosexuals and homosexuals, and people of different ages ranging from children to the very old.

Research on cross-cultural agreement in standards of facial attractiveness shows considerable agreement between Asian American and European American females (Wagatsuma and Kleinke 1979), among Chinese, Indian and English females (Thakerar and Iwawaki 1979), and between African and European Americans (Cross and Cross 1971). However, these studies all involve populations with considerable exposure to Western media and other Western influences.

Ontogeny of standards of attractiveness. Discrimination between attractive and unattractive faces develops very young. Langlois et al. (1987) have shown that infants as young as two to three months of age, given a choice between looking at photographs of women's faces rated attractive by adults, and women's faces rated unattractive, will spend more time looking at the attractive faces. This result holds not only for European-American infants looking at European-American faces, but also for the same infants looking at African-American women's faces rated attractive or unattractive by African Americans, and Asian-American faces rated by Asian Americans.

Facial and bodily attractiveness. Research in the United States suggests that ratings of overall physical attractiveness depend more on facial attractiveness than on bodily attractiveness (Berscheid 1981).

Who considers attractiveness important? Individuals vary in the importance they attach to physical attractiveness. Pheterson and Hourani (1976) find that men with high scores on a test of "sensation-seeking" give more weight to physical attractiveness than low scorers. "Sensation seekers" tend to be more sociable and extroverted, less neurotic and more psychopathic, and more sexually active than average (Zuckerman 1980). Simpson and Gangestad (1992) assess the relationship between attention to physical attractiveness and female "sociosexuality." Sociosexuality "concerns the willingness or lack thereof to have sex in a relationship prior to mutual investment in and commitment to the relationship." Simpson and Gangestad's "Sociosexual Orientation Inventory" contains questions about the subject's relevant past behavior and current beliefs. Women with high scores on the inventory report being more interested in a potential partner's looks, and less interested in his kindness, understanding, fidelity, or emotional stability than low scorers, and women with attractive partners tend to have high SOI scores.

There are also group differences in the importance attached to physical attractiveness. (I review some of the cross-cultural evidence below.) Young people are typically more interested in attractiveness than old people, and men are typically more interested than women. Both the age and sex differences in the importance attached to physical attractiveness track age and sex differences in sensation seeking: young people are more given to sensation-seeking than the old, men more than women (Zuckerman et al. 1980). In other words, sensation-seeking could be the variable that accounts for both within- and between-group differences in the importance attached to physical attractiveness. I will have more to say about the sex difference in Chapter 4.

Attractiveness and dating. An early study by Walster et al. (1966) helped to set off the current boom in social psychological research on physical attractiveness. The authors held a "computer-dance" at the University of Minnesota. They sold tickets to students who filled out questionnaires, and were guaranteed a dance partner, allegedly selected by computer but in fact assigned at random. The authors showed that physical attractiveness of partner, assessed when students bought their tickets, was the only significant predictor of liking partner and wanting to date partner again. There were no significant effects of partner's perceived social skills or intelligence. Brislin and Lewis (1968), again assigning partners at random at a dance at a university, got similar results, with strong effects of physical attractiveness and weak effects of ratings of partner's sociability and similarity of interest.

Studies of real-life dating situations also show consistent effects of attractiveness. For college students, Krebs and Adinolfi (1975) found that facial attractiveness correlated with dating frequency for females, but not for males. Berscheid et al. (1971) report significant effects of physical attractiveness on dating frequency for both sexes. Among participants in a video-dating service, Riggio and Wall (1984) found that more attractive individuals of both sexes were more often selected as dates. Folkes (1982) found that for 67 pairs who met through another video-dating service, couples similar in physical attractiveness were more likely to continue dating. Hill et al. (1976) and White (1960) also find that similarity in attractiveness within couples predicts duration and seriousness of involvement.

Just asking individuals how much importance they attach to physical attractiveness may give misleading results. Miller and Rivenbark (1970) present evidence that subjects are "either not fully aware or not fully honest about how important physical attractiveness really is to them."

Attractiveness and marriage. Physical attractiveness has consequences for marriage as well. Physically attractive women are more likely to marry. In an early study, Holmes and Hatch (1938) rated the facial beauty of several hundred female students at the University of California. Several years after graduation they found that 34% of the women rated beautiful had married, compared with 28% of the good-looking, 16% of the plain and 11% of the homely.

Attractiveness not only improves a woman's chances of marrying, it improves her chances of marrying an attractive partner. Sheperd and Ellis (1972) collected photographs of 36 wedding pairs, and had brides and grooms rated separately for attractiveness. They found a correlation of .39 between spouses' facial attractiveness. Several other studies have found significant correlations between facial attractiveness of spouses (Murstein 1976; Price 1979; McKillip 1983).

Attractive women are also more likely to marry successful men. Elder (1969) showed that physical attractiveness was associated with upward mobility for a sample of US American females born in the 1920s. The attractiveness, IQ and school performance of each girl was recorded during adolescence. Upward mobility was assessed by comparing father's occupational status in 1929 with husband's occupational status in 1958. The attractive girls were no more intelligent or achievement-oriented than the unattractive, but they were more upwardly mobile through marriage. The effect was stronger for girls of lower class origin ($r = .46$) than for girls of middle class origin ($r = .35$). The effect of attractiveness on upward mobility was stronger than the effect of IQ. It was also stronger than the effect of educational attainment for lower class but not middle class females. Wives with more education than their husbands were more likely to come from the less attractive group.

Taylor and Glenn (1976) found physical attractiveness of daughters of urban lower class men to be positively related to their husbands' occupational status for, though they did not find this relationship for middle class daughters or farmer's daughters.

Udry (1977) also showed that attractive women make upwardly mobile marriages; the effect was stronger for lower class white women and for black women than for middle class white women. Udry and Eckland (1984) found that ratings of female facial attractiveness from a high school yearbook were positively correlated with husbands' educational level and income, and with probability of being married. Male attractiveness, however, was negatively related to wife's educational attainment.

In summary, physically attractive women tend to marry up. The effect is weaker for middle class than for lower class females. It may be relevant here that middle class females are more likely never to marry; it may be that unattractive middle class females are more likely never to marry than unattractive lower class females. The relationship of male attractiveness to wife's social status is less studied.

Other effects of attractiveness. Attractiveness also has consequences outside of sexual relationships. For example, some studies show that attractive men and women have fewer same-sex friendships than others, both because they are likely to have more heterosexual opportunities and less time for other activities, and as a result of envy on the part of the less fortunate (Jackson 1992:136–38). (The disruptive effects of envy may also explain the finding that same-sex friends tend to be similar in attractiveness.) Several studies suggest that juvenile delinquents are less attractive than other boys; males who can't get ahead on the basis of their looks may be more likely to resort to violence (Cavior 1973).

But some of the consequences of attractiveness do not seem to follow simply from its importance in mating relationships. Adults often treat attractive children differently (usually better) than unattractive ones. While the present study considers attractiveness mainly in relation to mate value, non-sexual attractiveness and its consequences clearly deserve study in their own right.

ANTHROPOLOGICAL PERSPECTIVES

The ethnographic literature clearly demonstrates a great interest in physical attractiveness across a wide range of cultures. Good discussions, some including material on ornamentation, dancing and other sexual displays, and social consequences of attractiveness, can be found in Malinowski (1987[1929]), Berndt (1951), Weiner (1976), Gregor (1985), Munn (1986), Boone (1986), Grinker (1990), and Jankowiak (1993). But in spite of considerable descriptive material, the systematic comparative study of standards of physical attractiveness is a relatively neglected area of anthropology. By way of illustration, consider the Human Relations Area Files (HRAF), a massive compilation of ethnographic material for a representative sample of the world's cultures. Material for each culture is organized under standardized headings like "witchcraft beliefs" and "subsistence practices." Researchers interested in "ethnometeorology" or "religious orgies" will find appropriate headings in the HRAF; researchers interested in physical attractiveness will not. Material on this topic is scattered through several sections on sexuality.

This section will review the limited cross-cultural comparative material that does exist, focusing on three topics in particular: cross-cultural differences in standards of attractiveness, cross-cultural differences in the importance of attractiveness, and sex differences in the importance of physical attractiveness.

Cross-Cultural Differences in Standards of Attractiveness

Ford and Beach (1951:86) conclude in their pioneering review of the ethnography of human sexuality that

> [t]he cross-cultural evidence makes it clear that there are few if any universal standards of sexual attractiveness. Instead the physical characteristics which are regarded as sexually stimulating vary appreciably from one society to another. A thin woman is regarded as more attractive than a plump one in some societies; the reverse is true in others. Furthermore, there are great differences between cultures with respect to the particular bodily organs or characters that are considered critical determiners of beauty.

They note that criteria of female attractiveness recorded by ethnographers in different societies include a plump body build (in 13 societies in their sample), medium body build (5 societies), slim body build (5), broad pelvis and wide hips (6), narrow pelvis and slim hips (1), small ankles (3), shapely and fleshy calves (5), elongated labia minora (8), large clitoris (1), long and pendulous breasts (2), large breasts (9), and upright hemispherical breasts (2) (Ford and Beach 1951:88).

A major difficulty with ethnographic accounts of the sort reviewed by Ford and Beach is that ethnographers often have a strong bias toward recording differences rather than similarities between societies. For example, I will review evidence in Chapter 4 that attractiveness is universally perceived to decline with age, especially for females; ethnographers commonly mention this only in passing. Thus Ford and Beach are probably overinterpreting the available evidence in stating that "there are few if any universal standards of sexual attractiveness." However, there is certainly variation across societies, which any theory of attractiveness must accommodate.

Cross-Cultural Differences in the Importance of Attractiveness

There is also a great deal of variation across cultures in the reported importance of physical attractiveness in mate choice. Some of this variation seems to be related to the presence or absence of arranged marriage. Rosenblatt and Cozby (1972) show that there is a very strong and significant correlation ($r = 0.70$) between individual freedom of choice of spouse and choice on "impractical" grounds. In other words, when people choose spouses for other people, they are likely to choose on "practical" grounds, for traits like food getting or preparing skills, kinship connections, or rank. But when people choose their own spouses, ethnologists are likely to report that they give greater weight to "impractical" factors like physical attractiveness. (Rosenblatt and Cozby also show that societies with freedom of choice of spouse are likely to have more frequent and prominent heterosexual dances and other occasions for courtship. See also Rosenblatt 1974 and Rosenblatt and Anderson 1981.)

Since the societies most often studied by social psychologists and sociologists do not practice arranged marriage, while most of the societies in the ethnographic record (and presumably most of the societies in which human beings evolved) do, it may be worthwhile reviewing some of the factors involved in the custom. In most band and tribal societies in the ethnographic record there is a net transfer of goods or services from the family of the groom to the family of the bride (Murdock 1967). While long-term "pair-bonded" mateships, male provisioning of females and their young, and male sexual coercion of females are all found in some nonhuman animal societies, the coercive control of female mating by close kin, with the exchange of the reproductive capacity of female kinsmen for economic, political and reproductive assets, is uniquely human. In band and tribal societies it is usually wives, rather than husbands, who are bought or exchanged (or stolen), because women's reproductive capacities are often a limiting resource in a way that men's reproductive capacities are not. This point has been made not just by sociobiologists, but by mainstream cultural anthropologists, for example Meillassoux (1981), Goody (1976), and Robertson (1991). In the land-hungry peasant societies of Eurasia, the flow of resources is often in the other direction, with the bride's family setting up the new couple with a dowry.

But in these cases, the bride's family is not paying for the groom's reproductive capacity, but for his economic assets—the estate he stands to inherit. In either case, when kin groups stand to lose or gain economically, politically, or reproductively from the marriages of their members, they have an incentive to arrange those members' marriages.

Suzanne Frayser (1985), reviewing evidence from nearly 100 band, tribal and peasant societies, shows that arranged marriage is associated with both premarital and extramarital sexual restrictiveness for women. The presence or absence of institutions associated with sexual restrictiveness, including patrilocality, elaborate marriage ceremonies, brideprice (sometimes called bridewealth), and powerful fraternal interest groups is closely tied to the subsistence base. Paige and Paige (1981) divide societies into those with a low value resource base (gathering, hunting, fishing, and simple horticulture) and those with a high value resource base (pastoralism, complex horticulture, and agriculture). They show that the presence of brideprice correlates with the latter at $r = .57$. The absence of significant material consideration or bridal gifts is associated with the least productive and politically weakest societies in their sample.

Thus the limited evidence available suggests that the importance of physical attractiveness in mate choice is strongly related to freedom of individual choice of spouse, which is related to permissive sexual norms, and to a low value resource base and weak fraternal interest groups.

It is worth noting that the majority of societies in Rosenblatt and Cozby's and Frayser's samples are reported to give at least a limited say to individuals in their choice of marriage partners. Even in societies in which choice of marriage partner is strongly circumscribed by marriage rules allocating partners on the basis of kinship (commonly permitting or prescribing marriage to actual or classificatory cross-cousins or parallel cousins) there is generally enough ambiguity in the rules to give some scope to individual choice. Structure does not always trump sentiment (cf. Needham 1962); see, for example, Hiatt (1965) and Chagnon (1988). In other words, traditional societies in general, and hunting and gathering societies in particular, usually seem to give individuals at least some room for exerting sexual selection via mate choice.

There are other potential sources of cross-cultural variation in the importance given to physical attractiveness. In 1989 Buss published a cross-cultural survey on criteria of mate choice in 37 different population samples from 33 countries. Interview subjects were asked how much they valued a variety of traits in a potential long-term mate, including earning capacity, ambition/industriousness, youth, physical attractiveness, and chastity. The societies from which Buss's samples were drawn differ in important respects from those reviewed above. They are largely drawn from modernized populations with cash economies under the authority of centralized states and exposed to mass media. In other words the samples do not include the more isolated tribal societies studied by an earlier generation of anthropologists. They do, however, encompass a wide range of culture areas and social classes. Furthermore, the data in this sample are of higher quality than the scattered and impressionistic material reviewed in earlier cross-cultural studies.

Buss's study thus provides a particularly valuable opportunity to study why cultures differ in the importance they attach to physical attractiveness. A reanalysis of Buss's data (Gangestad and Buss 1993), in combination with an index of pathogen prevalence developed by Low (1990), shows that physical attractiveness is given more weight as a criterion of mate choice among populations in areas of high pathogen prevalence. This trend is even stronger when income differences and geographic region are controlled for. Chapter 6 reviews evidence that physical attractiveness is partly a function of health status; it is consistent with this line of evidence that especially wide variations in health status are associated with special attention to physical attractiveness.

Sex Differences in the Importance of Attractiveness

While Ford and Beach (1951) argue that there is a great deal of cross-cultural variation in standards of attractiveness, they also note:

> One very interesting generalization is that in most societies the physical beauty of the female receives more explicit consideration than does the handsomeness of the male. The attractiveness of the man usually depends predominantly upon his skills and prowess rather than upon his physical appearance. [p. 94]

The Buss study cited above also suggests sex differences in the importance attached to physical attractiveness may be a cultural universal or near universal. In virtually all populations sampled, males rated physical attractiveness (and youth) significantly more important in mate choice than did females. Females, by contrast, mostly rated earning potential and ambition/industriousness as more important in mate choice than did males.

In other words, human beings seem to be an exception to the general rule among animals that male attractiveness matters more than female attractiveness. In Chapter 2 I note that evolutionary theory predicts, and studies of nonhuman animals generally confirm, that the sex with the higher potential rate of reproduction (PRR) will be the more sexually selected sex. Human males have higher PRRs than human females, although the sex difference is less than among most mammals because biparental care is so important in our species. As predicted by the modern theory of sexual selection, human males are larger than females, attain sexual maturity at a later age, and senesce more rapidly. Violent competition is more common among human males than among females, and male sexual coercion of females is far more common than the reverse. In most respects, human females are more selective in their choice of sexual partners than human males. The importance attached to female (as opposed to male) physical attractiveness in our species is an anomaly; while there may be more overall variance in male than in female sexual attractiveness, variance in male attractiveness is less tied to somatic cues. Chapters 4 and 5 will explore some possible causes and consequences of this anomaly.

A review of the literature demonstrates that both social psychologists and cultural anthropologists have produced a considerable body of research on physical attractiveness. However, the theoretical foundations of the subject are still underdeveloped, with little in the way of explanation of why people have the standards of attractiveness that they do, why standards vary across cultures—to the extent that they do vary—or even why people experience physical attraction at all. Social scientists have generally studied physical attractiveness without relying on the theory of sexual selection, but they have not developed any alternative theory of comparable scope and predictive power.

CHAPTER 2

The Theory of Sexual Selection

NATURAL SELECTION AND SEXUAL SELECTION

"Sexual selection . . . depends on the advantage which certain individuals have over other individuals of the same sex and species, in exclusive relation to reproduction" (Darwin 1981[1871]:256). In this quotation from *The Descent of Man and Selection in Relation to Sex,* and in the rest of his introductory chapter on sexual selection, Charles Darwin calls attention to two features of sexual selection that distinguish it from more familiar cases of natural selection. First, he argues that only organs and behaviors adapted to promote the reproduction of one individual *at the expense of another* are products of sexual selection. By definition, characters shaped by sexual selection don't increase the total number of offspring produced; they only determine that individual A produces offspring *instead of* individual B. Second, adaptations produced by sexual selection are directly concerned with mating and fertilization, rather than survival of self or kin; they involve mating effort rather than somatic or parental effort. Darwin goes on to distinguish two forms of sexual selection: contests within one sex (usually males) over access to the other sex, and choice on the part of members of one sex (usually females) for particular members of the other sex.

The theory of sexual selection has had a checkered history (Cronin 1991). With a few exceptions, evolutionary biologists neglected the topic until the 1960s and 1970s, long after the triumph of the Modern Synthesis in the 1930s and 1940s, which united Darwin's theory of natural selection with Mendelian genetics. Sexual selection was neglected by the architects of the Modern Synthesis because sexual behavior, and social behavior in general, pose special problems for evolutionary theory. It was only beginning in the 1960s, with the development of sociobiology, that these problems were addressed in a sustained fashion. These problems result from the fact that in social evolution the fitness of a trait depends on its frequency. The performance of a given tail shape in flight will generally not depend on the frequency of that tail shape in the population; that is, its fitness is "frequency independent." In contrast the attractiveness of that tail to members of the other sex will depend on the preferences of the other sex, which will often depend in turn on the frequencies of different shapes of tail (i.e. its fitness is "frequency dependent"). Simple optimality modeling will not work in the case of frequency dependent selection; game theory is needed in cases where the strategy you adopt depends on the strategy I adopt, which depends on the strategy you adopt, and so on (Maynard Smith 1982; Parker and Maynard Smith 1990).

Frequency dependent selection presents a number of seeming paradoxes. There is no guarantee that organisms will progress toward optimal solutions. Instead, they may attain an evolutionary equilibrium in which no individual can gain by adopting a different strategy, even though all might be better off if all acted differently. Or they may enter an endless "arms race" in which each tries to get ahead of the others without anyone enjoying any long term gains. Frequency dependent selection may favor traits that increase the reproductive success of individuals but reduce the viability of groups and lower the productivity of ecosystems. It may favor the evolution of waste and extravagance, rather than efficiency, in sexual and other signals. (See the discussion of the handicap principle below.) Frequency dependent selection may result in coevolutionary positive feedback cycles that amplify arbitrary traits. (See the discussion of runaway selection below.)

Sexual selection's power to favor extravagant traits of no obvious utility in the "struggle for existence" led Darwin to classify *natural* selection and *sexual* selection as two separate processes. West-Eberhard (1991) follows Darwin, but suggests that the relevant distinction is one between *natural* selection and *social* selection. For Zahavi (1991), it is *natural* selection and *signal* selection that need to be distinguished. Sexual selection, social selection, and signal selection often have counterintuitive consequences because all are forms of frequency dependent selection.

The remainder of this chapter reviews aspects of the theory of sexual selection of likely relevance to sexual attraction in humans. I will make use of economic analogies throughout this chapter; economists have long been familiar with the idea that the individual pursuit of self-interest may have paradoxical social consequences. Economic analogies can make evolutionary theories more accessible (e.g. the comparison between runaway sexual selection and speculative booms), and they can also give insights into areas of social theory outside of economics proper (for example, the relevance of "handicap" theories of signaling to the study of ritual).

Mate Choice

Mate choice is the expression of mate preference. Before I consider the basis of mate preferences, I will consider how ecological circumstances and the machinations of own- and other-sex conspecifics may limit the potential for mate choice.

The Operational Sex Ratio

Males are usually the more sexually selected sex. Males typically compete more intensely for mates than do females, and commonly show greater development of secondary sexual characters; females are usually choosier than males about their sexual partners (Darwin 1981; Bateman 1948; Emlen and Oring 1977; Trivers 1972). Both this general rule, and the exceptions to it, depend on "the operational sex ratio (OSR) (the ratio of males that are ready to mate to females that are ready to mate) at the site and time when mating occurs" (Clutton-Brock and Parker 1992). When many males and few females are ready to mate at any one time, males are the more competitive sex, and females the choosier sex, and vice versa. The OSR is determined by the potential rates of reproduction of the two sexes, the adult sex ratio, and the spacing and timing of mating (Clutton-Brock and Parker 1992; Emlen and Oring 1977).

Potential reproductive rate. In most species, males are the more competitive sex, and females choosier, because potential rates of reproduction are greater for males than for females. For example, human males can, in principle, produce offspring at the rate of one every few weeks or months (Daly and Wilson 1978:59); human females can, at best, produce offspring every few years. In many species, female reproductive rates are limited by the energetic cost of producing eggs, which are commonly greater than the costs of producing sperm. Among mammals, the important limits on female reproductive rates come not so much from egg production as from pregnancy and lactation. In a typical mammalian species, each conception puts the female, but not the male, out of reproductive commission for an appreciable fraction of her expected life span. The result is that even if adult males and females are equally numerous, there are usually far more males than females ready to mate. This difference in the operational sex ratio resulting from differences in potential rates of reproduction commonly makes choosers of females, and beggars of males.

Adult sex ratio. Sex differences in numbers at birth, in rates of maturation and in mortality can all influence the adult sex ratio. These will have the most influence on the intensity of sexual selection in populations otherwise close to monogamy.

Spacing and timing of mating. The ecology of a population may keep potential rates of reproduction below the biological maximum. If females are scattered in space, then mating, for a male, may involve not just copulation, but time spent searching for a female and perhaps keeping other males away from her.

Timing of periods of sexual readiness may also affect the operational sex ratio. If only a fraction of reproductive-age females are in estrus at any one moment, then the ratio of males in breeding condition to females in breeding condition will be high. But if females synchronize their periods of estrus or if, as is the case in humans, females are sexually receptive throughout their ovulatory cycles, then the operational sex ratio will be lower. Ridley (1986) shows that troops of primate species in which many females are sexually receptive at the same time commonly have more adult males per adult female, presumably because males have more difficulty monopolizing females under these conditions, and male/male sexual competition is reduced.

Competition, Coercion and Choice

The operational sex ratio determines the relative intensity of sexual selection acting on males and females, but not the form of sexual selection. Darwin argued that sexual selection might take one of two forms: intrasexual combat (or the threat of it), or intersexual choice. Smuts and Smuts (1993) have recently argued that we need to add a third form of sexual selection to the list, sexual coercion. To the extent that males win the opportunity to mate by forcibly excluding rival males, or by coercing females, there will be little opportunity for females to exercise choice. In Chapter 1 I argue that while sexual competition and coercion often limit mate choice in humans, they seldom eliminate it altogether.

Monogamy and Mate Quality

It might seem that there would be no scope for sexual selection in populations in which individuals mate monogamously, and every individual finds a mate. However, if there are differences in mate value within both sexes, then females with high mate value will pair up with males of high mate value, and such pairs will have higher reproductive success than pairs with low mate value (Jones 1993; Burley 1986). Models of sexual selection often assume that one sex does the choosing, while the other is chosen. This is analytically simpler, and realistic for many species. However, the models discussed below also work, although sometimes not as strongly, in monogamous populations where both sexes exercise choice, and both are chosen (O'Donald 1980; Kirkpatrick and Price 1990).

MATE PREFERENCE

Mate Value and the Ultimate Bases of Physical Attraction

Sexually reproducing organisms are expected to have mechanisms for assessing the "mate value" of potential mates, just as heterotrophic organisms are expected to have mechanisms for assessing the nutritional value of potential food items. Following Kim Hill (personal communication) the mate value of individual i to individual j can be defined as the expected fitness from mating with i divided by the expected fitness from mating at random. Mate value will depend on the phenotype of the individual chosen as a mate (direct mate value), and on the genes that individual passes on to any resulting offspring (indirect mate value).

I will consider three ultimate bases for mate preferences:

1) *Direct mate value (phenotypic mate value)*. Direct mate value will depend both on the fecundity of a potential mate and on her ability and willingness to provide parental care for ego's offspring.

2) *Indirect mate value (genetic mate value)*. Indirect mate value will depend on the genetic contribution of a potential mate to offspring viability, fertility, and attractiveness.

3) *Sensory bias.* Evolutionary theory predicts adaptation, not perfection. Organisms may have nonadaptive mating preferences as a result of biases in sensory or cognitive mechanisms.

Direct Benefits: Good Phenotypes

I will consider two topics: What are the components of direct mate value? What are the outward signs of mate value actually used in mate choice?

Fecundity and potential parental investment. Successful mating involves both producing offspring and (in many species) providing parental care for them. Direct mate value thus will depend both on the fecundity of a potential mate and on her ability and willingness to care for ego and ego's offspring. Having high direct mate value and having high fitness are not synonymous, but there are as many ways of having high direct mate value as there are of being fit. Fecundity of a potential mate and potential parental investment may depend on age, health, nutritional status, social position, stage of reproductive cycle, and earlier reproductive history—to name just a few factors. It is impossible to do justice here to the vast literature on this topic; instead I will briefly discuss the difference between direct mate value and fitness, and leave further discussion of components of mate value in humans—including sex, age, health, and social position—to later chapters.

Organisms are designed by natural selection to make fitness-maximizing tradeoffs between somatic effort (SE), and reproductive/parental effort (RE and PE). The value of an individual as a mate will also depend on her levels of somatic and reproductive/parental effort; however, the combination of SE, RE and PE that maximize individual fitness usually will not be that which maximizes mate value. There is a consequent conflict of interest between males and females. For example, if a female is likely to switch mates between rearing one offspring and conceiving the next, then a male may be better off with a female who produces more offspring (high RE) or puts a great deal of effort into caring for the current brood (high PE) even if this reduces her chances of surviving to produce further offspring (low SE). As long as the characteristics associated with maximum mate value are different from those associated with maximum fitness, it will be adaptive to deceive potential mates about one's phenotype. I will return to this topic in Chapter 5.

Signs of mate value. Organisms assessing potential mates will rely on outward cues associated with mate value. In subsequent chapters I will have more to say about mate value cues that might be used by humans—including sex-typical face and body proportions, facial and bodily asymmetry, and quality and color of skin and hair. In this section I will consider the different ways that coadaptation of signals and preferences can overcome the problem of "false advertising."

Sexual selection for traits associated with mate value will favor organisms with high mate value, but it will also favor organisms bearing false advertisements—organisms that look as if they have higher mate value than they do. False advertisement, in turn, reduces the adaptive advantage of exercising mate choice. This does not imply that adaptive mate choice is evolutionarily unstable; rather, natural selection will favor organisms that rely on hard-to-fake cues to mate quality, assuming that some advertisements are harder to fake than others (Kodrick-Brown and Brown 1984).

The coevolution of sexual signals and sexual preferences is thus expected to lead to "honest advertising." Zahavi (1975) argues that the wastefulness and extravagance of sexual signals, which so impressed Darwin, is an expected result of selection for honest advertising—only individuals with high fitness and high mate value will be able to bear the handicap of exaggerated signals, less fit individuals will display more modest versions. There are actually several different versions of this "handicap principle."

Revealing handicaps. A revealing handicap need not be costly *per se,* but it makes its owner's faults more conspicuous—for example, a color pattern in an animal that makes it easier to detect weaknesses or deformities. Suppose organisms vary in mate value on a scale from 1 to 10. Then 10s should wear revealing handicaps to show that they have nothing to hide. Given that 10s are wearing handicaps, 9s should start wearing them as well, rather than risk being taken for having a lower mate value. But if 10s and 9s are wearing revealing handicaps, then 8s should as well, and so on. Everybody but 1s will gain by honestly advertising their value, given that everybody above them is doing the same.

Condition-dependent handicaps. Condition-dependent handicaps are handicaps that only organisms in good condition can produce. For example, if malnourished deer don't have enough calcium in their diets to produce large antlers, then large antlers may be a condition-dependent handicap, worth producing as a show of health even if costly.

"Pure" handicaps. If condition-dependent handicaps are ornaments that low quality individuals can't produce, then "pure" handicaps are ornaments that low quality individuals could produce but couldn't get away with. Pure handicaps can be adopted just as readily by low quality organisms as by high quality, but they are *disproportionately* costly for low quality organisms. Suppose there

are high quality males and low quality males, and females are better off mating with the former. Suppose males can be with or without a dangerous ornament—an ornament that greatly increases the risk of death when adopted by low quality males, and moderately increases the risk when adopted by high quality males. Under these conditions there may be an equilibrium at which females are able to use ornaments as an index of male quality, because high quality males have ornaments (the modest risk of an ornament is outweighed by the benefit of additional matings), while low quality males don't have ornaments (the high cost of an ornament outweighs the benefit of additional matings). The pure handicap is not just an effective signal that happens to be costly; it is an effective signal *because* it is costly.

A number of models show that revealing handicaps and condition-dependent handicaps can be stable forms of honest advertising (Iwasa and Pomiankowski 1991; Pomiankowski 1987). Early attempts to model pure handicaps were unsuccessful (Maynard Smith 1976; Davis and O'Donald 1976), but more recent work suggests a more favorable verdict (Grafen 1990a; Grafen 1990b). A great deal of research suggests that animal signals may often honestly advertise mate quality (Andersson 1994).

The theory of honest advertising may apply outside the sphere of sexual selection, and to learned as well as innate signals. Whenever signal producers and signal receivers have nonidentical interests, costly signals may be more honest signals. This applies to hostile transactions as much as to cooperative ones; thus Zahavi (1975) notes that males often use the same ornaments to intimidate other males that they do to woo females. And extravagant and costly signals may be used to signal commitment to a relationship as well as quality. Extravagant and wasteful displays are as much a feature of human cultures as they are of animal societies. The economically "irrational" aspects of ritual and display that have attracted so much attention from social scientists may be in part a predictable and individually optimal result of signal selection acting on cultural variation.

Indirect Benefits: Good Genes

Heritable viability and fecundity. In many species, males probably differ little in their direct mate value to females, because securing enough sperm for fertilization is not a problem for females, and because males give nothing in the way of parental care. Yet in such species there are commonly strong female mate preferences, and males commonly display exaggerated secondary sexual characteristics as a result of female choice (see, for example, Borgia 1986; Bradbury and Gibson 1983). Why should females be choosy in a world of uniformly improvident males? One possible explanation is that males differ in their genetic quality—a female may give her offspring a better chance of surviving and reproducing by picking a mate with good genes. "Good genes" mate choice might also be involved in extra-pair copulations in populations in which males and females pair off to raise offspring but females sometimes cuckold their mates.

There are several difficulties with this superficially attractive idea. One is that there is a potential circularity in the definition of good genes. If females in a population prefer males with long tails then genes for long tails will be "good genes" simply by virtue of the fact that males with these genes will attract more mates. The potential positive feedback between genes for traits and genes for choices will be discussed below under Heritable Attractiveness: The "Runaway" Effect.

Another difficulty is that there is no point in trying to avoid potential mates with bad genes if nobody has bad genes, and quantitative genetic theory suggests that natural selection should be very efficient at weeding out bad genes. Except under special circumstances, reviewed below, there may be considerable variation in fitness, but there should be little *heritable* variation in fitness (Reeve and Smith 1990). Suppose there is an aerodynamically optimal tail length. Let us begin by assuming that tail length in some species of bird is under pure genetic control, that genes interact additively (e.g., there is no dominance or recessiveness), that there is no pleiotropy (tail length genes do not affect other characters), that the optimal tail length varies little over time and space, and that mutations affecting tail length are rare. Under these circumstances, tail length will evolve to an equilibrium value (or values, if there are frequency dependent effects) at which all individuals will have equal fitnesses, and there is no point in choosing a mate on the basis of tail length.

Suppose we relax the assumption that tail length is under pure genetic control, and allow that environment may affect tail length. Under these circumstances, tail length may vary, and there may be differences in *direct* mate value related to tail length, if, for example, poorly nourished individuals have shorter tails, but there will still be no heritable variation in tail length, and no "good genes" advantage to choosing a short-tailed mate. If we relax the assumption about pleiotropy, and assume, for example, that genes for long tails have some negative side effects, then there may be heritable variation in tail length at equilibrium, but there will be no heritable variation in *fitness,* since the adaptive advantages of choosing a long-tailed mate will be canceled out by the adaptive disadvantages of the side effects. If we relax the assumption about additivity, then there may be genetic differences in fitness, but these differences will not be heritable, since they will depend, not on the possession of particular genes, but on the possession of particular gene combinations which will be broken up by meiosis.

Some authors have been led by this line of reasoning to strong skepticism about the idea of mate choice for "good genes." Perhaps mate choice has some non-obvious direct benefit—for example, fertility backup or avoidance of venereal disease—even in those species in which males provide no parental care (Taylor and Williams 1982; Balmford and Read 1991; Sheldon 1994).

However, another line of argument suggests that natural populations may have significant heritable fitness variation as a result either of arms races with other species (especially parasites) which never reach equilibrium, or of mutation, or of constant changes in the physical environment. Heritable variation in fitness can persist indefinitely if the fitness of an organism is positively correlated with the fitness of its offspring, but negatively correlated with the fitness of more remote descendants—in other words, if success breeds success in the short run, but failure in the long run. A great deal of attention has been focused lately on the possibility that coevolutionary "arms races" between parasites and hosts may maintain the heritable variation necessary for "good genes" sexual selection (Hamilton and Zuk 1982; Hamilton and Axelrod 1990). Suppose that parasites are biologically specialized for infesting hosts with common genotypes, and less well adapted to attack rare-genotype hosts. In this case, hosts with common genotypes will decline in number, and those with rare genotypes will increase. This in turn will put selection pressure on parasites to improve their adaptations for dealing with once-rare-now-common host genotypes. Under a wide range of parameter values, the result will not be an equilibrium point, but a cycle in which host and parasite gene frequencies are constantly changing (Hamilton and Axelrod 1990).

This version of the "good genes" theory was proposed by Hamilton and Zuk (1982), and they and other researchers have presented a variety of supporting evidence. One prediction of the Hamilton-Zuk theory is that sexual ornaments should be more developed in populations where average levels of parasite infestation are high. This prediction has been tested in 109 North American passerine bird species (Hamilton and Zuk 1982), 526 neotropical bird species (Zuk 1991), and 113 European passerine species (Read 1987), with positive although not always significant results. Another prediction is that within populations, individuals with heavier parasite loads should have less showy ornaments, and be less attractive to members of the other sex. Again, a number of studies have produced generally positive results. Finally, the Hamilton-Zuk theory predicts that when females are allowed to choose their mates, their offspring will enjoy higher fitnesses than the offspring of females given no such choice. Research to date gives some, although not overwhelming support to this prediction (see *American Zoologist* 1990, 30(2), a special issue on parasites and sexual selection).

Mutation provides another possible source of heritable variation in fitness. Until recently the conventional wisdom held that, although mutation might be the ultimate source of the variation needed for natural selection, it was not an important cause of change in gene frequency in its own right. The measured rates of mutation for genes of visible phenotypic effect is so low, typically 10^{-6} per gene per generation, or lower, that mutation was presumed to contribute little to trait variance. However, complex traits like fitness and mate value are bound to be affected by mutations at a huge number of loci. Furthermore, improved techniques for measuring mutation suggest that for every mutation with an easily detectable phenotypic effect there are dozens or hundreds more with weak phenotypic effects. The total effect of such mutations may be considerable, even if their individual effects are minute. A number of experiments with captive populations suggest that in the absence of natural selection, genetic load resulting from the accumulation of deleterious mutations can increase rapidly (Kondrashov 1988; Pomiankowski et al. 1991; Lande 1975; Partridge and Barton 1993; Houle and Hoffmaster 1992).

Finally, although this possibility has been less studied, changes in the physical environment of a population may occur frequently enough to produce heritable variation in fitness even in the absence of host-parasite coevolutionary "arms races." Endler's review of the literature on natural selection in the wild indicates that "the frequent statement that selection is usually weak in natural populations is without merit.... Selection coefficients ... above 0.1 are quite common.... Selection differentials can be as high as in animal and plant breeding experiments" (Endler 1986:222). More work needs to be done to integrate the abundant literature on natural selection in the wild reviewed by Endler with studies of mate choice.

Much of the evidence that has been cited in support of the Hamilton-Zuk hypothesis is also consistent with other hypotheses; for example, one might expect that organisms carrying a high genetic load would be especially vulnerable to parasites regardless of whether that load was a product of coevolutionary cycles between parasite and host or of accumulated mutations or of changes in the physical environment. So more research is needed to determine both the level and the sources of heritable variation in fitness. Evidence for substantial heritable variation in fitness in natural populations would affect our view of the evolutionary process in many ways. The implicit assumption of many treatments of evolution is that most populations most of the time are at equilibrium. The Hamilton-Zuk theory, the mutational theory and the literature reviewed by Endler suggest a more dynamic, nonequilibrium view—less Olympian and more Sisyphean—in which populations are constantly scaling adaptive peaks without ever getting to the top.

Heritable attractiveness: the "runaway" effect. Runaway sexual selection is a version of "good genes" sexual selection, but it is enough of a special case that it deserves separate treatment. I will introduce the concept of runaway sexual selection by way of a comparison with what may be a more familiar phenomenon: "speculative booms" in market economies. Speculative booms are a form of self-fulfilling prophecy. They begin when speculators buy a product in the hope of being able to resell it for a higher price. Let enough such speculation take place, and the price of the product will indeed increase, encouraging more speculation, and further price increases. The resulting spiral may push the price of the product well above what would be expected simply on the basis of the product's real value in consumption and production.

The Dutch tulip craze of the 1630s, which pushed the price of some bulbs as high as $50,000 (measured at today's gold exchange rates) is perhaps the most famous example of an alleged speculative boom (cf. Garber 1989 for an alternative interpretation of "Tulipmania"). More recent candidates include the stock market bubbles of 1929 and 1987, and the overheated real estate market of the 1980s. In real world markets it is difficult to prove that a particular price bubble represents a genuine speculative boom, because it is difficult to be sure what the "real" (nonspeculative) price of a product should be (Hedrick and Flood 1990). However, speculative booms also occur in "experimental economies" when researchers pay experimental subjects to play artificial markets in which nonspeculative exchange values *are* known (Smith and Suchanek 1988).

Runaway sexual selection is a genetic version of a speculative boom. I have already discussed how mate choice can influence both offspring *number* (direct benefits) and offspring *viability* (indirect benefits via good genes). However mate choice can also influence offspring *mating success* via its effects on offspring attractiveness. If long-tailed males are especially attractive to females then a female with an especially strong preference for long tails may have more second generation descendants than average, because she is likely to choose especially long-tailed mates, and thus to produce especially long-tailed sons (assuming that tail length is heritable), who are likely to have more offspring than average (given the existing preference for long-tailed mates) (Fisher 1958). This has been called the "sexy son" effect (Weatherhead and Robertson 1979) and it will produce an increase in the frequency of trait-preference genes if there is any genetic basis to female preferences. The result will be mutually reinforcing increases in male tail lengths and female preferences for long tails. Both speculative booms and runaway sexual selection involve a positive feedback between traits and preferences. Just as speculators who bet on the future popularity of a stock may raise both the price and the popularity of the stock, members of an operationally scarce sex who bet on the attractiveness of a given trait in the course of mate choice may increase both the average levels of the trait and (by increasing the frequency of trait-preference genes) its attractiveness.

Runaway sexual selection can also be regarded as a kind of "selfish gene" effect, in which a gene spreads because it leads organisms carrying it to help other carriers. Males with long tails are more likely than average males to have had (1) fathers with long tails and (2) mothers attracted to males with long tails, and are thus more likely to have inherited both genes for long tails and genes for preferring long tails. This means that females who choose long-tailed mates, who are more likely than average to be carrying genes for preference for long tails, are giving an extra boost to the replication of genes for long tail preference carried by those mates. (Readers may recognize this as a version of the "green beard" effect; Richard Dawkins [1987:199-212] presents this interpretation of the runaway theory at greater length.)

The theory of runaway sexual selection was initially proposed by R. A. Fisher, one of the first biologists to look for an adaptive explanation for mate preferences rather than simply taking them as given. He presented a verbal argument that runaway sexual selection could lead to exponential increases in traits and trait preferences (Fisher 1958). Since that time a number of mathematical models have confirmed that runaway exaggeration of sexually selected traits is possible (Kirkpatrick and Price 1990; Lande 1981; O'Donald 1980; Pomiankowski 1987). The possibility of runaway sexual selection is thus not just an artifact of particular modeling assumptions.

Granted that episodes of runaway sexual selection can get started, how do they end? Sexual selection can push trait measures away from their ecological optima, but can it keep them away indefinitely, or do episodes of runaway sexual selection follow the same boom-and-bust cycle as speculative bubbles? This issue is not completely settled. Below I summarize some results to date, but conclusions should be treated as provisional.

Early models suggested a range of possible outcomes to episodes of runaway sexual selection. In Lande's (1981), Kirkpatrick and Price's (1990) and O'Donald's (1980) models, viability selection pushes traits toward ecologically optimal dimensions while sexual selection pushes them toward extravagance, and there is a whole range of possible equilibria at which these two forces are in balance. In these models sexual selection may result in wildly exaggerated male traits maintained by strong female preferences, or weakly exaggerated male traits maintained by weak female preferences, or some intermediate combination; the particular stable combination of trait preferences and trait values attained will depend on initial conditions.

This conclusion, that the balance struck between sexual selection and viability selection is largely a matter of historical accident, has been undermined by a series of recent papers by Andrew Pomiankowski and coworkers (Iwasa and Pomiankowski 1991; Pomiankowski 1987a, 1987b; Pomiankowski et al. 1991). Earlier models assumed that there was no direct cost to mate choice, although females choosing mates with exaggerated traits would lose indirectly, by having less viable offspring. More realistically, however, exercising mate choice rather than mating at random is sure to involve some cost in time, energy, and risk of predation, infection and harassment, as discussed above, and documented in Pomiankowski (1987a). When such direct costs of mate choice are incorporated into models of sexual selection, the range of equilibria reported in previous models collapses to a single point. Episodes of runaway sexual selection begin in Pomiankowski's model as in the other models with a mutually reinforcing increase in traits and preferences. As in other models the runaway eventually comes to an end, but in contrast to other models the initial boom is followed by collapse; in the long run the only stable state is one in which the trait and the preferred value of the trait are at the ecological optimum.

These results suggest that, as long as there are costs to mate choice, runaway sexual selection can lead only to passing "boom-and-bust" episodes of character exaggeration. However, more recent work (Pomiankowski et al. 1991) offers a loophole if mutations affecting sexually selected traits are "biased." Models of sexual selection (and selection in general) which incorporate a mutation term often assume that mutation is unbiased on average—changing the *variance* of a trait but not its *mean*. But biased mutation is likely when traits are costly or complex, because random changes in physiological functioning are more likely to degrade costly or complex traits than to exaggerate them (see Pomiankowski et al. 1991 for a review). And as long as mutations act, on average, to erode a trait, sexual selection can favor stable preferences for exaggerated versions of that trait even when there are direct and indirect costs to mate choice.

Current models of runaway sexual selection thus suggest several likely patterns. First, runaway sexual selection may result in transient "boom-and-bust" episodes, in which initial modest trait preferences resulting from sensory bias, genetic drift or handicap selection are first amplified and then collapse. Second, runaway sexual selection may result in enduring preferences for any traits that are subject to mutational erosion in their exaggerated form.

The theory of runaway sexual selection has been severely criticized by many biologists who argue that sexually selected traits are overwhelmingly viability markers. (See the volume by Bradbury and Andersson [1987] for both defense and criticism of the runaway theory.) Partly these criticisms are based on the growing body of theory and evidence which supports the viability marker theory for many traits. But partly the criticisms are based on a feeling that appeals to runaway sexual selection, whatever their theoretical merits, are methodologically suspect. The theory that sexually selected traits have evolved as signals of viability predicts that such traits should be well designed to advertise relevant aspects of quality. If selecting parasite-free mates, or faithful mates, or fertile mates is an important adaptive problem, then sexually selected traits should honestly advertise these qualities. By contrast, the theory that female A selects a mate with more of trait X in order to have a son with more of trait X who will be chosen by females B, C and D, in order that their sons will have more of trait X, and so on, seems to make virtually no concrete predictions about what trait X will look like. Alan Grafen puts this criticism of runaway theories forcefully: "To believe in the Fisher-Lande [runaway] process as an explanation of sexual selection without abundant proof is methodologically wicked" (Grafen 1990).

Because the runaway theory offers little guidance concerning which traits are likely to be affected by sexual selection and how, testing the theory is likely to require quantitative genetic evidence regarding correlations between female preferences and male traits. Several recent studies involving insects and fish provide evidence that males with exaggerated sexually selected features are likely to have both sons with exaggerated features, and daughters with a preference for such features (Pomiankowski and Sheridan 1994). These experiments are consistent with runaway sexual selection. Further research will determine whether alternative explanations can be ruled out.

Sensory Bias

Mate preferences may show nonadaptive "esthetic" biases as a by-product of the way animals' perceptual systems are wired. I will give just a few examples here; Ryan (1990) reviews many others.

Male tungara frogs (*Physalaemus pustulosus*) attract females by calling. Their calls consist of a chuck portion and a whine portion, and synthetic calls that omit the chuck are less attractive. Males of other species in the same genus produce calls consisting of whines only. However females of these other species are actually more attracted to *pustulosus*-type calls containing chucks! Such a preference cannot be adaptive in their current environments since females are never exposed to calls with chucks. Is it possible that the ancestors of non-*pustulosus* males produced calls with chucks and that current female preferences are an evolutionary vestige? Probably not, according to Ryan et al. (1990). *P. pustulosus* apparently split off from other members of its genus only recently; it is far more likely that males in one species (*P. pustulosus*) added a chuck to their repertoire than that males of a number of different species independently and in parallel dropped the chuck. In other words, it is likely that *P. pustulosus* males have recently hit upon the chuck to exploit a preexisting female sensory bias.

Nancy Burley (1986) stumbled onto another case of sensory bias. She put colored bands on the legs of zebra finches she studied, for purposes of identification, and discovered that these bands influenced mate choice. Females were especially attracted to males with a great deal of red and orange in their leg bands, and especially averse to males with a great deal of green. Males were especially attracted to females with black leg bands. Further experimentation showed that a red or white "hat" glued to a male's head made him more attractive, while a yellow, blue or especially green hat made him less attractive. Attractive individuals mated earlier than unattractive ones, and had more extra-pair copulations, while the mates of attractive birds worked harder and had a higher mortality rate.

It is important to note that while mate preferences in these cases are possibly (for Ryan's frogs) or certainly (for Burley's finches) not adaptations, they are nonetheless explicable as by-products of adaptation. For example, the attraction that female zebra finches show to red leg bands and red hats is probably a result of a general attraction to red. Male zebra finches have red beaks and orange cheek patches which probably advertise their health; healthy males in many bird species advertise their condition by producing extra red and orange carotenoid pigments (Zuk 1992; Hill 1990; Hill 1991). The aversion to green is an aversion to a color that to the finch visual system, as to the human, is the opposite of red.

It seems likely that adaptations for complex perceptual discriminations will commonly have nonadaptive biases built into them, and I have followed West-Eberhard (1991) in putting "sensory bias" on an equal footing with adaptive varieties of sexual selection. But in many other treatments of sexual selection, sensory bias is largely ignored. There are probably several reasons for this. First, many evolutionary biologists are strongly committed to adaptationism, and resistant to the idea that organisms may often fail to maximize their inclusive fitnesses. Second, the mathematical tools most often used to model sexual selection—optimization theory and quantitative genetics—make it difficult to incorporate sensory bias except in a *post hoc,* theoretically unmotivated fashion. All of the models of sexual selection that I have reviewed so far assume that organisms are choosing between mates that vary in a simple one-dimensional trait such as tail length, which is perceived with 100% accuracy. These models obscure the complex information-processing that must be involved in real-world perceptual discrimination. But new modeling tools may make such complexity more tractable. The increasing availability of computer power has made it practical to supplement optimization and equilibrium theories of evolution with techniques like genetic algorithms and neural networks which simulate not just the end results but the dynamics of natural selection and trial-error learning.

Consider, for example, a recent simulation by Enquist and Arak (1993) which models the evolution of nonadaptive preferences as by-products of adaptation. The authors present a "neural network"—a simple computer model of a retina and nervous system—with a long-tailed shape representing a mate of the right species, with a short-tailed shape representing a mate of the wrong species, and with random shapes. They make small random changes in the network, and save those versions of the network that respond strongly to the right shapes and weakly to the wrong ones. By reiterating this trial-and-error process in a simulation of natural selection they produce a network that distinguishes almost perfectly between mates of the right species (presented in a variety of orientations) and other stimuli. However, there are a few shapes—especially shapes that present the distinguishing features of the correct stimulus in an exaggerated form—to which the network responds even more strongly than to the stimulus to which it was selected to respond! A further simulation shows that this nonadaptive sensory bias toward "supernormal stimuli" can persist, and result in the evolution of exaggerated traits, even when these traits carry a moderate fitness cost.

Williams (1992) gives a graphical version of a similar argument in a recent book, suggesting that preferences for exaggerated stimuli may be a nonadaptive by-product of *asymmetrical fitness functions.* For example, if reproductively immature males have shorter tails than mature males, then a female preference for males with longer than average tails may be adaptive if it leads females to avoid matings with juveniles—better to err on the long side than on the short. But as a by-product, females may show a nonadaptive preference for mature males with long tails over mature males with short or average tails. Given heritable variation in male tail length, the result over time will be the evolution of exaggerated male tail length through female choice.

Ethologists since the time of Tinbergen have been familiar with the phenomenon of the *supernormal stimulus*—animals often respond more strongly to an exaggerated version of a stimulus than to a normal one. Responsiveness to supernormal stimuli shows up in contexts where strict adaptationist explanations, like the handicap effect and runaway selection, are unlikely. Here sensory bias is the likely explanation, with adaptations for distinguishing between categories (edible/inedible, same species/other species) spilling over incidentally into sensory biases in favor of exaggerated stimuli within categories. Preferences for supernormal stimuli may result from learning as well as natural selection. Staddon (1975) notes that animals trained by reinforcement learning to show a response to a stimulus commonly show an even stronger response to a version of the stimulus that exaggerates its distinguishing features—a phenomenon called "peak shift." Ten Cate and Bateson (1989) note an analogous phenomenon in the case of imprinting.

Various authors have suggested that attention to novelty (the converse of habituation) may be another source of sensory bias. (See West-Eberhard 1983, as well as Hartshorne 1956, for an application of the argument to the evolution of bird song.) Animal suitors, like human advertisers, will often find that they can exploit potential customers' attentiveness to novel stimuli for their own ends. Ryan (1990) argues that preferences for supernormal and novel stimuli both exemplify the same phenomenon—preference for greater sensory stimulation, which is a by-product of mechanisms adapted to distinguish relevant signals from background noise.

On a theoretical level, information processing considerations suggest that perfect perceptual systems are no more likely to exist than computers that play a perfect game of chess. At a practical level, there are numerous cases in the natural history literature of cross-species exploitation of sensory biases by predators and parasites. These cases, for which adaptive explanations like the handicap effect and runaway selection can often be ruled out, argue that dishonest advertising is likely to be prevalent within species as well. That there is selection for detecting dishonest advertisements does not mean that such advertisements will never succeed, but only that when they succeed they will probably be sophisticated, or of low cost to the receiver, or of recent evolutionary origin.

Furthermore, what starts out as a dishonest advertisement exploiting the sensory biases of others may turn into an honest advertisement when it becomes more common. The first mammal to display piloerection (hair standing on end) in a confrontation may have won by fooling her opponent about her size. But in a population where all organisms display piloerection, nobody will be fooled by the display and everybody will make an accurate estimate of the size of opponents.

Learning, Imitation and the Proximate Bases of Physical Attraction
Evolutionary biologists commonly distinguish between "proximate causes" (how genes and environments interact to produce phenotypes) and "ultimate causes" (why organisms have the genes they do rather than some other genes). Up to this point this chapter has been concerned with ultimate causes, with the *evolution* rather than the *individual development* of standards of physical attractiveness. However, in many organisms, including humans, standards of physical attractiveness are influenced by learning and imitation, and these proximate bases of attraction need to be considered as well.

Innateness, imprinting and reversible learning. Learning theory in psychology has gone through a massive theoretical shift in the last generation, with the collapse of behaviorism, and the rise of more evolutionarily oriented theories. In behaviorist theory, the contribution of evolution to learning was to make certain stimuli innately reinforcing (e.g. sugar, genital contact), and to produce a limited number of unlearned pairings between stimulus and response (e.g. between food in the mouth and salivation). With these modest innate foundations, animals could be taught to "emit" virtually any physically possible behavior ("operant") in response to virtually any reinforcer (operant conditioning), and to associate virtually any perceptible conditioned stimulus with virtually any unconditioned stimulus (respondent, or Pavlovian, conditioning).

There is now overwhelming evidence, however, that organisms learn some stimulus-operant and stimulus-stimulus associations much more readily than others, because "selection acts to favor those individuals that possess the least costly learning abilities permitting successful reproduction in the environment in which the population is evolving. Nothing is gained, and much may be lost, by an individual that possesses ecologically surplus learning abilities" (Johnston 1982:96). In Edward O. Wilson's words, "the process of learning is not a basic trait that gradually emerges with the evolution of larger brain size. Rather it is a diverse array of particular behavioral adaptations" (Wilson 1975:156). In other words, mate-choice learning mechanisms are likely to be complex, to differ adaptively between sexes and between species, and to operate differently from food-choice and other learning mechanisms.

One form of "prepared learning" that has been extensively studied in relation to mate choice is sexual imprinting (reviewed in Immelman 1972). Early experience during a juvenile "sensitive period" commonly has irreversible effects on adult mate choice. Imprinting is not universal; for example male ducks learn to court females of their own species by imprinting on their mothers, while female ducks choose males of the right species with no learning. Imprinting is often guided by innate templates; for example, while zebra finches exposed only to bullfinches between 13 and 40 days of age will reach adulthood with an irreversible preference for bullfinches as sexual partners as adults, zebra finches exposed to both bullfinches and zebra finches during their sensitive period will grow up to prefer zebra finches.

Imprinting may be generally adapted to track intermediate frequencies of environmental change. When the environment changes little on an evolutionary time scale, organisms will adapt via "hard-wired" innate responses, and when the environment changes frequently over the course of one individual's lifespan, organisms will adapt via reversible learning. An innate template which can be overridden by imprinting if nothing in the local environment exactly fits may be adaptive in species whose members share an overall similarity in morphology, but in which microevolution often pushes traits in local populations a standard deviation or so away from the species average.

Copying and informational cascades. Adaptation is costly. Natural selection shapes adaptive behavior through death and reproductive failure. Individual reinforcement learning shapes adaptive behavior through less costly, but still painful, trial and error. Learning through imitation may avoid some of this pain, but it carries its own costs. Both sensory bias and learning through imitation result from constraints on information. Sensory bias occurs when internal constraints on information processing result in imperfect discrimination. And copying may be an adaptation to environments in which an animal's own experiences are likely to misinform it about the real payoff structure.

Copying of mate choice may be common in birds and mammals with "leks." Leks are small areas where males gather to establish territories and display, and females arrive to select mates. After mating, females go elsewhere to raise the resulting offspring without male assistance (Bradbury and Gibson 1983). There is commonly a strong degree of female agreement about which males are desirable and which undesirable. Male physical characteristics and territory location explain some of this agreement, but recent evidence suggests that females are also copying other females.

The study of female copying in mate choice is still relatively new, and many studies showing correlated female choice are more suggestive than conclusive since they do not rule out other explanations—for instance, that being chosen by one female changes a male's behavior in ways that make him more attractive to other females. Probably the most thorough study of copying to date is Dugatkin's on the Trinidadian guppy (*Poecilia reticulata*). Female guppies choose males more often when those males have artificial models of females nearby (or had them nearby on previous trials), and this preference isn't a result of changes in male behavior, preferences for specific sites, or "schooling" with other females (Dugatkin 1992). Studies of deer and black grouse have shown that females are more attracted to males whom they observe mating with other females. With the grouse, this greater attraction persists even after the other females leave the male's territory, so females are not simply seeking out the company of other females (Pruett-Jones 1992).

There are likely to be costs to copying the choices of other females. In some lekking species, females choosing popular males must wait their turn before mating, and are subject to harassment from less popular males. This raises the question of what (if anything) females are getting out of copying. Gibson and Höglund (1992) note that copying can either reduce the costs of mate choice or raise its benefits by improving discrimination. Three economists (Bikchanandi et al. 1992) have recently taken up the topic. They assume that a series of females arrives sequentially to choose mates. A female can inspect potential mates and make her choice accordingly, or she can copy the choices of earlier arrivals. If individual experience is an imperfect guide to mate quality, then a female will be better off with a non-zero probability of copying the choices of others, even when others' choices contradict her own experience. Bikchanandi et al. show that if it is optimal for the nth female to copy regardless of her own experience, then it will be optimal for all subsequent females to copy. The result is an "informational cascade," in which the choices of the earliest arriving females eventually lead all subsequently arriving females to choose one male. In the model there is a fairly high probability that this cascade will settle on the wrong male; when individuals strike an individually optimal payoff between learning on their own and copying others there is only a modest improvement over individual learning alone. The individually optimal mix of trial and error learning and copying is not the socially optimal mix; individuals that copy are "free-riding" on non-copiers, with the result that at the population level the net gains from copying are modest. Rogers (1988) comes to a similar conclusion in his model of individual learning versus cultural transmission. An old saying has it that "Fifty million Frenchmen can't be wrong," but models of copying and informational cascades suggest that the probability of fifty million Frenchmen being wrong is only moderately smaller than the probability of one Frenchman being wrong.

Bikchanandi et al. note that informational cascades are likely to be fragile. Let even a few nonconformists break with the norm established by a cascade and, if they suffer no apparent ill effects, the whole cascade may collapse. This means that incorrect cascades may not be locked into place for all time. But in a changing environment with imperfect information there will still be a fair chance that the norm of the moment is off-track.

Wade and Pruett-Jones (1990) demonstrate that one of the consequences of copying is to raise the variance in male reproductive success beyond what it would be if females were simply reliably discriminating between high and low quality males.

So far studies of mate choice and copying have focused on copying of preferences for individuals rather than preferences for traits, although it is the latter that is most relevant to the study of physical attraction, particularly in species where male parental care limits polygyny.

SEXUAL SELECTION AND MACROEVOLUTION

The theory of speciation was a central topic in the revolution in evolutionary theory known as the Modern Synthesis, the revolution that united Darwin's theory of natural selection and Mendel's gene theory. Two of the classic works of the Modern Synthesis, Dobzhansky's *Genetics and the Origin of Species* (1937) and Mayr's *Animal Species and Evolution* (1963), feature speciation in title and text. The founders of the Modern Synthesis paid particular attention to the problem of speciation because earlier critics of the theory of natural selection like Bateson and Goldschmidt often argued that while natural selection might account for variation within species, other processes must be involved in the production of new species.

In the view of Dobzhansky and Mayr, species (at least among sexual organisms) are defined by reproductive isolation —two populations belong to different species if they are unable or unlikely to interbreed when inhabiting the same geographic area. Dobzhansky and Mayr divide reproductive isolating mechanisms into pre-mating (those that prevent mating between species) and post-mating (those that prevent fertilization or survival or reproduction of hybrid offspring, assuming that mating takes place.) In principle, this definition of species (the Biological Species Concept) decouples speciation from ecological adaptation. Whether or not two populations belong to the same species has no necessary relationship to their overall morphological similarity or degree of ecological divergence. And in fact many cases are known of polytypic species whose members have different morphologies and occupy different ecological niches in different parts of their range, while there are many other cases where populations that are morphologically and ecologically almost indistinguishable are assigned to different species by virtue of differences in mating habits that ensure reproductive isolation (so-called sibling species).

Since the biological species concept makes speciation partly a matter of mate choice, the theory of sexual selection should have occupied a prominent role in the Modern Synthesis. Curiously, however, the topic was relatively neglected. As late as 1972, when a volume was published to commemorate the centenary of *The Descent of Man, and Selection in Relation to Sex,* many contributors were skeptical about the importance of sexual selection (Campbell 1972). But the advent of sociobiology brought a renewed focus on sexual selection in the 1970s, and a variety of work appeared arguing for the importance of sexual selection in speciation (Lande 1981; West-Eberhard 1983).

The review of the origins of mate preferences above suggests a number of processes that might lead to rapid divergence in sexual signals between populations. Runaway sexual selection may turn small differences between populations in sexually selected traits and trait preferences into immense differences. The evolution of male signals that exploit female sensory biases may lead to counter-adaptations in female signal discrimination which have new biases open to exploitation. There may be sensory biases toward novelty *per se*. And in species dependent on social learning, copying the mate choices of others may result in nonadaptive informational cascades with potential selective consequences. West-Eberhard (1983) argues that for these reasons sexual (and other social) signals are likely to diverge rapidly, leading eventually to speciation, even when ecological differentiation is modest. Lande (1981) backs up this argument mathematically with a model of speciation resulting from runaway sexual selection.

Divergent sexual selection is suspected as a cause of high rates of speciation in several groups of organisms. Anuran frogs have a more complex auditory neuroanatomy than other frogs, which allows them to make more sophisticated acoustical distinctions. Their mating calls are more elaborate than those of other frogs and they have higher rates of speciation, apparently as a result of rapid divergence in species-typical mating calls (Ryan 1986). Oscine birds (songbirds) have an anatomical specialization, the syrinx, that allows them to produce particularly elaborate songs. Oscines have high rates of speciation, probably at least in part as a result of rapid song divergence between populations (Fitzpatrick 1988; Raikow 1986).

Divergent signal selection may also be important in primate macroevolution. In a recent review of primate differentiation, Groves (1989) identifies two common patterns. On the one hand, among groups of related species or subspecies that occupy a variety of habitat types—for example baboons—differentiation between species or subspecies is generally the result of adaptation to differences in habitat. On the other hand, among related species or subspecies occupying a single habitat type, differentiation is apparently less related to ecological differences. Instead, these groups commonly conform to a "centrifugal" pattern, in which populations at the center of the geographic distribution evolve more quickly, while more peripheral populations evolve more slowly and are closer to ancestral character states. The result is that populations at opposite ends of a distribution are often more similar to each other, because they share ancestral traits, than they are to central populations (Brown 1957).

Groves seems to be unaware of the work of West-Eberhard and others on differentiation through divergent sexual selection. He appeals to orthogenetic laws to explain differentiation in the absence of habitat differences. However, in many of the cases of centrifugal speciation (and subspeciation) that Groves cites, the chief characters distinguishing populations are almost certainly social signals (e.g. guenons; see Kingdon 1980). The most plausible explanation for this pattern is disruptive signal selection (including sexual selection), with populations in the center of a group's distribution changing signals more rapidly, perhaps partly as a result of more intense social competition.

SEXUAL SELECTION AND HUMAN EVOLUTION

Signal Selection and Human Differentiation
In the remaining chapters of this work, the evolutionary focus will largely be a focus on *microevolution,* on showing how mechanisms of mate choice may have been affected directly or indirectly by natural selection. But here I will briefly consider some of the *macroevolutionary* issues which the study of physical attractiveness raises for physical anthropology. Darwin believed that "of all the causes which have led to the differences in external appearance between the races of man . . . sexual selection has been by far the most efficient" (Darwin 1981[1871]:384). Some of the population differences that Darwin cited in support of this view, like differences in the form of scalp hair and in the distribution and abundance of face and body hair, seem comparable to signal differences in other primate species, and may very well result from disruptive sexual selection (or other forms of signal selection). On the whole, however, humans seem to fit better the pattern of groups like baboons in which population differences in morphology are largely adaptations to habitat differences. Differences in skin color seem to be largely adaptations to differing intensities of ultraviolet radiation (Harrison et al. 1988), differences in body build and nose form largely adaptations to different temperature and humidity regimes (Ruff 1991; Weiner 1954), differences in jaws and teeth largely adaptations to different diets (Rosenberg et al. 1987).

Thus despite tremendous morphological variation, all living human populations undoubtedly belong to a single reproductively integrated species. Mating signals and standards of sexual attractiveness have not diverged to the point of making cross-population mating impossible or even unlikely. I will discuss several possible explanations of why it is that the expansion of humans from one corner of Africa to the farthest reaches of the globe has resulted in morphological differentiation but not in speciation.

Lack of time or lack of isolation. A number of lines of evidence suggest that human population differentiation is fairly superficial (Cavalli-Sforza et al. 1988; Howells 1989; Nei and Roychoudhury 1982; Turner 1986). Eighty-five percent of protein polymorphism in the human species is within-population variation, only 5% is variation between populations of geographic races, and only 10% is variation between races. One interpretation of these results is that the ancestors of modern humans left Africa only in the last 100,000 years or so, replacing Neanderthals and other extra-African groups with little or no admixture. In this scenario, disruptive signal selection might have proceeded far enough in regional populations descended from *Homo erectus* to make interbreeding unlikely between African emigrants and groups like Neanderthals. But after the success of modern *Homo sapiens* there may simply not have been enough time for disruptive signal selection to produce more than slight differentiation between populations. Another possibility is that human population differentiation has been kept at relatively low levels by strong interregional gene flow.

Weakness of disruptive sexual selection. Natural selection has managed to produce considerable morphological differentiation between regional populations of our species, so the lack-of-time and lack-of-isolation arguments cannot be the complete explanation for why modern *Homo sapiens* remains a single reproductively integrated species. Another factor may be that the potential for disruptive sexual selection is reduced in typical human mating systems. As I discuss in Chapter 1, factors like monogamy and arranged marriages may limit the potential for sexual selection in our species. Furthermore, as I will document in subsequent chapters, criteria of physical attractiveness apparently include markers of age and health that probably operate similarly across populations, so that to the extent that sexual selection does occur in our species it may not be strongly disruptive.

Disruptive sexual selection without genetic divergence. Finally, when disruptive sexual selection does take place in human populations, it may not have the same evolutionary consequences that it does in some other species, because of the role of social learning. Social learning may be important both in the acquisition of standards of physical attractiveness and in the development of techniques of adornment. Darwin's account of sexual selection in humans is full of accounts of extravagant and costly adornments which members of different populations find attractive—filed teeth, lip plugs, tattoos, and so on—and modern accounts by cultural anthropologists provide many other examples (Polhemus 1988). Such exaggerated displays may have the same ultimate functions among humans as among other animals—the advertisement of physical condition and social position, the exploitation of the sensory biases of others—but their evolutionary consequences must be very different, since they are acquired adaptations, not genetic adaptations.

Perhaps the best nonhuman analogy for such adornment is found among bowerbirds (Borgia 1986). Male bowerbirds attract females by building elaborate "bowers" that they decorate with colorful objects. (They often steal these objects from the bowers of other males.) Females inspect the bowers of a number of males and mate with the male with the most elaborate and colorful bower. After mating, females build inconspicuous nests and brood their eggs on their own. There are several species of bowerbirds, and in those species that produce the most elaborate bowers males have the drabbest plumage. In other words, bower-building —part of the "extended phenotype" of the birds—has become a replacement for bright feathers. By the same token, human dependence on learned standards of attractiveness and artificial modification of phenotypes means that cultural divergence of sexual signals between populations may far outrun genetic divergence.

Sexual Selection and Physical Attractiveness: A Preview of Hypotheses

An evolutionary perspective on human behavior suggests that human beings, like members of other species, are likely to have adaptations for assessing the "mate value" of potential sexual partners, using visual and other cues, and that standards of physical attractiveness may reflect the operation of these adaptations. This does not imply that standards of physical attractiveness will always be unresponsive to environmental variation. Human beings are likely to have *both* relatively "canalized" or "hardwired" responses to visual stimuli that have been consistently associated with high mate value throughout human evolutionary history *and* relatively flexible learned responses to stimuli that have been associated sometimes with high mate value and sometimes with low. In other words, standards of physical attractiveness are likely to have both species-typical and population-specific components, and these components may be predictable given knowledge of human biology and local circumstances (Symons 1979). The remaining chapters of this work consider several likely clusters of criteria of physical attractiveness, both species-typical and population-specific.

1) *Species-typical criteria: age, sex and fecundity.* The shape of the curve of natural fertility versus age is remarkably constant over a wide range of noncontracepting populations, even though the absolute level of fertility varies tremendously. Fecundity is one component of mate value (along with potential parental investment and genetic quality), and one might expect that human beings would have a relatively invariant response to signs of age insofar as these are related to changing mate value via changing fecundity. (While potential for parental investment is also likely to change with age, it is less certain whether: (a) age of a potential mate is a better predictor of her PPI than her past performance, and (b) there is a robust, species-typical relationship between PPI and age, and consequently selection pressure for "canalized" response to age-related changes in PPI.)

Age, fecundity and attractiveness are the subject of Chapters 4 and 5.

2) *Species-typical criteria: health, symmetry, and averageness.* Levels of all three ultimate components of mate value—fecundity, potential for parental investment, and genetic quality—are likely to be lower, on average, among individuals in poor health. Signs of ill-health may vary to some extent between populations, but some characteristics, including asymmetry, and departure from average proportions, may be universal indicators of poor health and low mate value. These characteristics are the subject of Chapter 6.

3) *Population-specific criteria.* Changes in fecundity with age, and increases in fluctuating asymmetry, and dysmorphology as a result of genetic load, stress

and infection, are well studied areas of human biology, and obvious places to look for species-typical criteria of physical attractiveness. By contrast, the adaptive basis, if any, of population-specific standards of attractiveness is a more speculative topic. If natural selection favors different physical types in different environments, it will be adaptive for individuals to vary their standards of attractiveness accordingly. For example, fat stores may be selectively advantageous in environments subject to episodic food shortage, and disadvantageous in environments requiring considerable physical movement; one might expect that esthetic responses to fatness would vary among populations depending on social learning and on individual assessments of the consequences of being fat or thin, rather than developing in a uniform fashion within the human species. It might also be adaptive to adopt local standards of attractiveness insofar as attractiveness is heritable and attractive mates produce attractive children—the "sexy son" effect (Laland 1994). But more study is needed of ongoing natural selection and sexual selection in different populations to assess the importance of these forces.

Whatever their ultimate adaptive basis, population-specific standards of attractiveness may be influenced by correlations between social status and physical appearance; individuals may track local variation in the physical correlates of high mate value by giving extra weight to the appearance of high-status individuals in arriving at a standard of attractiveness. Chapter 7 uses evidence from multiracial societies to assess the impact of social status (among other factors) on somatic ideals.

CHAPTER 3

Five Populations

The study of physical attractiveness in relation to the theory of sexual selection is a relatively new field. In particular, there is little quantitative research on standards of attractiveness in non-Westernized populations. This chapter introduces an investigation of physical attractiveness across cultures which began in 1989 and continues today. Research to date embraces five populations: Brazilians, US Americans, Russians, Ache Indians, and Hiwi Indians. This selection of populations makes it possible to address topics sometimes slighted in the social psychology literature on attractiveness. The two indigenous South American populations are relatively isolated from the outside world, making it possible to test some potential universals of attractiveness. Brazil's stratified and racially mixed population makes it possible to examine physical attraction in relation to social status.

SITES AND ITINERARY

Brazilians

I have spent more time doing research in Brazil than in any other place. In this chapter I give a brief introduction to the cultural geography of Brazil; Chapter 7 covers race and attractiveness in Brazil at greater length.

Brazil is an amalgam of several cultural traditions occupying a particular place in the world political economy. In parts of Amazonian Brazil, American Indian influences are important; in much of Southern Brazil the influence of nineteenth and twentieth century immigration from Europe, the Middle East, and Japan has been overwhelming. But in the state of Bahia in the Brazilian Northeast (*nordeste*), the dominant cultural influences derive from Africa and Portugal. Until 1763 the colonial capital of Brazil was the city of Salvador (*Salvador da Bahia de Todos os Santos*), and during most of this time the economic heart of Brazil lay in the sugar-producing slave plantations of the Bahian coastal zone. Gilberto Freyre's (1964) account of the world the Brazilian slaves and slaveholders made is still unsurpassed, although his claims for the egalitarian and democratic character of Brazilian race relations are now generally viewed with some skepticism.

With successive economic booms from the eighteenth to the twentieth centuries—in mining, coffee growing, and industry—Brazil's economic center of gravity moved to the south, first to Rio de Janeiro and then to São Paulo. Slavery lingered on, not abolished until 1889, and the sugar plantations continue to employ a large share of Bahia's rural population, although mechanization in the last several decades has pushed many people off the land. But the fusion of Portuguese and African culture under conditions of radical inequality has left its mark on today's Bahia. In particular, Brazilian sexual culture is a contradictory hybrid of Mediterranean ideals of female honor and chastity and the African diaspora tradition of matrifocal households and female sexual and economic independence. The opposition between these traditions runs parallel to the opposition in Brazilian culture between the house (*casa*) and the street (*rua*). The *casa* is the domain of patrimonial authority and female propriety, the *rua* the domain of license, roguery and sexual transgression (*sacanagem*), with the latter finding its fullest expression during *Carnaval*. DaMatta (1990, especially pages 73–81) and Parker (1991) provide further discussion. The Bahian coastal zone in particular, memorialized in the novels of Jorge Amado, is renowned for its carnivalesque spirit, its sensuality and musicality.

However winning the friendliness, charm and exuberance of Bahians, these qualities must also be considered as survival and reproductive strategies forged under conditions of extreme inequality, in a society where personal ties, both within classes and to upper class patrons, can be a matter of life and death (see Scheper-Hughes 1992, especially pages 98–127.) The Brazilian economy has passed through a number of boom and bust cycles in the past five centuries. By the time of my fieldwork, the Brazilian economic "miracle" of the 1960s and 1970s and the political "opening" of the 1970s and 1980s had terminated in a morass of recession, hyperinflation, and corruption, and the air was heavy with economic and political pessimism.

I worked at three sites in Bahia in and around the city of Salvador:

1) The Federal University of Bahia (UFBA) is the leading university in Bahia, drawing students from throughout the state. UFBA has a number of campuses throughout Salvador. My research was carried out among students at the Philosophy Faculty (*Faculdade da Filosofia*). Students, who are majoring in philosophy, psychology and the social sciences, reside off campus and attend courses at the Faculty during the day. Students must pass a statewide exam, the *vestibular*, to be admitted to the school, and are generally aiming for master's or doctor's degrees. Most are of middle class background, and most give their ethnicity or race (*etnía, raça*) as mixed (*mestiça, parda*).

2) "Campo Alto" is the name used for the second of my Brazilian study sites, a lower class community (*favela*) in the northern suburbs of Salvador. Brazilian cities have experienced massive growth in the last several decades, driven by increases in population and by migration from the countryside. Large numbers of the destitute and homeless camp out in the center of Salvador, and much for-

merly vacant land in and around the city is now occupied by squatters. As a result, "suburb" (*subúrbio*) has a very different connotation in Brazil than in the US. The Salvadoran *subúrbio* (or *periferia*) is a zone of slum housing extending nearly 20 kilometers from the city center along the polluted western, bay side of the Salvadoran peninsula. Meanwhile, the apartment buildings, houses and shops of the middle class and rich extend along the eastern, oceanic side of the peninsula (the *orla marítima*) as far as the village of Arembepe. The social geography of the metropolitan area is represented in miniature in the main city bus station (*Terminal Lapa*), where buses bound for the *orla* leave from the sunny upper deck, while buses bound for the *subúrbio* depart from the gloomy, smog-choked deck below.

Campo Alto began as a squatter community, but by now most residents have traded in their plywood shacks for more substantial houses of brick and tile, to which they generally have legal title. Campo Alto is by no means the most desperate section of the *periferia*. While most residents are working class or without fixed employment, some hold down middle class jobs, and own consumer goods like cars and VCRs, and have remained in the community because of personal and family ties. But recent economic hard times in Brazil have taken their toll. A certain fraction of the young men in the Campo Alto have always had a reputation as "bad guys" (*malandros*), but until recently (or so I was told) they generally limited their assaults (from pickpocketing to armed robbery) to the wealthier parts of town. Many residents now say that economic problems and neighborhood crime have taken a turn for the worse in the last several years.

3) Arembepe is described at length in Kottak's *Assault on Paradise* (1992). When Kottak began working there in 1962, it was a relatively isolated fishing village. Since then, road connections with Salvador have been improved, and the town is now a two-hour bus trip from downtown Salvador. "Summer people" have rented or bought some of the nicer beach front property, and many residents (*Arembepeiros*) now live in two satellite communities outside of Arembepe proper. Arembepe never experienced the sharp class divisions of much of the rural *nordeste,* and there is less poverty, less obvious malnutrition, and far less violence than in Campo Alto. Many of the poorest members of the community live in the *Loteamento Luis Caetano,* a series of lots provided by the government. Interview subjects in Campo Alto frequently told me that they wanted to move somewhere else; when I brought up the subject with Arembepeiros, most of them told me they thought themselves fortunate to live in Arembepe.

In addition to the fieldwork at the three sites discussed above, I also did a brief pilot study, described in the next section, near the center of Salvador.

US Americans

Physical attractiveness in the United States has been the subject of an enormous number of studies (see Chapter 2). For reasons of convenience, the University of Michigan was an obvious choice for one site in my cross-cultural study.

Russians

My research in Russia was carried out at the Russian State University of the Humanities (*Rossiskii Gosudarstvennyi Gumanitarnyi Universitet*) in Moscow. Under Soviet rule the university was mainly devoted to training historical archivists; it is now transforming itself into a center for general research in the humanities. Students at the University at the time of my research were drawn from all over the former Soviet Union. Most were studying for the equivalent of master's degrees or doctorates and were in their early to mid-twenties. Most were of Russian or other Slavic nationality, but my sample included a large minority of Jews, ethnic Germans, and Central Asians.

I employed an interpreter for research in Russia.

Ache Indians

The Ache Indians of Paraguay are an isolated population of former hunter-gatherers who have been studied by anthropologists for more than twenty years. They are the subject of a forthcoming book by Kim Hill, on which I rely for much of the information in this section. At the time of first contact, which ranged from the 1960s to the 1970s for different bands, the Ache lived scattered over a wide area in the forests of eastern Paraguay. Since first contact they have settled in five communities—Puerto Barra, Ypetimi, Cerra Moroti, Chupa Pou, and Boijawa—and now spend less time as forest hunters. (Average time spent foraging in the forest outside the settlements was down to about 10% by 1990–1991.) By now all Ache have seen Paraguayan nationals and visiting foreigners, but the only outsiders whom the Ache are likely to see on a daily basis are a small number of missionaries and anthropologists.

According to a common stereotype in the anthropological literature (see, for example, Lee 1966), hunter-gatherers typically live in small nomadic bands with fluid membership. Male dominance, male-male violence, and polygyny are only weakly developed in comparison with horticulturalists and pastoralists. Corporate kin groups are also weak or absent, kinship tends to be bilateral, and postmarital residence flexible. Men may or may not do brideservice for their wives' families, but they do not pay bridewealth, or pay very little. A number of anthropologists question just how well this model, based on studies of just a few groups, especially the !Kung San of Namibia, really fits the majority of hunter-gatherers. Studies of other populations, such as Australian aborigines, archeological evidence (Binford 1980), and cross-cultural surveys (Ember 1983) all suggest a wide range of variation among hunter-gatherers. However, the Ache *do* conform closely to the classic hunter-gatherer model.

Both in the forest and in their settlements, the Ache lead fairly uninhibited sexual lives. Girls lose their virginity around the time of puberty, and choose their husbands without much parental interference. Divorce and extramarital intercourse are common; women have a mean of 11 husbands during the course of a lifetime, and women asked to name the possible fathers of their children name a mean of 1.97 men per child. (This figure refers to possible biological fathers (genitors), whom the Ache distinguish from fictive fathers).

I visited four Ache settlements in the course of my fieldwork, and collected data in the following three:

1) *Puerto Barra.* The smallest settlement, population about 50, is also the most isolated and least acculturated. The Puerto Barra Ache belong to a different division of the Ache (the Nyacunday) than most of the others in this study, and when they were first contacted in the early 1970s had had no contact with other Ache groups in living memory. A US missionary family (the Fosterwalds) in full-time residence at Puerto Barra has been particularly successful in protecting the Ache of Puerto Barra from outside encroachment, and they are in better shape economically than any other Ache group.

2) *Ypetimi.* More than other Ache groups the Ache at Ypetimi have tried to go it alone without outside help. Their current economic position is precarious. Ypetemi is home to many Southern (Ypety) Ache who feel some degree of separate identity from the majority Northern Ache. The population of Ypetimi numbers about 100.

3) *Chupa Pou.* Chupa Pou and Cerra Moroti are the two largest Ache communities, each with over 300 residents. In addition to hunting, they grow manioc and raise livestock. A Paraguayan Catholic missionary is in occasional residence, and tries to help the Ache in their dealings with the outside world. The central square in Chupa Pou is about 8 kilometers down a dirt road from a bus stop and a small general store.

Hiwi Indians

The Hiwi Indians of Venezuela, like the Ache, were isolated hunter-gatherers until recently. Hiwi (or Cuiva) social organization, however, presents a strong contrast with the Ache. The Hiwi practice preferential cross-cousin marriage. Marriages are long-lasting, extramarital intercourse probably infrequent, and relations between the sexes formal. The Hiwi fall on the restrictive end of the permissive/restrictive scale in their sexual attitudes.

Hiwi photographic ratings were carried out by Kim Hill. The number of raters is small, and results from the Hiwi accordingly need to be taken with caution, but I will show below that the Hiwi nevertheless seem to have a shared standard of attractiveness.

Itinerary

Research at the sites described above was carried out according to the following itinerary:

- Salvador, Brazil, June-August 1989: pilot study on physical attractiveness.

- Ann Arbor, Michigan, April-June 1990: interviews, measurements, photographs among university students.
- Eastern Paraguay, July-September 1990: interviews, measurements, photographs among Ache Indians in three communities.
- Salvador, Brazil, October 1990-July 1991: interviews, measurements, photographs among university students and urban lower class Brazilians.
- Ann Arbor, Michigan, October-December 1991: ratings of photographs among university students.
- Moscow, Russia, February 1992: ratings of photographs among university students.
- Arembepe, Brazil, May-July 1992: life history interviews and photographs in a rural community.

RESEARCH METHODS: PHOTOS AND INTERVIEWS

Quantitative data collection involved 1) taking photographs and measurements of subjects, and administering questionnaires or conducting interviews, 2) collecting judgments of the attractiveness of photographs and other research instruments, and 3) measuring positions of a series of facial landmarks with a computer scanner. Different methods of data analysis are discussed as needed in each chapter. This study was approved by the Human Subjects Committee of the University of Michigan.

Photography, Anthropometry, Questionnaires
The following photographic samples were collected in the course of research:
- Brazilian pilot study sample: 30 Salvadoran females, ages 17 to 25.
- US samples: 60 female and 35 male undergraduate students at the University of Michigan, Ann Arbor.
- Ache samples: 41 Ache females and 42 Ache males at Ypetimi and Chupa Pou settlements.
- Brazilian university samples: 51 female and 25 male post-secondary students at the Faculdade da Filosofia, Universidade Federal da Bahia.
- Arembepe sample: 102 female residents of Arembepe.

The method of recruitment of photographic subjects was different for each population sample. In the pilot study I positioned myself in several public places (Praça Dois de Julho—better known as Campo Grande; Praça da Piedade; the Barra shopping center and at the Barra beach). At each location I waited until a set time, and then approached the nearest female who seemed to be in her late teens or early twenties, avoiding women who seemed to be busy or in a hurry. I asked each woman if I could take her photograph, explaining that I was doing research on perceptions of physical variation in Brazil, and attempting to answer any questions she had. (My Portuguese was too limited at that point to give any very complicated explanation.) After taking each photograph I asked the subject her age, and recorded the circumstances and number (roll and frame) of the photograph. There was probably some bias toward physically unattractive subjects among those who declined; two women stated explicitly that they were too unattractive or unphotogenic to be photographed. Given the neighborhoods I worked in, there must also have been some bias toward upper class subjects (relative to the population of the city as a whole), but it is probably fair to say that the sample spans the whole range of physical types common in Salvador. I worked with an inexpensive camera, and under varied lighting conditions, with the result that 11 of my photographs were of low quality and had to be excluded from the final sample.

The data collection protocol for US, Ache, and Brazilian university photographic samples was more elaborate. Below I describe first the different procedures by which subjects were recruited in each population, then the standard data collection protocol used for each subject, then some of the special conditions that affected the protocol in each population.

During the 1990 Winter term at the University of Michigan I recruited students (32 females, 24 males) by making several announcements before a large introductory anthropology course. Would-be subjects signed up in class for appointments. During the spring and early summer I recruited more subjects (28 females, 11 males) by posting flyers around campus. In each case, subjects were offered $6.00 for 40 to 50 minutes of their time.

My impression at the time was that students recruited in class would have been perceived as more attractive than those recruited by flyer. Analysis of data collected later seems to bear this out, at least for females; all relevant groups of raters (Brazilian, US, Russian and Ache) gave US females from the first group a slightly higher average attractiveness rating than those from the second. Some degree of sampling bias is inevitable in research of this kind. Limiting one's sample to a select population, like students in introductory psychology classes, and using semi-coercive methods to ensure a representative sample (i.e. making participation in experiments a condition for passing the course) is no panacea; there is no guarantee that such a sample will not be biased relative to larger populations of interest like university students in general. If it is true (as I suspect) that unattractive individuals are less likely to participate in research on physical attractiveness, the main consequence will be a restriction in the range of variation of sample physical attractiveness. Such restriction will reduce correlations of physical attractiveness with other variables of interest (type II error); it should not produce spurious correlations (type I error). I found a similar female bias in Brazil, but not among the Ache. My experience in giving talks on physical attractiveness is that women are more likely than men to ask questions and to want to find out more about the subject, a reflection possibly of the fact that being attractive or unattractive is more consequential for women than for men.

In Paraguay I set up a photographic/anthropometric station at central locations in each of the three settlements where I collected data (Puerto Barra, Ypetimi, Chupa Pou). Kim Hill and I asked Ache both at this central point and in their homes if they were willing to be photographed and measured.

In Brazil, at the Federal University of Bahia, I set up my photographic apparatus in one corner of a student dining area, next to a display table used by student groups. I passed out flyers describing my work to students visiting that end of the commons, and asked them if they would like to volunteer. Subjects were paid approximately $4.50 for 40 to 50 minutes of their time.

The subject protocol itself involved the following:

1) *Introduction.* US and Brazilian university subjects were asked to sign a consent form. This step was omitted for Ache subjects, who are largely illiterate.

2) *Photography.* Subjects were asked to sit in a chair facing a camera. The camera stood at a distance of 313 centimeters from a wall, which was white, or covered with a white oilcloth backdrop. Subjects were covered below the neck with a pale yellow scarf to eliminate cues from bodies and clothing. They were asked to hold a 15 cm wide box in position with their heads against the wall, which served both to put their faces at roughly a standard distance from the wall and the camera, and to keep their heads fixed. I moved their heads around with my hands into a standard position. I placed the sagittal (front to back) plane of the head perpendicular to the wall with the help of a T-square. I used an angle meter to ensure that the line from mid-brow (glabella) to mid-chin (gonion) was held vertical, and to put the transverse plane of the head 10% above Frankfurt horizontal. (At Frankfurt horizontal a line running from porion to orbitale is set horizontal. This is a standard position used in photographing and measuring heads and skulls in physical anthropology. Living subjects are more comfortable with their heads 10% above this angle.) A vertical black thread, visible through the viewfinder of the camera, and barely visible in the photos, was also used to ensure that subjects' heads were vertical and directly in front of the camera.

After positioning the head I moved to the camera, adjusted the camera height to center the focus frame (a black frame visible in the viewfinder) on the subject's eyes, put the camera in focus with the automatic focus button, repositioned her head if it had moved in the meantime, and took two photographs. Afterward I took one left profile photograph with the sagittal plane of the head parallel to the wall and 25 cm from it, and the head once again 10% above Frankfort horizontal. After completing these photographs I wrote down the film roll number, frame number, and subject ID number of each shot.

The positions of the camera tripod and chair were kept fixed by marks on the ground (made with tape or pegs driven into the ground). I also checked the distance of the camera from the wall at least once a day. I left a white card positioned to appear near the edge of the photograph on the subject's left. This card bore a test pattern of four squares, each 10 cm on a side, and a smaller piece of paper affixed with paper clips and marked with the subject's ID number and the date.

The camera used for these photographs was a tripod mounted Canon ES 750 with automatic focus and a 70 to 120 mm lens set at a focal length of 120 mm. The film was 24 exposure 400 ASA from Agfa. US subjects were photographed with an automatic flash in space provided indoors by the Evolution and Human Behavior Program of the University of Michigan. Ache and Brazilian subjects were photographed in natural light. Photographs were developed by the photographic supply service at the University of Michigan and by commercial developers in Paraguay and Brazil.

3) *Anthropometry.* I collected a number of head and body measurements from each subject. Measurements were made with calipers, stadiometer, tape measure, scale, and skinfold calipers following guidelines in Farkas (1981) and Frisancho (1990). Each measurement was repeated once. Facial measurements include: nasion/gonion; nasion/l.exocanthion; nasion/r.exocanthion; l.exocanthion/l.porion; r.exocanthion/r.porion; gonion/l.porion; gonion/r.porion; l.porion/r.porion; inion/glabella. Body measurements include: height; weight; biacromial breadth; biilliac breadth; midchest circumference; lower chest circumference (females only); waist circumference; hip circumference; l.triceps circumference; l. triceps skinfold.

4) *Questionnaires.* Questionnaires were administered to US and Brazilian university subjects, but not to Ache subjects, for whom a large data base already exists. The following information was solicited: birth date; age; number and ages of siblings; marital status; father's and mother's employment and income; parental marital status; ethnicity (as specifically as possible, including country of origin of ancestors if possible); estimate of height and weight; eye and hair color; recent weight changes; exercise frequency; use of acne medication, hair dye, makeup, permanent; time since last haircut; use of glasses or contact lenses; tanning; electrolysis; relevant medical problems; age at menarche (females only); age at first shaving (males only); waist, inseam, shirt, dress (females only), shoe size; best and least liked features of own face; best and least liked features of own body; length of relationship with boy/girlfriend.

5) *Skin color.* In the US I used a reflectometer to measure reflectances at three wavelengths, amber, green and blue, on the forehead and on the inside of the left arm. In both Paraguay and Brazil there were problems with the power supply. In Paraguay I measured the skin colors of a large sample of Ache separately from the collection of photographic data and other anthropometric measurements.

Rating Pictures

Ache and Hiwi raters were recruited by visiting people in their houses and asking them to participate. Photographs of US subjects were rated by residents of Chupa Pou; photographs of Ache and Brazilian subjects by residents of Puerto Barra.

Brazilian university raters were approached in the same manner as Brazilian university photographic subjects (see above). Brazilian raters in Campo Alto were recruited by going from door to door. Photographs of US and Ache subjects were rated by a mixture of Brazilian university students and residents of Campo Alto; photographs of the Brazilian university sample were rated by residents of Campo Alto.

US raters were recruited by asking for volunteers in an Introduction to Biological Anthropology class.

Russian raters were recruited by approaching potential raters in the school buildings and dormitories of the Moscow State University of the Humanities.

Other researchers working in the United States and other industrialized societies have asked raters to give numerical scores to photographs. (The Likert scale, running from 1 to 7, is often used.) But Kim Hill and I had to use a different procedure among the Ache and Hiwi, because they would have had difficulty understanding numerical ratings. For the sake of consistency I used the same procedure with the other groups as well. For each rater we laid out nine photographs at a time in a 3 × 3 square. We covered up the second and third columns, and asked the rater to pick the most attractive face from the three in the first column. (Portuguese: *rosto mais bonito;* English: most attractive face; Russian: *samoe krasivoe litso;* Ache: *cha'a gatuvi* = best face; Hiwi: *wohune/pehenowa* = pretty/handsome face.) Then we covered up this photograph and asked for the most attractive face from the remaining two. We put the most attractive photograph at the top of the column, the second in the middle, the last at the bottom. We repeated this procedure with the second and third columns, leaving each column sorted by attractiveness. Then we applied the same procedure to the rows, so that the rater sorted the top row (with the three top ranking pictures) from most to least attractive, then the middle row (with the three middle ranking), then the bottom row (with the three bottom ranking). The result was to sort the pictures roughly from 1 to 9. We wrote down the initial order, the order after the column sort, and the order after the row sort. For each rater we laid out 3 × 3 squares, selecting photos at random from a single population sample of the other sex, until there were fewer than nine photographs left.[1]

To avoid unconscious cueing we made a point of not looking at the photographs or at the raters while they were choosing. Although we did not explicitly ask raters to assess individuals in photographs as potential sexual or marital partners, many raters, especially Ache and Brazilians of both sexes, made spontaneous comments along these lines.

Only a few individuals had any difficulty following these instructions. Some old Ache and Hiwi seemed confused by the task, and didn't pick any photographs, or left them all in order. One Brazilian majoring in philosophy had unanswerable questions about the meaning of "attractiveness." Another Brazilian rater treated the interview as a joke, and seemingly tried to pick the least attractive photos while making fun of the researcher. A few raters in each population had to quit in the middle of the session. All these rankings were discarded.

In addition to photographs, most raters were tested on two other instruments:

1) A series of line drawings (9 of each sex) running from thin to obese. Raters were asked to pick the male and female with the best body. No analysis of these data is attempted in the present work.

2) A silhouette of a female seen from the side (see Figure 5.3). Raters were asked whether they thought the figure would be most attractive if her breasts were larger, smaller, or of the same size, and similarly for buttocks and thighs. Results for this instrument are presented in Chapter 5.

The Ache (but not Brazilians, US Americans or Russians) seemed to have trouble interpreting the silhouette (but not the line drawings).

Scanning Faces

At the University of Michigan, using a Macintosh II computer and an Apple scanner belonging to the Department of Anthropology, I measured the $\{x, y\}$ coordinates of 80 points on 252 photographs, including full facial and profile views. A partial list of points measured is shown in Figure 3.1, and listed in Table 3.1. (Points not used in this analysis are not included.) As each point was measured I wrote down its $\{x, y\}$ coordinates. When I had a full set of landmark coordinates for several faces, I copied the numbers into an Excel file. I checked for transcription errors by computing the Euclidean distances between each point and a number of other points, and checking any distance that seemed discrepant.

Only a fraction of the points measured were actually used in the analyses presented in this work. In particular, coordinates from profile photographs are still unanalyzed. This is a potentially important data set; many of the points measured in profile coincide with points measured in full face view, so it should be possible to assign three-dimensional coordinates to these points. Assuming that photographic raters can use cues from shade and texture to extract three-dimensional information from two-dimensional photographs, it should eventually be possible to figure out how three dimensional variations in facial proportions affect ratings of attractiveness.

To estimate measurement error, I remeasured 18 photographs, three from each sample, and calculated correlations between test statistics for these remeasurements and test statistics for the original measurements of the same pho-

Figure 3.1. Facial landmarks measured for this study. (Landmarks measured but not used in this work are omitted.) See also Table 3.1.

tographs. Error variance as a portion of total variance based on these remeasurements is equal to $1 - r$, where r is the correlation between original and remeasured test statistics. Error variances for various indices of facial proportions are given in Chapters 5 and 6.

RESULTS AND DISCUSSION: COMPARING STANDARDS OF ATTRACTIVENESS

Within Groups

Table 3.2 presents the results of a test for within-group agreement in standards of attractiveness. I use a nonparametric test (Kendall's tau) because the rank data are uniformly rather than normally distributed. The numbers in Table 3.2 are not Kendall's taus themselves, but Kendall's taus converted into average Spearman's rank correlations by the formula $r_s = (kW - 1)/(k-1)$, where r_s is the mean of Spearman's rank correlations between all possible pairs of ratings, k is

Table 3.1 List of facial landmarks used for this study

ABBREVIATION	SCIENTIFIC NAME	DESCRIPTION
LATERAL		
obi	otobasion inferius	juncture of ear with cheek
zy	zygion	lateralmost protrusion of cheek
ch	cheilon	outside corner of mouth
al	alare	lateralmost extension of nose
en	endocanthion	inside corner of eye
pi	palpebrale inferius	center of lower eyelid
ex	exocanthion	outer corner of eye
ps	palpebrale superius	center of upper eyelid
E1		eyebrow closest to mid-face
E2		eyebrow farthest from mid-face
CENTRAL		
gn	gonion	bottom of chin
CL		junction of chin and lower lip
li	labiale inferius	bottom center of lower lip vermilion
sto	stomion	center of labial fissure
ls	labiale superius	upper center of upper lip vermilion
sn	subnasale	bottom center of nose
g	glabella	bony prominence between eyebrows

the number of raters, and W is Kendall's tau. Thus, for example, the value of .30 given for US females rating US males means that if two raters were picked at random from among the 18 US American females who rated photographs of US males, the mean expected Spearman's r between the two would be .30. Significance levels are calculated from the two-tailed chi-squared approximation for W, although it needs to be kept in mind that this approximation is inaccurate for $k < 7$ (Howell 1987:270).

Information from Table 3.2 can be combined with figures for individual error variance (generated by Monte Carlo simulation, see note 1) to estimate the extent of within-group agreement. Given an average Spearman's correlation coefficient of r_s', shared standards of attractiveness will account for r_s' of rank variance while individual variation plus error variance will account for $1 - r_s'$. Since the proportion of variance due to measurement error is around .26, shared standards of attractiveness will account for $r_s'/(1 - .26) = 1.35 \cdot r_s'$ of the remaining rank variance. Since average Spearman's r's are mostly in the .2 to .4 range, shared standards of attractiveness account for around .25 to .55 of non-measurement-error variance, while individual idiosyncrasy and inconsistency account for the rest. It is important to keep in mind that these figures are for *rank* variance only, not for variance in absolute attractiveness.

Table 3.2 Within-group agreement (mean Spearman's *r*) in standards of attractiveness within groups of raters (Kendall's tau converted to average Spearman's *r*). Numbers in parentheses are numbers of raters.

Photographs of	Rated by	Photographs of Females	Males
		N=51	N=23
Brazilians	Brazilians(19,11)	.19 **	.25 **
	US Americans(12,20)	.36 **	.44 **
	Russians(11,14)	.33 **	.27 **
	Ache Indians(11,13)	.24 **	.24 **
	Hiwi Indians(4,4)	.38 **	.20 **
		N=52	N=31
US Americans	Brazilians(20,23)	.16 **	.26 **
	US Americans(11,18)	.30 **	.30 **
	Russians(12,14)	.27 **	.29 **
	Ache Indians(20,21)	.28 **	.24 **
	Hiwi Indians(0,0)	n.a.	n.a.
		N=41	N=42
Ache Indians	Brazilians(17,16)	.19 **	.25 **
	US Americans(12,15)	.27 **	.43 **
	Russians(12,12)	.27 **	.39 **
	Ache Indians(15,15)	.21 **	.21 **
	Hiwi Indians(7,4)	.26 **	.62 **

These numbers show that there is significant within-group agreement in standards of facial attractiveness for all combinations of rater and photographic samples (even when just four Hiwi women are rating just 23 Brazilian men). No population in this study is without a shared standard of attractiveness. While individual taste is not of negligible importance, there must be some process operating within each of the population samples in this study to produce some degree of agreement in standards of attractiveness.

I have not controlled for age in this analysis, because the variables involved are not normally distributed, but it is unlikely that age-related changes in physical attractiveness could account for the within-group agreement found in this study: University of Michigan and Brazilian photographic subjects span a very small age range, and Ache subjects were divided into groups of similar ages (see discussion in Chapter 4). And I will demonstrate below that there is also significant agreement *between* populations even with age partialed out.

There is no evidence in Table 3.2 that populations with heavy exposure to magazines, movies and television (Brazil, US and Russia) show more within-group agreement than societies with little exposure (Ache and Hiwi).

Between Groups

For each photographic subject for each population of raters I have calculated mean attractiveness by averaging rankings given to that subject by all raters in the population. Because these average attractiveness ratings are used extensively through the rest of this study, the following should be noted:

1) For the US sample I include only subjects of predominantly European ancestry except in Chapter 7. All populations of raters tested with US photographs give significantly lower attractiveness ratings to African American subjects, and some give lower ratings to Asian Americans. There is no evidence in the US sample that different European American ethnic groups are perceived by any group of raters to differ in attractiveness (based on Wilcoxon rank sum tests on mean attractiveness ratings for Northern Europeans compared to other whites and for Jews compared to gentiles). In Chapter 7, I discuss the significance of differences in perceived attractiveness of different racial groups.

2) In most of the analyses that follow, I use mean attractiveness ratings controlled for age by least squares regression. This has little effect on ratings of US and Brazilian photographic subjects, since the age range in these samples is limited. A more complicated procedure was used for ratings of Ache subjects. For both male and female Ache I divided the photographs into four groups, roughly on the basis of age, with 9–12 photographs in each group. Descriptive statistics for these subgroups are presented in Table 3.3. Each of these subsamples was presented separately to raters to avoid ranking subjects of widely disparate ages against one another. In order to carry out correlational tests between attractiveness ratings and various independent variables for each sample as a whole, I converted correlations from each subsample into Fisher's z's, took the mean of the results, and applied the inverse of Fisher's z transformation.

Table 3.3 Descriptive statistics for the subgroups into which Ache photographs were divided for this study.

	N	median age	mean age	age range
FEMALE				
Ypetimi	9	19	21.8	14-31
Young Chupa Pou	10	19	20.2	14-33
Med. Chupa Pou	11	29	29.6	22-40
Old Chupa Pou	12	42	42.8	37-51
TOTAL	42	28	29.1	14-51
MALE				
Ypetimi	12	26	30.2	16-54
Young Chupa Pou	11	20	21.1	16-33
Med. Chupa Pou	10	32	29.2	19-38
Old Chupa Pou	11	43	46.2	27-60
TOTAL	44	28.5	31.7	16-60

Table 3.4. Age-corrected agreement across populations about facial attractiveness. Off diagonal numbers show agreement in mean rankings). Boldface diagonal numbers are Cronbach's alphas (reliabilities). Boxes enclose two clusters of agreement, Western and Indian. Numbers in parentheses are numbers of photos/raters.

Photographs of

Brazilians

Rated by	Females(51)					Males(23)				
	Braz	US	Rus	Ache	Hiwi	Braz	US	Rus	Ache	Hiwi
Braz(19,11)	*.98*					*.79*				
US Americans(12,20)	.68 **	*.87*				.70 **	*.94*			
Russians(11,14)	.68 **	.79 **	*.85*			.72 **	.56 *	*.85*		
Ache Indians(11,13)	.32 *	-.07	.04	*.87*		.12	-.28	-.13	*.51*	
Hiwi Indians(4,4)	.25 +	-.03	.08	.57 **	*.71*	.33	.26	.40 +	.21	*.58*

US Americans

Rated by	Females(52)					Males(31)				
	Braz	US	Rus	Ache	Hiwi	Braz	US	Rus	Ache	Hiwi
Braz(20,23)	*.78*					*.87*				
US Americans(11,18)	.59 **	*.86*				.44 *	*.89*			
Russians(12,14)	.66 **	.78 **	*.82*			.71 **	.64 **	*.88*		
Ache Indians(20,21)	.15	.15	.19	*.90*		-.07	-.05	-.13	*.88*	
Hiwi Indians(0,0)	n.a.	n.a.	n.a.	n.a.	*n.a.*	n.a.	n.a.	n.a.	n.a.	*n.a.*

Physical Attractiveness and the Theory of Sexual Selection

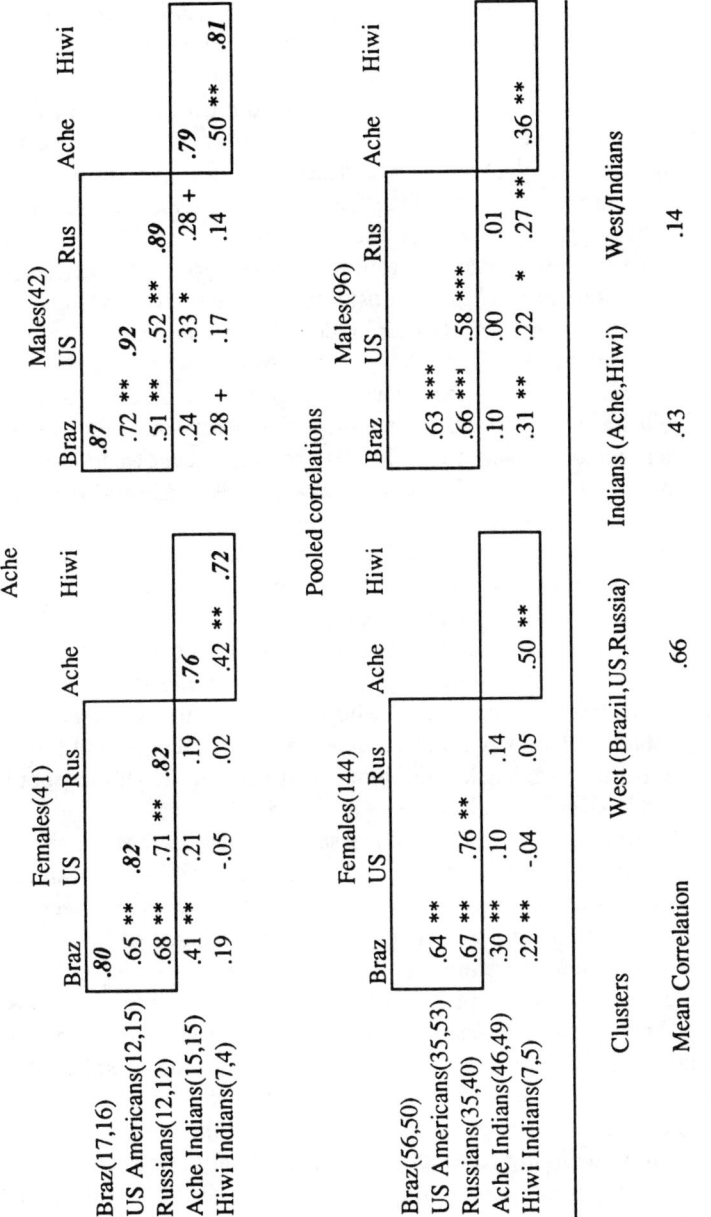

The alternative procedure would have been to rate Ache of all ages together, and then partial out age. The disadvantage of this alternative procedure would have been that after age was controlled for there would have been little variance in attractiveness left to be explained by other independent variables. This is not to say that the procedure used in this study is without problems. When a picture is always ranked together with a small number of other pictures, its attractiveness may be systematically under- or overstated, depending on the attractiveness of the rest of the subsample. And when the independent variable being tested is correlated with age (as are most of the independent variables considered in Chapters 4 to 6) moderate errors in estimating the slope of the attractiveness-versus-age regression line may cause substantial changes in correlations between age-controlled attractiveness and other independent variables.

Whatever procedure we use, we have to accept that whenever one independent variable—age—accounts for a large part of the variation in a dependent variable, it will be more difficult to measure the effects of other independent variables. There is no real way to avoid this problem except to collect a sample with a limited range of ages, which was not a practical possibility with the Ache.

3) I use parametric statistics throughout whenever a Lilliefors test on the variables involved (or transformations of those variables—e.g. logarithms) shows no significant ($p < .05$) departure from normality. Both average attractiveness ratings and age-controlled attractiveness ratings are close to a normal distribution, judging by a Lilliefors test. There seems to be no consistent tendency toward right or left skewing—that is, there is no more or less agreement about who is especially attractive than about who is especially unattractive.

I have calculated Cronbach alphas, a measure of the reliability of the average attractiveness ratings, for each combination of rater and sample population. These are given in the diagonal elements of Table 3.4.

With age partialed out, how much do samples of different populations of raters agree in their judgments of physical attractiveness? Table 3.4 shows rank correlations in age-corrected ratings of physical attractiveness between samples of raters. Two sets of boxes (solid lines) set off two clusters of agreement. The larger boxes, with three correlation coefficients in each box, set off what I call the Western cluster, including raters from Brazil, the United States and Russia. There is very strong and significant agreement among the members of this cluster in standards of physical attractiveness for all population samples rated. The average correlation between members of the Western cluster is .64. The smaller boxes, with zero or one correlation coefficients in each box, mark off what I call the Indian cluster, including Ache and Hiwi raters. The average correlation here is .42. Finally, outside the two sets of boxes, Table 3.4 gives correlations between different populations across the two clusters. Even in these cross-cluster comparisons there seems to be some agreement, with a number of correlations being significantly positive, and none significantly negative. The average correlation across clusters is .14.

These results have some implications for hypotheses about criteria of facial attractiveness:

First, standards of attractiveness vary across populations. This is certainly not news. Darwin (1981[1871]), Westermarck (1921) and Ellis (1926), relying on missionaries' and travelers' accounts, all reported such variation across populations, and modern ethnographers commonly second such reports (Ford and Beach 1951).These results do not disprove the existence of specialized naturally selected mechanisms for assessing attractiveness, any more than linguistic variation disproves the existence of naturally selected mechanisms for processing syntax and phonology. However, they do argue that theories of the psychology of attractiveness need to be tested across a range of cultures, if they are to have any claims to be theories of *human,* and not merely industrial Western, psychology.

Second, shared culture probably cannot completely account for similarities in standards of physical attractiveness across populations. Shared culture might be responsible in part for similarities in standards of attractiveness within the Western cluster on Table 3.4. But it is hard to see how similarities between Ache and Hiwi Indian standards could have anything to do with shared culture; Ache and Hiwi cultures have been developing independently for many thousands of years. On the other hand, something like the Face Averaging Device discussed in Chapter 6 would make sense in this case; two physically similar groups like the Ache and Hiwi could have similar ideal composites even without culture contact. More complicated mechanisms—such as setting the ideal face equal to the average face subject to some transformation—would also work.

The results of this chapter suggest that judgments of attractiveness are similar within and, to some extent, between cultures. The following chapters will consider some of the psychological mechanisms that might account for this agreement.

NOTE

1. The sorting procedure introduces three sources of random noise into the ranking process:
    1) Within each 3 × 3 square, the most attractive picture will always end up at the top, and the least attractive at the bottom, but other pictures may end up one or more ranks above or below where they should be, depending on where they start out.
    2) A photograph that ends up by chance in a square in which the other eight faces are especially attractive or unattractive will receive an unrealistically low or high rank.

3) The ranking technique gives a relative rather than an absolute measure of attractiveness. It is impossible to tell whether the difference in attractiveness between two pictures with adjacent ranks is large or small.

I used a Monte Carlo simulation to estimate the likely measurement error from sources 1 and 2. Using the Excel 4.0 spreadsheet package, I produced a series of columns of random numbers, and sorted each using the procedure outlined above (3 × 3 squares sorted by columns then by rows). Then I calculated the Spearman's rank correlation coefficient between the rank order produced by the sorting procedure and the true rank order. For ten simulations using 54 random numbers per simulation the mean correlation between experimental and true rank was .86 (range .74 to .96), giving a mean individual error variance as a fraction of total variance of .26 ($= 1 - .86^2$). This does not take into account error introduced by using rankings and rank correlations rather than absolute attractiveness (source 3 above). This is an estimate of the experimental error for *individual* rankings; when individual rankings are averaged to produce group rankings these errors will tend to cancel out.

CHAPTER 4

Age, Mate Value and Attractiveness

Age (and the physical cues associated with it) are important to this study for several reasons. First, one component of mate value, fecundity, depends strongly on the age of a potential mate. Second, the relation between fecundity on the one hand, and age on the other, has probably been relatively invariant through most of human evolutionary history, so that emotional responses to age cues may be relatively "hard-wired" in our species. Third, age-related differences in fecundity may be especially relevant to understanding *physical* attractiveness because *physical* cues—including facial proportions, skin color and body shape—may be particularly reliable indicators of such differences.

In this chapter I will review theory about the relationship between age and mate value, and set forth evidence that age does function as expected as a basis of mate choice.

AGE, FECUNDITY AND MATE VALUE: THEORY

Menopause and Marriage

Two features of human reproduction have major consequences for the relationship between age and mate value in our species.

Menopause. Human females are probably the only primates, and among the few animals, who have a long period of post-reproductive life. Human female fecundity begins to decline fairly rapidly at around age 35, and typically reaches zero by around age 45–50. A large proportion of females survive past this age in traditional societies—around 40%, given a life expectancy at birth of 35 years (Coale and Demeny 1983:45). Male fecundity declines more slowly; Goldman and Montgomery (1989), reviewing data from several traditional societies, report fertility declines of about 10% for men between 45 and 50, compared to younger men, and about 20% for men over 55, after controlling for age of wife and duration of marriage. (Throughout this chapter, I will use "traditional" to mean pre-demographic-transition.)

The evolution of menopause is not well understood. Several sociobiologists have argued that menopause might be a result of kin selection; women's reproductive systems might shut down at the age at which, historically, the inclusive fitness benefits of raising grandchildren exceeded those of producing new children. However, data from the Ache (Hill and Hurtado 1991) and other populations (Rogers 1993) on the costs and benefits of pregnancy and child-rearing do not support this or related adaptationist hypotheses.

Whatever the evolutionary basis for menopause, it has important consequences for mate choice. Menopause must increase the level of male/male sexual competition by increasing the ratio of males in breeding condition to females in breeding condition. More important, for purposes of this chapter, menopause means that under a traditional demographic regime the age-related variance in mate value will be much greater for females than for males. This is true for both long-term and short-term mate value.

Long-term pairbonds. In traditional societies, the interval between the conception of a child and her attainment of independence (more than a dozen years) is much longer than typical interbirth intervals (commonly two to four years). In other words, human beings have overlapping broods. These encourage the formation of long-term mateships—*de jure* or *de facto* marriages. When one man fathers a number of children in succession with one woman, conflicts between parents over the allocation of resources among children are reduced. By contrast, Daly and Wilson (1988) show that, in the United States, living with a stepparent is far and away the biggest risk factor for infanticide and child homicide—presumably a reflection of conflicts over resource allocation. They review evidence that stepchildren fare poorly in a wide range of societies.

This is not to say that human beings never switch mates between one child and the next. Fisher (1989) argues that many societies show signs of a "four year itch"—a peak in divorce rates after four years of marriage. Given typical interbirth intervals, this peak is expected if couples who have one child together sometimes split up before starting another child. But pair-bonds in humans are nonetheless usually more enduring than in species where no dependent offspring remain in the nest from one breeding season to the next.

The result is that human beings often choose mates on the basis of long-term prospects, rather than immediate conditions. Several researchers (Symons 1979; Thornhill and Thornhill 1983) suggest that insofar as future fertility is a consideration in mate choice, human beings should be adapted to choose partners on the basis of reproductive value (a measure of potential lifetime reproduction) rather than fecundability (a measure of potential immediate reproduction). I will show below that the calculation of long-term mate value in relation to age is more complicated than this, because in traditional societies an individual has a good chance of dying or becoming infertile before the end of a partner's reproductive career.

Below I discuss how short-term mate value and long-term mate value change with age. As discussed in Chapter 2, mate value has several components including mate's ability and willingness to invest in ego and ego's offspring, mate's expected fecundity, and mate's heritable fitness. In this chapter I will focus particularly on age-related changes in mate's *expected fecundity* because it seems likely that physical appearance will be a particularly good indicator of such changes. Where mate's *parental investment potential* is concerned, mate's social position and past economic performance may be better predictors than age-related changes in mate's physical appearance. More research is needed to determine how realistic these assumptions are (they are probably more realistic for women's mate value than for men's), but they offer at least a starting point for analysis.

Short-Term and Long-Term Mate Value

Although there is tremendous variation in birth and death rates across human populations, demographers have uncovered some robust invariants in the relation between birth and death rates and age. Research shows that without knowing more than the life expectancy in a given population, it is possible to make fairly accurate estimates of the survivorship to different ages. For example, where the average life expectancy is 35, about 62% of females will survive to age fifteen, 50% to age 35, and 42% to age 45. In other words, the *level* of mortality is strongly affected by the environment, but the *shape* of the curve of mortality versus age and sex more nearly reflects the invariant biology of *Homo sapiens,* with mortality rates high in infancy, declining through childhood and into adolescence, and increasing at an accelerating rate over the course of adulthood. By the same token, Henry (1961) shows that the *shape* of the curve of female marital fertility versus age varies little across a number of "natural fertility" (noncontracepting) populations, in spite of considerable variation in *levels* of fertility. Barring exceptional circumstances—for instance, homicide, including warfare, which may cause unusually high death rates in particular age/sex classes—we can rely on "model life tables" (Coale and Demeny 1983), which give expected vital rates for different age classes as a function of given life expectancies, to calculate the values of evolutionarily important variables given plausible assumptions about the range of life expectancies in traditional societies. Below I discuss mate value as a function of age for two extreme scenarios, very short-term sexual relationships, and lifelong marriages.

Short-term mate value. Obviously many factors affect how mate value varies with age, but for this chapter I will consider mainly the effects of life expectancy and fecundity. In this case, the short-term mate value of an individual of age x is equal to expected fertility from mating with that individual divided by expected fertility from mating with a random adult of the opposite sex. Tables 4.1 and 4.2, and Figures 4.1 and 4.2 give female and male short-term mate values using Henry's (1961) figures for age-specific female fertility, and Goldman and Montgomery's (1989) figures for age-specific male fertility. Henry does not give figures for females at ages 15–19; for this age range I used Howell's figures for

Table 4.1 Age and short-term mate value (female).

Age x	Fertility M(x)	Age distrib. L(x)	Mate Value MV(x)
0-4	0	3.70103	0
5-9	0	3.27883	0
10-14	0	3.16619	0
15-19	.132	3.04842	0.68
20-24	.435	2.90329	2.24
25-29	.407	2.73967	2.10
30-34	.371	2.56595	1.91
35-39	.298	2.38466	1.54
40-44	.152	2.20107	0.78
45-49	.022	2.01714	0.11
50-54	0	1.81681	0
55-59	0	1.58552	0
60-64	0	1.31245	0
65-69	0	1.00272	0
70-74	0	0.6832	0
75-79	0	0.38328	0
80-84	0	0.15923	0
85-89	0	0.04392	0
90-94	0	0.00629	0
95+	0	0.00035	0

	average M(x)		var MV
	.194		0.789

$M(x)$ = fertility at age x, from Henry and Howell. See text.
Average $M(x)$ – fertility of average adult female (x > 14), assuming age structure given by $L(x)$; $L(x)$ = age distribution, West Model life table 7, $e(x) = 35$; $MV(x)$, short term – fertility of female of age x/average MV; var MV = variance in adult female MV (x > 14), assuming age structure given by $L(x)$.

!Kung fertility, after correcting for the low overall fertility among the !Kung. Goldman and Montgomery's figures for male age-specific fertility in monogamous relationships controlling for age of wife and duration of relationship show a 10% decline in fertility going from 20–24 year-olds to 45–49 year olds, and a further 10% decline going to 55–59 year olds. For this analysis, I assume male fecundity is proportional to 0 at 10–14, 1 at 20–24, .9 at 45–49, .8 at 55–59, and 0 at 75–79, filling in the gaps with linear interpolation. Denominators (fertilities from mating at random) were calculated by averaging fertilities over all adults (age 15–19 and older) assuming the age distribution associated with a female life expectancy of 35 ($L(x)$ in Coale and Demeny's Model West Life Table; Coale and Demeny 1983:45). While there is room for argument about the details of the relationship between age and fecundity (James 1979; Menken 1986; Weinstein et

Table 4.2 Age and short-term mate value (male).

Age x	Fertility M(x)	Age distrib. L(x)	Mate Value MV(x)
0-4	0	3.54864	0
5-9	0	3.13989	0
10-14	0	3.04176	0
15-19	.500	2.94085	.62
20-24	1.000	2.80458	1.23
25-29	.980	2.6425	1.21
30-34	.960	2.46962	1.18
35-39	.940	2.28195	1.16
40-44	.920	2.0757	1.13
45-49	.900	1.85276	1.11
50-54	.850	1.6107	1.05
55-59	.800	1.34861	.99
60-64	.600	1.06751	.74
65-69	.400	0.77444	.49
70-74	.200	0.49678	.25
75-79	0	0.25932	0
80-84	0	0.09669	0
85-89	0	0.023268	0
90-94	0	0.003	0
95+	0	0.00014	0
average M(x)	.811	var MV	0.081

M(x) is proportional to fertility at age x, from Goldman. See text.
Average M(x) is proportional to fertility of average adult male (x > 14), assuming age structure given by L(x); L(x) = age distribution, West Model life table 7, e(x)=32.5; MV(x), short term = fertility of male of age x/average MV; var MV = variance in adult male MV (x>14), assuming age structure given by L(x).

al. 1990), the general shape of the curve, and the differences between males and females, are not in dispute.

Long-term mate value. Several authors (Symons 1979; Thornhill and Thornhill 1983) have suggested that long-term mate value of an individual is equal to her reproductive value—reproductive value being a measure of the expected lifetime reproductive success of an organism. But reproductive value is not quite the same as mate value, since under a traditional demographic regime an individual has a good chance of dying or becoming infertile before the end of a

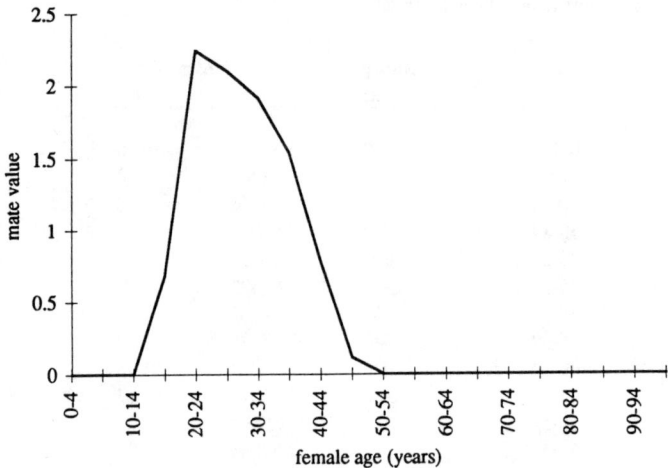

Figure 4.1. Age and short-term mate value (female).

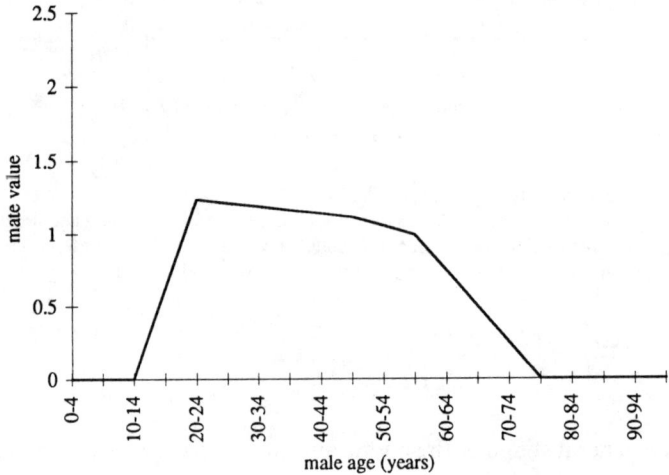

Figure 4.2. Age and short-term mate value (male).

mate's reproductive career. Below I present an equation for mate value as a function of fertility allowing for both age of mate and age of ego.

The mate value of an individual of age x to an individual of age y in a relationship lasting z years is

$$V_{x,y,z} = \frac{\sum_{t=0}^{z} \dfrac{m'_{x+t} \cdot m_{y+t}}{m_{ave}}}{\sum_{t=0}^{z} m_{y+t}} \qquad (4.1)$$

where m'_w is fertility at age w for mate's sex, m_w is fertility at age w for ego's sex, and m_{ave} is average fertility for ego's sex.

Long-term mate value is thus the mate value for a relationship lasting z years, times the probability that the relationship lasts z years (and no more), summed over all z. In other words,

$$V_{x,y} = \sum_{z=0}^{\infty} L_{x,y,z} \cdot V_{x,y,z} \qquad (4.2)$$

where $L_{x,y,z}$, the probability that a marriage between an x-year old mate and a y-year old ego will last z years and no longer, is,

$$L_{x,y,z} = \frac{l'_{x+z}}{l'_x} \cdot \frac{l_{y+z}}{l_y} \cdot \left[1 - \left(\frac{l'_{x+z+1}}{l'_x} \cdot \frac{l_{y+z+1}}{l_y}\right)\right] \qquad (4.3)$$

where l'_w is the probability of survival from birth to age w for mate's sex and l_w is the probability for ego's sex. The definition of long-term mate value given in Equation 4.2 assumes that the population growth rate is zero. Changing this assumption would require the addition of a discount factor.

Figures 4.3 and 4.4 show female and male long-term mate value as a function of age of mate and age of ego given a female life expectancy of 35, based on Equation 4.2 using age-specific death and birth rates following Coale and Demeny, Henry, Goldman and Howell, as described above. The same data are presented in Tables 4.3 and 4.4.

This analysis of course oversimplifies in many respects; for example, it mea-

Table 4.3 Age and long-term mate value (MV) of females as a function of age of female and age of partner. For a male of 25 to 29 years, a female of 30 to 34 years has 1.44 times the long-term mate value of an adult female picked at random. "var MV" is variance in adult female MV (x > 14), assuming age structure given by L(x) in Table 4.1. Compare with variance in male mate value in Table 4.4.

Age of female (years)	Age of male (years)														
	0–4	5–9	10–14	15–19	20–24	25–29	30–34	35–39	40–44	45–49	50–54	55–59	60–64	65–69	70–74
0–4	1.95	2.47	1.59	1.06	0.83	0.73	0.60	0.46	0.31	0.18	0.08	0.02	0.00	0.00	0.00
5–9	2.71	3.56	2.43	1.65	1.36	1.27	1.14	0.98	0.80	0.58	0.37	0.20	0.06	0.00	0.00
10–14	2.41	3.69	2.96	2.09	1.74	1.68	1.59	1.47	1.32	1.13	0.88	0.64	0.42	0.17	0.00
15–19	2.39	3.17	3.02	2.49	2.20	2.16	2.12	2.06	1.98	1.86	1.71	1.51	1.33	1.10	0.70
20–24	2.45	2.61	2.52	2.44	2.43	2.43	2.42	2.42	2.41	2.39	2.36	2.34	2.31	2.29	2.31
25–29	1.77	1.71	1.83	1.91	1.95	1.96	1.98	1.99	2.02	2.05	2.08	2.10	2.12	2.13	2.16
30–34	1.28	0.92	1.10	1.33	1.43	1.44	1.46	1.49	1.53	1.58	1.66	1.74	1.81	1.88	1.97
35–39	0.89	0.42	0.46	0.73	0.86	0.87	0.89	0.91	0.95	1.00	1.07	1.18	1.27	1.40	1.58
40–44	0.40	0.17	0.11	0.25	0.34	0.34	0.35	0.36	0.38	0.40	0.44	0.50	0.56	0.64	0.80
45–49	0.06	0.03	0.01	0.03	0.04	0.04	0.05	0.05	0.05	0.05	0.06	0.07	0.08	0.09	0.12
50–54	0.00	0.00	0.00	0.00	0.00	0.00	0.00	0.00	0.00	0.00	0.00	0.00	0.00	0.00	0.00
55–59	0.00	0.00	0.00	0.00	0.00	0.00	0.00	0.00	0.00	0.00	0.00	0.00	0.00	0.00	0.00
60–64	0.00	0.00	0.00	0.00	0.00	0.00	0.00	0.00	0.00	0.00	0.00	0.00	0.00	0.00	0.00
65–69	0.00	0.00	0.00	0.00	0.00	0.00	0.00	0.00	0.00	0.00	0.00	0.00	0.00	0.00	0.00
70–74	0.00	0.00	0.00	0.00	0.00	0.00	0.00	0.00	0.00	0.00	0.00	0.00	0.00	0.00	0.00
75–79	0.00	0.00	0.00	0.00	0.00	0.00	0.00	0.00	0.00	0.00	0.00	0.00	0.00	0.00	0.00
80–84	0.00	0.00	0.00	0.00	0.00	0.00	0.00	0.00	0.00	0.00	0.00	0.00	0.00	0.00	0.00
85–89	0.00	0.00	0.00	0.00	0.00	0.00	0.00	0.00	0.00	0.00	0.00	0.00	0.00	0.00	0.00
90–94	0.00	0.00	0.00	0.00	0.00	0.00	0.00	0.00	0.00	0.00	0.00	0.00	0.00	0.00	0.00
95+	0.00	0.00	0.00	0.00	0.00	0.00	0.00	0.00	0.00	0.00	0.00	0.00	0.00	0.00	0.00
var MV	0.94	1.39	1.30	1.03	0.93	0.92	0.91	0.90	0.88	0.86	0.83	0.81	0.79	0.79	0.79

Table 4.4 Age and long-term mate value (MV) of males as a function of age of male and age of partner. For a female of 25 to 29 years, a male of 30 to 34 years has 1.09 times the long-term mate value of an adult male picked at random. var MV is variance in adult male MV (x > 14), assuming age structure given by L(x) in Table 4.2. Compare with variance in female mate value in Table 4.3.

Age of male (years)		Age of female (years)								
		0–4	5–9	10–14	15–19	20–24	25–29	30–34	35–39	40–44	45–49
0	4	0.83	0.87	0.57	0.33	0.17	0.07	0.01	0.00	0.00	0.00
5	9	1.15	1.32	1.03	0.68	0.44	0.29	0.13	0.03	0.00	0.00
10	14	1.14	1.37	1.28	1.00	0.74	0.62	0.44	0.24	0.07	0.00
15	19	1.26	1.35	1.33	1.23	1.09	1.03	0.94	0.82	0.67	0.59
20	24	1.32	1.31	1.28	1.25	1.24	1.23	1.21	1.20	1.19	1.18
25	29	1.20	1.20	1.18	1.17	1.17	1.16	1.15	1.15	1.15	1.14
30	34	1.08	1.09	1.08	1.08	1.09	1.09	1.09	1.09	1.10	1.10
35	39	0.95	0.96	0.97	0.98	1.00	1.01	1.02	1.03	1.05	1.05
40	44	0.81	0.82	0.84	0.87	0.90	0.92	0.94	0.96	0.99	1.00
45	49	0.68	0.67	0.71	0.74	0.79	0.82	0.85	0.88	0.92	0.94
50	54	0.56	0.51	0.55	0.61	0.65	0.69	0.73	0.77	0.82	0.85
55	59	0.45	0.38	0.40	0.45	0.51	0.54	0.58	0.64	0.70	0.75
60	64	0.31	0.25	0.25	0.30	0.34	0.36	0.39	0.43	0.49	0.53
65	69	0.20	0.15	0.14	0.17	0.20	0.21	0.23	0.26	0.30	0.33
70	74	0.09	0.08	0.05	0.06	0.08	0.09	0.09	0.11	0.13	0.15
75	79	0.00	0.00	0.00	0.00	0.00	0.00	0.00	0.00	0.00	0.00
80	84	0.00	0.00	0.00	0.00	0.00	0.00	0.00	0.00	0.00	0.00
85	89	0.00	0.00	0.00	0.00	0.00	0.00	0.00	0.00	0.00	0.00
90	94	0.00	0.00	0.00	0.00	0.00	0.00	0.00	0.00	0.00	0.00
95 +		0.00	0.00	0.00	0.00	0.00	0.00	0.00	0.00	0.00	0.00
var MV		0.15	0.17	0.16	0.14	0.12	0.11	0.10	0.09	0.09	0.09

sures mate value only in terms of offspring produced, without taking into account effects of age and marital status on parental ability and willingness to keep offspring alive. Nevertheless this analysis supports some conclusions:

1) *Both short-term and long-term mate value vary more with age for females than for males.* We can calculate variance in mate value if we know age-specific mate values and the age structure of the population. Tables 4.1 through 4.4 include figures for variance in mate value among adults (= more than 14 years old) of both sexes assuming the age structure associated with female life expectancy of 35 in a Model West Life Table. For short-term mateships age-related variance in adult female mate value is almost 10 times greater than age-related variance in adult male mate value (9.7 = .79/.081). For long-term mateships age-related variance in adult mate value is 6 to 10 times greater for females

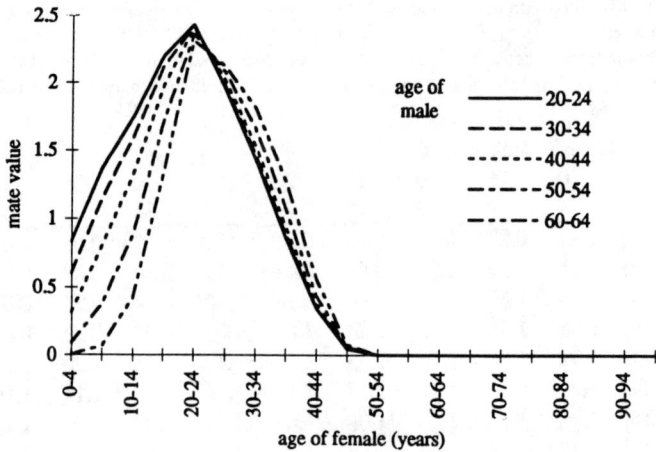

Figure 4.3. Age and long-term mate value (MV) of females as a function of age of female and age of partner.

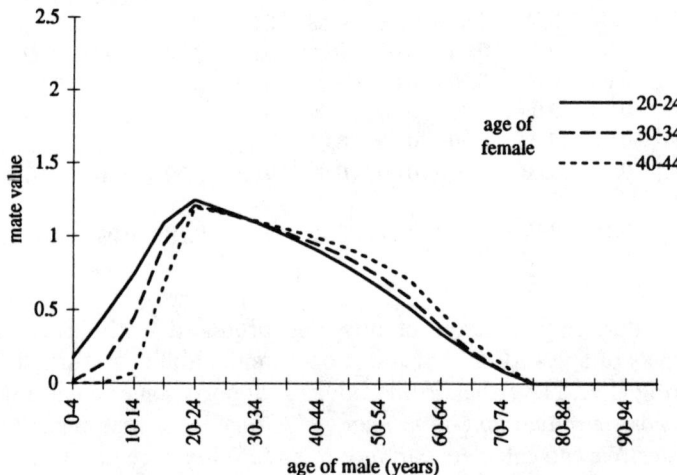

Figure 4.4. Age and long-term mate value (MV) of males as a function of age of male and age of partner.

than for males. (The exact value depends on the age of ego.) This means that selection on individuals to assess age-related changes in fecundity in adults of the other sex will operate more strongly on males than on females, especially where short-term mateships are involved. The reproductive consequences of having a mate of one age rather than another are much greater for males than for females.

Thus, other things being equal, there is stronger selection pressure on males than on females to discriminate between potential mates on the basis of cues related to aging, relative to other cues. This may explain the nearly universal finding that human males, to the extent that they show any discrimination in their choice of partners, are more interested than human females in the physical appearance of a potential mate. If male fecundity declined with age as quickly or more quickly than female fecundity, humans might follow the more common animal pattern of predominantly female choice for male attractiveness.

> Nature is not a feminist. If nature were a feminist women would have no biological clock and no menopause. Instead of being born with all the eggs we'll ever have, women would produce new eggs until we were eighty. . . . Men would run out of sperm when they were fifty whereupon everyone would approve as we dumped worn-out flabby husbands and scooped up young dudes and started a whole new life, a whole new family. [Heimel 1993:145]

2) *Contrary to Symons, and Thornhill and Thornhill, even with lifelong mateships, the age of maximum mate value is not the age of maximum reproductive value.* It is at age 15 to 19 that a female's expected future reproduction attains a maximum in traditional societies. But given the life expectancies typical of such societies, a male is likely to die before the end of his wife's reproductive career. Such realities make 20- to 24-year-old females a better reproductive bet for all but the youngest males. This is not to say that males may not try to acquire much younger females as wives. In extreme cases, for instance, the Tiwi of Northern Australia, females may be promised as mates even before they are born. But early betrothal under such conditions seems to result from efforts to preempt rival claimants for a female's sexual and reproductive powers, not from physical attraction to juveniles (Hart and Pilling 1960). In other words, it reflects availability rather than attractiveness.

3) *Age of maximum mate value is not the whole story. The rate at which an individual's long-term mate value rises to or declines from its maximum value is also important, and depends on the age of both partners.* Thus female long-term mate value is a function of male age. In a population where female life expectancy at birth is 35, a 20–24 year old male will have a life expectancy of 31 years, while a 50–54 year old male will have a life expectancy of just 14 years. The older male is thus more likely to die before the end of a young wife's reproductive career, and has more to lose in a marriage to a girl not yet at her peak fecundity. For a

young male, a 20–24 year old female has 1.2 times the long-term mate value of a 10–14 year old (1.2 = 1.35/1.13); for an old male, the 20–24 year old has 3.5 times the long-term mate value (3.5 = 2.1/.59). Naturally this assumes an extreme definition of a long-term mateship—one lasting until the death of one of the partners. Allowing for divorce would reduce, but not eliminate, this discrepancy between young men and old men.

By the same token, male long-term mate value is a function of female age. Although male fecundity does not decline with age as dramatically as female fecundity, a young woman who has a long potential reproductive career ahead of her will experience an appreciable loss of reproductive value if she is married for life to an old man. The same point does not hold as strongly for an old woman near the end of her reproductive career.

One likely consequence of age interactions in mate value is assortative mating for age, since young men have less to lose than old men in marriage to a preadult partner, and young women have more to lose than old women in marriage to an old man. At the same time, given the more rapid decline in female mate value with age, older males are likely to have more success in attracting younger partners than will older females, so that assortative mating for age is likely to coexist with an increasing age difference between male and female partners with increasing age.

In summary, to the extent that physical attraction results from the operation of adaptations for assessing age-related changes in mate value consequent on changes in fecundity, both male and female, both young and old, should show an attraction for young adult features, but the attraction should be considerably stronger among males than among females, particularly in short-term mateships. Where long-term mateships are concerned, a young woman has more to lose than an old woman in marriage to an old man; and an old man has more to lose than a young man in a long-term mateship with a woman not yet at peak fecundity.

AGE AND ATTRACTIVENESS: EVIDENCE

This analysis suggests a number of hypotheses about age and sexual selection in humans. Evolutionary theory suggests that organisms will have canalized or "hard-wired" responses to features of the environment that vary little, while they will have adaptively variable responses to variable features of the environment. The shapes of the curves of mortality and fertility with respect to age are sufficiently invariant in traditional societies that we can anticipate some species-wide automatic emotional responses to signs of age, including an attraction to young adult features, operating more strongly in males than in females. At the same time, the behavioral consequences of these emotional responses are likely to vary from one society to another depending on variations in the costs and benefits and perceived moral legitimacy of acting on one's feelings of attraction.

In spite of a considerable literature devoted to the claim that human sexuality and standards of physical attractiveness are culturally constructed, there does not seem to be *any* evidence from *any* society that seriously challenges the proposition that physical attractiveness is perceived to decline from young adulthood to old age, especially for females. Kligman (1993) notes that markers of aging include "wrinkles, sags, bags, blotches and splotches, fleshy nevi, pigmented lentigines, dilated sprays of vessels, seborrheic keratoses, actinic keratoses, and yellow, leathery, loose skin." In no known society are these signs of aging considered to add to a woman's beauty, or, beyond a certain point, to a man's. "The correlation of female age and sexual attractiveness is so intuitively obvious that ethnographers apparently take it for granted—as they do the bipedalism of the people they study—and the significance of female age tends to be mentioned only in passing, in discussions of something else" (Symons 1979:188).

Symons cites passing references to the effects of aging on female attractiveness in ethnographies of the Kgatla, prerevolutionary China, the Yanomamö, and the Tiwi. Additional references can be found in ethnographies of Trobriand Islanders (Malinowski 1987[1929]; Weiner 1976) and Gawa (Munn 1986) of Melanesia, Mende of Sierra Leone (Boone 1986), Mehinacu of Amazonia (Gregor 1985), and modern Chinese (Jankowiak 1993) to name just a few. A number of social psychological studies (reviewed in Jackson 1992) have documented such age-related declines in physical attractiveness and have demonstrated the expected sex differences as well.

Buss's review of human mate preferences in 37 cultures (Buss 1989, summarized in Chapter 2) provides further evidence. In every culture sampled, males have a significant preference for women younger than themselves, while females prefer older men. Males, on average, prefer an age difference of 2.66 years, females of 3.42 years (p. 9). Males from non-Western cultures prefer larger age differences than Western males (p. 43). Buss (p. 9) cites data from the *Demographic Yearbook of the United Nations* showing that in all countries sampled men are older on average than their wives, with an average age difference of 2.99 years. These data "yield evidence that stated preferences are reflected in actual mating decisions, [and] they provide . . . support for the evolution-based hypothesis that males both prefer *and* choose females displaying cues to high reproductive value."

Kenrick and Keefe (1992) examine age preferences stated in a sample of United States singles advertisements and Asian Indian marital advertisements, as well as actual ages at marriage in the US and in an isolated Philippine fishing village. Their study demonstrates an interaction of age and sex both in stated preferences and in actual marriages. Throughout their lives, women prefer and/or marry men averaging 0–10 years older than their own age. Young men prefer and/or marry women 0–5 years younger than their own age. Old men prefer and/or marry women considerably younger than their own age, but older than the preferred or actual mates of younger men. The interaction between sex and age is consistent with that predicted by models of changes in long-term mate value as a function of mate's age and ego's age.

Data from this study support the proposition that attractiveness declines with age among adults. Table 4.5 presents correlations between ages of photographic subjects and mean ratings of attractiveness for different combinations of photographic subjects and raters. Since the photographic samples used in this study differ in how wide a range of ages they span, I also present slopes of least squares regression lines to make it easier to compare different samples. The regression coefficients are expressed in terms of standard deviations of age-controlled physical attractiveness ratings. In other words, a coefficient of -.05 indicates that attractiveness declines by .05 standard deviations per year.

The United States photographic samples have the most limited age ranges (18–25 for females, 18–30 for males). Not surprisingly, the correlations between age and attractiveness in these samples are low. There is a greater range of ages in the Brazilian photographic sample (17–34, 19–32), and correlations with attractiveness are consistently (and in some cases significantly) negative for both sexes.

The format for the Ache photographic subjects (presented in the bottommost set of rows) differs somewhat from that for the other two groups, since there are two sets of attractiveness ratings for each subject. In the segregated set, Ache were divided into four separate subgroups, roughly segregated by age, and rankings reflect relative standing *within* a subgroup. In the mixed set, rankings derive from Ache from all four age groups mixed together, and reflect standing relative to *all* other same-sex Ache in the sample (see Chapter 3 for further discussion). I present two columns of regression slope coefficients for each sex. The first is based on calculating the regression of attractiveness within subgroups on age separately for each of four subgroups and averaging the resulting slopes.

The second column for each sex in Table 4.5 is based on calculating the regression of attractiveness on age for the mixed sample. These columns are shaded, because they offer the best estimate of differences in physical attractiveness over widely varying ages. The mean change in attractiveness for the mixed Ache samples is -.052 standard deviations/year for females and −.030 standard deviations/year for males. If attractiveness declined linearly with age at these rates—a reasonable approximation over the age range in question—then a woman who was of average attractiveness at age 20 would be one standard deviation less attractive at age 39. She would be as attractive as a twenty year-old in the 16th percentile of attractiveness, which is to say less attractive than five sixths of twenty year-olds. A twenty-year-old man would experience a similar decline in

Table 4.5 Age and facial attractiveness. Pearson's correlations between age and ratings of attractiveness, and slopes of least squares regressions of attractiveness on age. Numbers in parentheses are numbers of photographs or raters of both sexes.

Photos of	Rated by	Photographs of Females		Photographs of Males	
	mean age =	23.0		24.0	
	age st dev=	3.76		3.34	
	age range=	17-34		19-32	
		correl	regress slope	correl	regress slope
Brazilians	Brazilians(19,11)	-.38 **	-.11 **	-.40 +	-.12 +
(51,23)	US Americans(12,20)	-.07	-.02	-.36 +	-.08 +
	Russians(11,14)	-.22 +	-.06 +	-.10	-.02
	Ache Indians(11,13)	-.18	-.05	-.17	-.05
	Hiwi Indians(4,4)	-.10	-.03	-.54 **	-.17 **
	mean age =	20.1		21.3	
	age st dev=	1.38		2.84	
	age range=	18-25		18-30	
		correl	regress slope	correl	regress slope
US Americans	Brazilians(20,23)	-.15	-.11	.13	.05
(52,31)	US Americans(11,18)	-.12	-.09	.18	.08
	Russians(12,14)	-.16	-.12	.20	.08
	Ache Indians(20,21)	-.16	-.10	-.05	-.02
	Hiwi Indians(0,0)	n.a.	n.a.	n.a.	n.a.
	mean age=	29.1		31.7	
	st dev age=	10.54		12.96	
	age range=	14-51		16-60	
		regress slope segregated	mixed	regress slope segregated	mixed
Ache Indians	Brazilians(17,16)	-.05	-.06 **	-.05	-.05 **
(41,42)	US Americans(12,15)	-.03	n.a.	-.04	n.a.
	Russians(12,12)	.03	-.03 *	-.04	-.04 **
	Ache Indians(15,15)	-.14	-.07 **	-.03	-.02 *
	Hiwi Indians(7,4)	-.09	n.a.	-.01	-.01

attractiveness by age 53. Regression coefficients vary enough between populations of raters that these estimates are fairly rough.

AGE AND ATTRACTIVENESS: NATURE, NURTURE, AND MECHANISMS

In the preceding sections of this chapter, I discussed how mate value would have varied with age under the demographic regime to which most human beings were subject until a few centuries ago, and to which human nature must still be largely adapted. I argued that age-related changes in physical attractiveness seem to track age-related changes in mate value. While the fit between theory and evidence is close, the case for the fecundity-tracking theory of attractiveness and age will also depend on the relative success of rival theories in accounting for the evidence, and on the success of mechanistically oriented researchers (neurologists, endocrinologists, behavior geneticists and others) in tracking down the "hardware" responsible for esthetic responses to age cues.

Age and Attractiveness: Beyond Fecundity?

Fecundity is only one component of mate value. Other components may also vary with age. In particular, several authors (Brownmiller 1984; Wolf 1992) argue that male preferences for youthful (and otherwise physically attractive) mates are an expression of male domination; men are attracted to young women because young women are more vulnerable and easily dominated than old ones. "Youth and (until recently) virginity have been beautiful in women since they stand for experiential and sexual ignorance. Aging in women is 'unbeautiful' since women grow more powerful with time" (Wolf 1992:14). Gowaty (1992:231–40) puts an evolutionary spin on this argument:

> There should be strong selection on males to control females' reproduction through direct coercive control of females.... Evolutionary thinkers, whether informed by feminist ideas or not, are not surprised by one of the overwhelming facts of patriarchal cultures, namely that men ... seek to constrain and control the reproductive capacities of women.... I argue that shaved legs and underarms, madeup faces, and exaggerated thinness are neotenic characteristics that signal juvenilization and its attendant dependence and subordination.... Juvenilization decreases the threat some men may feel when confronted with women; many men are comfortable around women whom they can clearly dominate and are profoundly uncomfortable around women whom they cannot so clearly dominate. The hypothesis that femininity signals ability to be dominated through juvenilization is an alternative to, but not necessarily mutually exclusive of, other evolutionary hypotheses that posit that femininity signals, sometimes deceptively, reproductive value and fertility.

Yet ethnographic evidence commonly suggests that young women at their peak attractiveness are not especially manipulable. Both Mehinacu and Ache men often complain that young women, far from being easy to push around, set a high value on themselves and are "stingy with their vaginas" (Gregor 1985; Kim Hill, pers. comm.). The fickleness and sexual reluctance of young women as compared to old is a common complaint among Brazilian men as well. Berry and McArthur's (1986) research on social perception of age-related craniofacial changes also fails to support the equation of sexiness with vulnerability. They presented subjects with a series of outline profile drawings representing individuals ranging from juvenile to adult and collected ratings of perceived social characteristics of each drawing. The drawing which was perceived as being the weakest and least threatening was the most juvenile-looking. (Subjects judged this drawing to represent a 4 year old.) The drawing perceived as sexiest was intermediate in "juvenility." (It was judged to be 23 years old.) In other words, the level of juvenility that maximizes perceived vulnerability does not maximize perceived sexiness. Kenrick and coworkers (1994) show that for teenage males, the age of an ideal sexual partner is older than their own age, which is more consistent with the hypothesis that men are concerned with cues to female fecundity than with the hypothesis that men prefer younger, more easily dominated females.

Thus both ethnography and social psychology suggest that female attractiveness cannot simply be equated with powerlessness, and that something more than changes in perceived vulnerability is involved in age-related changes in physical attractiveness. However, nothing in evolutionary theory rules out the possibility that markers of female submissiveness may be attractive to men and the topic certainly deserves more research.

Possible Mechanisms

Presumably our understanding of the psychological mechanisms involved in the production of adaptive behavior will pass through the same three stages as our understanding of the mechanisms of heredity. In stage 1, Darwin and other evolutionists knew that there were "laws of heredity," but didn't know much about them. In stage 2, indirect evidence gathered by Mendel and others demonstrated the existence of genes, but little was known about their physical constitution. During part of stage 2, Darwinians and Mendelians regarded their theories as incompatible rather than complementary. Finally, in stage 3, the physical basis of heredity, including the double helix structure of the gene and the genetic code, was worked out.

Our understanding of evolution and human behavior seems to be somewhere around stage 2. Indirect evidence suggests the existence of domain-specific psychological adaptations. But little is known about the physical basis of these adaptations. And like the early twentieth-century Darwinians and Mendelians, some behavioral ecologists and evolutionary psychologists regard their respective theoretical perspectives as conflicting rather than complementary. The future is likely to see a movement to stage 3, with rapid progress in understanding the genetic, endocrinological and neurological bases of adaptive behavior.

The study of the psychology of sensation-seeking is one possible road to a mechanistic understanding of why physical attractiveness is perceived to vary with age. As was noted in Chapter 1, individuals with high scores on tests of sensation-seeking also tend to place particular stress on the physical attractiveness of potential mates. Insofar as physical attraction is based on the assessment of age-related changes in mate value, the models presented above suggest, first, that men should be more interested in physical attractiveness than women, and that (for long-term mateships) the young should show more attraction to youthful features than the old. Sensation-seeking varies across sex and age categories in a fashion consistent with these expectations. We know something about the physical basis of sensation-seeking. It correlates with high levels of testosterone in both sexes, and with low levels of the neurotransmitter monoamine oxidase (Zuckerman et al. 1980). So far physiologically minded studies of sensation-seeking have not focused on physical attraction or attraction to youthful characteristics *per se,* but this seems like a promising avenue for research.

Comparisons of heterosexuals and homosexuals may also contribute to understanding the mechanisms involved in age preferences. Homosexual men resemble heterosexual men and homosexual women resemble heterosexual women in the importance they attach to the age of a potential partner, suggesting that sexual orientation and age preferences may under the control of separate systems (Jankowiak et al. 1992).

CHAPTER 5

Signs of Age and Fecundity

Chapter 4 presented the argument that human beings probably have adaptations for assessing age-related changes in the fecundity of potential mates. Chapter 5 carries the argument a step further, considering how somatic cues like facial proportions, skin color and body shape may signal age and fecundity. The chapter considers the possibility that adaptations for choosing a mate of a particular sex and age may lead incidentally to nonadaptive biases in the choice of a mate from among those individuals who fall *within* the "right" sex and age class. It seems likely that adaptations for complex perceptual discriminations will usually have nonadaptive biases built into them, and there is a growing interest in the possibility that some mate preferences are adaptive by-products, rather than adaptations in their own right. In particular, sensory bias may lead to preferences for "supernormal stimuli," stimuli that present the distinguishing features of a target stimulus in exaggerated form (Enquist and Arak 1993; Ryan et al. 1990; Staddon 1975; ten Cate and Bateson 1989). How much sensory bias toward exaggerated age- and sex-typical features contributes to variation in attractiveness within age/sex classes will depend both on the shape of fitness curves and on the strength of constraints on accurate age and sex assessment. In Chapter 4 I argued that there is more age-related variance in the mate value of adult females than of adult males. If age-related cues "spill over" to affect within-cohort attractiveness, this might explain why female attractiveness is more important than male attractiveness even within age groups.

FACIAL PROPORTIONS

Below I consider: 1) typical age-related changes and sex differences in facial proportions, and 2) how age and sex-related differences in facial proportions relate to attractiveness.

Facial Proportions, Age and Sex
There are differences not only in size but in shape between the faces of juvenile and adult humans, between women and men, and between young and old adults.
  1) *Juvenile vs. adult facial proportions.* In human beings, as in other mammals,

the neurocranium—the portion of the skull housing the brain, but also including the contiguous orbital region—grows rapidly early in development, while the facial skeleton proper—including the nasal and masticatory complex—attains its maximum rate of growth only later. As a result, juvenile mammals present a characteristic "cute" appearance, with relatively large eyes, high foreheads, and reduced snouts. Lorenz (1970) argued that this combination of features constitutes a releaser for parental behavior. Animals like cats and dogs which have been bred by human beings to serve as pets commonly retain juvenile cranial features into adulthood, in comparison with their wild relatives. (The retention of traits from early stages of the life cycle into later stages of the life cycle, in comparison with ancestors or with other members of the population, is known as neoteny—"holding on to youth." See Gould 1977 for discussion and further refinement of terminology.)

Mark et al. (1988) review a number of studies showing that a simple mathematical transformation, "cardioidal strain," has a powerful effect on perceived age of faces. Cardioidal strain maps each point $\{x, y\}$ on a figure onto $\{x', y'\} = \{x \cdot (1 - k \cdot y/r), y \cdot (1 - k \cdot y/r)\}$, where $r^2 = x^2 + y^2$, and k measures the magnitude of the transformation. A shape subjected to positive ($k > 0$) cardioidal strain shows downward and outward expansion in features located toward the bottom, no change in features located toward the sides, and downward and inward contraction in features located toward the top. Negative cardioidal strain produces the reverse transformations. Drawings of the faces of children or young adults subjected to a positive cardioidal strain transformation are perceived as older and less cute; pictures subjected to a negative transformation are perceived as younger and cuter. Full facial and profile drawings of the heads of birds, monkeys, and dogs, and even front and side drawings of Volkswagen Beetles, can be made to appear more or less "mature" or "cute" by subjecting them to positive or negative cardioidal strain. Figure 5.1 shows the effects of positive and negative cardioidal transformation on a square grid and on a line drawing of a face.

Attraction to "cute" proportions may not be learned: even at four months of age infants orient preferentially toward pictures of infant rather than adult faces, although it is not known whether infantile facial proportions are the relevant cue (McCall and Kennedy 1980). In Chapter 1 I cited research (Langlois et al. 1987) showing that infants as young as two months of age orient preferentially toward attractive rather than unattractive female faces. If female attractiveness is partly a matter of neoteny, then infant preferences for attractive female faces may be part of a more general attraction to faces or facelike stimuli manifesting low cardioidal strain.

Neotenous facial proportions in children may be a releaser for parental behavior. McCabe (1988) reviews studies showing that subjects report a greater willingness to provide nurturance for children with a high ratio of neurocranial to lower facial features. She also cites research conducted at several localities

Physical Attractiveness and the Theory of Sexual Selection 85

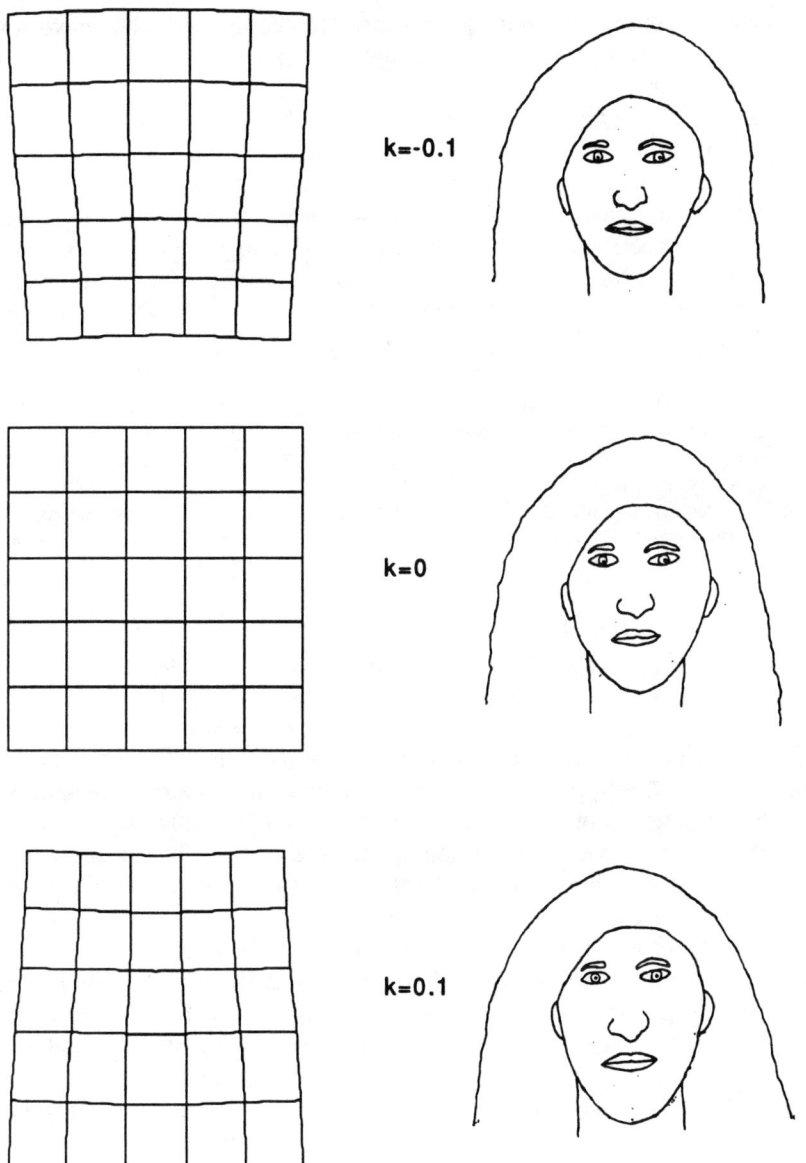

Figure 5.1. The effect of negative (top row) and positive (bottom row) cardioidal transformations on a 5 × 5 grid and on a face.

showing that abused children under court protection (ages 3–6) have lower ratios of neurocranial to lower facial dimensions than age-matched nursery school control groups.

2) *Female vs. male facial proportions.* In human beings, many of the traits that distinguish juvenile from adult faces also distinguish female from male faces. In other words, male faces undergo a more thorough remodeling over the course of adolescence than female faces. During adolescence, a male will develop heavier brows, a more protrusive nose and midface, and a larger chin and jaw. Adult male faces are not only larger but longer, more protrusive (that is, not as flat), and more robust than children's faces or adult female faces. These differences affect the appearance of the eyes and cheekbones.

> Because of the greater . . . protrusiveness of the male forehead and nose, the eyes appear more deep-set. In the female the eyes appear . . . "closer to the front" of the face. Female cheekbones also "look" much more prominent for the same reason; that is, the malar protuberances seem more apparent because the nose and forehead are less prominent. Indeed, high cheekbones are a classic feature of femininity, much emphasized by beauty analysts. Of course the malar protuberances are not actually "higher," they are just more conspicuous. [Enlow 1990:8]

Measurements of photographs in the present study support the proposition that adult facial proportions are more neotenous in females than in males. When I looked at the ratio of median female measurements to median male measurements in each of three populations of photographic subjects, the distances between landmarks around the eyes and eyebrows consistently produced some of the highest ratios (typically > 1), while vertical distances along the midline of the face consistently produced some of the lowest (typically < .9). In other words, the size of the eyes in relation to the height of the face strongly distinguishes between females and males; female faces are more neotenous than male faces.

3) *Young adult vs. old adult facial proportions.* Skeletal growth greatly slows down with the attainment of adulthood, but changes in facial morphology continue. "Beginning at age 25, the eyebrows steadily descend from a position well above the supraorbital rim to a point far below it; sagging of the lateral aspect of the eyebrows makes the eyes seem smaller" (Larrabee Jr. and Makielski 1993:14). Cartilaginous tissues also continue to grow: ears get bigger, and noses get longer, wider, and more protrusive. With the loss of connective tissue, the vermilion, or red zone, of the lips gets thinner (Enlow 1990; Larrabee Jr. and Makielski 1993; Susanne 1977).

Facial Proportions and Attractiveness.

Studies in several Westernized countries suggest that neotenous/feminine facial proportions are an important component of female facial attractiveness.

McArthur and Berry (1983), working in the United States, Riedl (1990), working in Austria, and Fauss (1988), working in Germany, all artificially manipulating the sizes and positions of facial features, show that the ideal female face has a more "neotenous" (juvenile) appearance—larger eyes and more reduced vertical dimensions—than the average female face, while the ideal male face is closer to the average male face. Cunningham (1986) shows that photographs of female faces rated attractive by US raters have unusually large eyes, wide cheekbones, narrow cheeks, and small noses, chins and jaws. Johnston and Franklin (1993) use a "genetic algorithm" to allow subjects to generate attractive female faces by a process analogous to artificial selection, repeatedly asking subjects to assign attractiveness ratings to faces, and then producing a new generation of faces by adding small random "mutations" to the most attractive faces, and repeating the process of selection. They show that attractive female faces had significantly smaller eye-chin lengths, smaller lower facial features, fuller lips, and narrower mouths than average US undergraduates. Perrett et al. (1994), working with both English and Japanese subjects, constructed a composite of digitized photographs of 60 Caucasian English females, a composite of the most attractive 15 females (as rated by English raters), and an attractiveness "caricature" that exaggerated the features distinguishing the second composite from the first. They used the same techniques to generate three images based on photographs of Japanese females as rated by Japanese males. Both within and across populations, caricatures were rated most attractive, composite attractive faces second, and composite average faces last. Attractive faces had higher cheekbones, a thinner jaw, larger eyes relative to the size of the face, and shorter vertical distances between jaw and mouth, and mouth and nose.[1]

One limitation of the studies reviewed above is that they are confined to societies strongly influenced by Western ideals of physical attractiveness. (The Westernization of Japanese standards of attractiveness is reviewed in Chapter 7.) Below I report three tests of the hypothesis that neoteny is a component of female facial attractiveness as well as data on neoteny and attractiveness among males. The research reported below includes a test of the neoteny hypothesis in two societies (Ache, Hiwi) not strongly affected by Western somatic ideals. Because there are no strong grounds in theory or in previous research for expecting facial neoteny to contribute positively or negatively to male attractiveness, I use two-tailed statistical tests for males and one-tailed tests for females.

Eyes, Noses, Lips: Age Predictors as Attractiveness Predictors

Aging is expected to change the relative size of the major facial features—eyes, noses and lips. Table 5.1 gives the correlations and partial correlations of measures of size of facial features with age for Ache females and males. These measures were selected based on discussions cited above on typical age-related changes in facial proportions. They include:

Table 5.1 Correlations of relative sizes of major facial features with age and with one another among Ache women and men.

		Age	EW/FH	NH/FH
Ache females	EW/FH	-.15		
	NH/FH	.24 *	.06	
	LH/FH	-.40 **	-.15	-.50 **
Ache males	EW/FH	-.52 **		
	NH/FH	.11	-.24	
	LH/FH	-.65 **	.32 *	-.31 *

EW/FH	Eye Width/ Face Height
NH/FH	Nose Height/ Face Height
LH/FH	Lip Height/ Face Height

Eye Width (EW = mean of D[l.endocanthion, l.exocanthion] and D[r.endocanthion, r.exocanthion]),
Nose Height (NH = D[glabella, subnasale]), and
Lip Height (LH = D[labiale superius, labiale inferius])

where D[a,b] is the Euclidean distance between landmarks a and b, and l. and r. are left and right. All measures were standardized by dividing them by Face Height (FH = D[glabella, gonion]). (See Table 3.1 and Figure 3.1 for definitions of landmarks.) All three measures are associated with age in the expected directions. Two other measures, Eye Height and Cheek Width, were not significantly associated with age and dropped out of both age regressions, and have been eliminated from this analysis.

Do facial proportions that distinguish young females from old ones also distinguish attractive females from unattractive ones within samples of females of similar ages (as the "sensory bias" hypothesis would suggest)? Table 5.2 reports the partial correlations of attractiveness ratings with logarithms of eye width, nose height, and lip height (all corrected for face height) for Brazilian, US and Ache females and males. Of the four age predictors presented in Table 5.2, only EW/FH functions consistently as a predictor of attractiveness, although the other variables generally give results in the predicted direction (that is, cues associated with increased age are associated with decreased attractiveness when age is controlled for.)

Simply piling up a list of age predictors and reporting their correlations with attractiveness is an inefficient way of testing the neoteny hypothesis. A better way begins by combining information from multiple age cues into an age-predictor equation using multiple regression. I used the stepwise multiple linear regression routine in Systat 2.2 to construct an equation that would predict age among the Ache as a function of the variables above. Both *p to enter* and *p to discard* in the stepwise regression are set at .15. The resulting equation is

Table 5.2. Mean and standard deviation of measures of facial proportions, and their correlations with ratings of attractiveness. Numbers in parentheses are numbers of male and female raters.

Photos of	Rated by		Males rating females			Females rating males		
			EW/FH	NH/FH	LH/FH	EW/FH	NH/FH	LH/FH
		mean=	.210	.589	.125	.185	.585	.135
		stdev=	.014	.030	.020	.018	.033	.027
Brazilians	Brazilians(19,11)		.39 **	.01	.24 +	-.09	-.19	.17
N=49,20	US Americans(12,20)		.19	-.14	-.07	-.35	-.41 +	.42 +
	Russians(11,14)		.32 *	.13	.12	-.10	-.43 +	.27
	Ache Indians(11,13)		.43 **	-.29 *	.23	-.07	-.15	.10
	Hiwi Indians(4,4)		.28 *	-.19	.21	.03	-.47 *	.53 *
		mean=	.225	.581	.121	.202	.574	.118
		stdev=	.018	.024	.022	.013	.025	.022
US Americans	Brazilians(20,23)		.23	-.26 +	.17	.00	.18	.04
N=51,35	US Americans(11,18)		.30 *	.04	-.04	-.03	.02	-.15
	Russians(12,14)		.21	-.20	.03	.07	.09	.05
	Ache Indians(20,21)		.25 +	.10	.13	-.11	-.04	-.01
	Hiwi Indians(0,0)		n.a.	n.a.	n.a.	n.a.	n.a.	n.a.
		mean=	.189	.599	.128	.177	.607	.118
		stdev=	.013	.035	.023	.013	.032	.029
Ache Indians	Brazilians(17,16)		-.12	.00	.10	.12	-.26	.19
N=41,36	US Americans(12,15)		-.09	.19	.08	.22	-.29 +	.18
	Russians(12,12)		-.22	.31	-.03	.13	-.43 **	.14
	Ache Indians(15,15)		.15	-.02	.00	.21	-.17	.14
	Hiwi Indians(7,4)		.19	-.32 *	.49 **	.31 +	-.11	.01

EW/FH	Eye Width/ Face Height
NH/FH	Nose Height/ Face Height
LH/FH	Lip Height/ Face Height

$$\text{PredictedAge1} = -141 \cdot \log[\text{EW/FH}] - 62 \cdot \log[\text{LH/FH}] - 128 \qquad (5.1; \text{females})$$

The variance accounted for (R^2) is .23**.

This equation predicts female age as a function of Eye Width and Lip Height; Nose Height drops out of the regression. However, an equation with nearly the same predictive power can be produced by excluding Lip Height from the regression:

$$\text{PredictedAge2} = -108 \cdot \log[\text{EW/FH}] + 139 \cdot \log[\text{NH/FH}] - 17 \qquad (5.2; \text{females})$$

The variance accounted for (R^2) is .17*.

For Ache males, the regression of age on Eye Width, Nose Height and Lip Width yields the equation:

$$\text{PredictedAge3} = -146 \log[\text{EW/FH}] - 61 \cdot \log[\text{LH/FH}] - 136 \qquad (5.3; \text{males})$$

The variance accounted for (R^2) is .55**.

In this case, however, excluding Lip Height from the regression produces no new age predictor equation. Thus the regression produces two age predictor equations for females and one for males. The measurement error variance (as a fraction of total variance) associated with the three predicted ages is .10, .08, and .10.

Given that a neotenous face is one in which the morphological apparent age is less than the chronological age, the age predictor equations above can be combined with information about actual ages to produce indices of neoteny:

$$\text{Neoteny1} = \text{Age} - \text{PredictedAge1} \qquad (5.4; \text{females})$$
$$\text{Neoteny2} = \text{Age} - \text{PredictedAge2} \qquad (5.5; \text{females})$$
$$\text{Neoteny3} = \text{Age} - \text{PredictedAge3} \qquad (5.6; \text{males})$$

An individual with neotenous facial proportions—large eyes, small nose, full lips—has a lower *predicted* age (Equations 5.1–5.3), and a higher index of neoteny (Equations 5.4–5.6), than one of the same age with less neotenous facial proportions.

Table 5.3 reports the correlations between attractiveness ratings (controlled for age) and these indices of neoteny. All correlations involving photographs of Brazilians and US Americans, and some correlations involving photographs of all three samples, are sufficiently close to pool (Sokal and Rolf 1969:520–23). Pooled correlations for females are shaded; they provide consistent support for the hypothesis that neoteny is a component of female facial attractiveness.[2]

Students and Models

I carried out a second test of the neoteny hypothesis incorporating measurements of a new sample of facial photographs, the US model sample. This sample comprises 1) photographs of ten models displayed on the covers of *Cosmopolitan* and *Glamour* magazines between 1989 and 1993 (five from each magazine), and 2) photographs of ten male models displayed in advertisements in *Esquire* and *GQ*, selected from magazines on file at the Ann Arbor Public Library. Models not facing directly toward the camera, models with their lips parted, celebrities and non-Caucasians were excluded. I used calipers to measure face height, right and left eye width, nose height, and lip height. The mean and standard deviation of these measurements, and the comparable figures for my sample of University of Michigan undergraduate females are presented in Table 5.4. For females, all differences between models and undergraduates are in the

Table 5.3. Means and standard deviations of three indices of facial neoteny, and their correlations with ratings of attractiveness. Numbers in parentheses are numbers of male and female raters subjects.

Photos of	Rated by	Males rating females		Females rating males	
		Neoteny1 (Eqn 4.4)	Neoteny2 (Eqn 4.5)	Neoteny3 (Eqn 4.6)	
	mean=	-1.0	-1.6	-1.3	years
	stdev=	7.5	5.5	7.1	years
Brazilians	Brazilians(19,11)	.37 **	.24 *	-.23	
N=49,20	US Americans(12,20)	.06	.04	-.17	
	Russians(11,14)	.23 +	.11	-.05	
	Ache Indians(11,13)	.38 **	.45 **	-.02	
	Hiwi Indians(4,4)	.25 *	.25 *	.35	
	mean=	-.2	-.1	-1.6	yrs
	stdev=	7.8	4.5	7.7	yrs
US Americans	Brazilians(20,23)	.34 *	.36 **	.03	
N=51,35	US Americans(11,18)	.20 +	.28 *	-.13	
	Russians(12,14)	.23 +	.26 *	.08	
	Ache Indians(20,21)	.25 +	.18	-.07	
	Hiwi Indians(0,0)	n.a.	n.a.	n.a.	
	Brazilians(39,44)	.36 **	.30 **	-.10	
Pooled samples	US Americans(23,38)	.13 +	.16 +	-.15	
(Brazil + US)	Russians(23,28)	.23 *	.18 *	.02	
N=100,55	Ache Indians(31,34)	.32 **	.32 **	-.05	
	Hiwi Indians	n.a.	n.a.	n.a.	
	mean=	.2	-.2	-.4	yrs
	stdev=	9.2	9.6	9.3	yrs
Ache Indians	Brazilians(17,16)	-.10	-.13	.00	
N=41,36	US Americans(12,15)	-.05	-.16	.14	
	Russians(12,12)	-.19	-.29	.01	
	Ache Indians(15,15)	.07	.12	.21	
	Hiwi Indians(7,4)	.38 **	.24 +	.07	
	Brazilians(56,50)	n.a.	n.a.	-.07	
Pooled samples	US Americans(35,53)	n.a.	n.a.	-.07	
(All)	Russians(35,40)	n.a.	n.a.	.02	
N=141,91	Ache Indians(46,49)	.25 **	.26 **	.03	
	Hiwi Indians(7,5)	.31 **	.24 **	.23 *	

Table 5.4. Facial proportions and predicted ages of students and models of both sexes. Asterisks show results of t-tests on mean differences between students and models

	Students		Models	
	Mean	St.Dev.	Mean	St.Dev.
FEMALES				
EW/FH	.23	.019	.24	.012 *
NH/FH	.58	.024	.49	.034 **
LH/FH	.12	.022	.17	.015 **
PredictedAge1 (yrs)	20.2	8.0	7.4	3.1 **
PredictedAge2 (yrs)	20.2	4.5	6.8	3.8 **
MALES				
EW/FH	.20	.013	.20	.014
NH/FH	.57	.025	.47	.025 **
LH/FH	.12	.022	.12	.018
PredictedAge3 (yrs)	22.8	8.3	23.1	5.8

EW/FH   Eye Width/ Face Height
NH/FH   Nose Height/ Face Height
LH/FH   Lip Height/ Face Height
PredictedAges from Equations 5.1-5.3

right direction—models are relatively neotenous, with large eyes, small noses and full lips. A *t*-test on log-transformed variables shows that all differences are significant.

Table 5.4 also includes figures for predicted age, according to Equations 5.1–5.3 above. These figures confirm the neotenous facial proportions of female models; predicted ages are just 6.8 and 7.4 years! This does not imply that models have the same facial proportions as 7 year olds, because Equations 5.1–5.3 presume, incorrectly, that the rate of facial growth is constant. But it does provide strong support for the proposition that attractive female faces represent a "supernormal stimulus," presenting in exaggerated form the features that distinguish young women from old ones.

Cardioidal Strain and Facial Attractiveness

Figure 5.1 shows the effect of negative and positive cardioidal strain on a line drawing of a facial photograph of a Brazilian female. I carried out a third test of the neoteny hypothesis using similarly transformed drawings of female and male US Americans. From the US American sample I selected photographs of the three most attractive females, three females of median attractiveness, and the three least attractive females. I made line drawings of all nine photographs, and produced two new drawings for each one of the original drawings via cardioidal strain, using polar coordinate graph paper. For each trial, a rater was presented with one original and two transformed drawings of a single face, and asked to rank them from most to least attractive. I followed the same procedure for nine drawings of male faces. Raters were drawn from an intermediate level anthropology class, and each set of drawings was rated by at least four raters.

Figure 5.2 presents the results. Positive cardioidal strain ($k = 0.1$) had a consistent negative effect on attractiveness for both males and females (for both sexes, $p < 0.01$, binomial test). Negative cardioidal strain ($k = -0.1$) had a positive effect on female attractiveness and a negative effect on male attractiveness, relative to untransformed faces. Results were marginally significant for females ($p = 0.06$, binomial test) and nonsignificant for males ($p = 0.11$); the sex difference in the results was highly significant ($p < 0.01$).[3] There seemed to be an interaction between the attractiveness of the original drawing and the effect of negative cardioidal strain; negative cardioidal strain increased the attractiveness of the least attractive females, decreased the attractiveness of the least attractive males, and left the attractiveness of others unaffected. In other words, making faces "cuter" (more neotenous) via negative cardioidal strain increased attractiveness only up to a point.

Summary of Results, and Discussion

In humans, mate value declines with age beginning in early adulthood. It declines more quickly for females than for males. Consequently we expect human beings, especially males, to have adaptations for assessing age-related changes in mate value. Regardless of whether age-related changes in physical attractiveness (especially for females) result from such adaptations or from other causes, it is possible that particularly attractive faces are those that present age-related cues in an exaggerated, or supernormal form. Large eyes in relation to face height, small noses, and full lips, are markers of youth and femininity. The results presented in this chapter suggest that these features are indeed criteria of female attractiveness even when age is controlled for. Specifically:

1) Women with facial proportions suggesting a younger age than their actual age are perceived as more attractive by male raters from five populations.

2) A sample of facial photographs of US female models has significantly more neotenous proportions than a sample of facial photographs of US female undergraduates.

3) Female faces artificially transformed to make them more and less neotenous are perceived as correspondingly more and less attractive.

4) Associations between facial neoteny and male attractiveness are weak and/or inconsistent.

Thus, this analysis provides consistent support for the proposition that neoteny is a component of female facial attractiveness. However more research will have to be carried out in a wider range of populations before this associa-

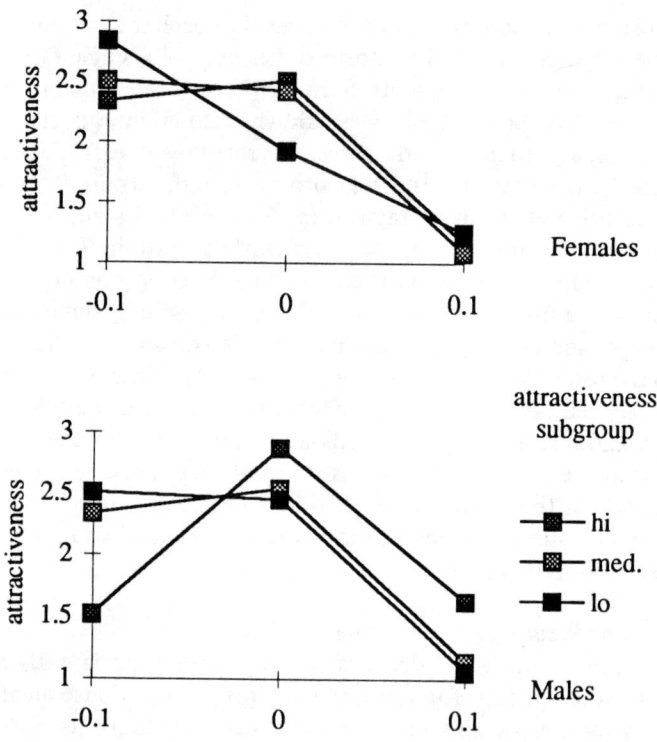

Figure 5.2. The effects of negative and positive cardioidal transformations on the perceived attractiveness of faces of both sexes (including faces previously rated attractive medium, and unattractive).

tion can be accepted as a human universal. If such research continues to support this association, a number of topics will remain to be addressed.

Fecundity, nubility and supernormal stimuli. Why should a male assessing females around their age of maximum fecundity be most attracted to those displaying exaggerated markers of youth? One possible answer to this question is that males prefer females of maximum reproductive value rather than maximum fecundity; female reproductive value peaks earlier than female fecundity. However, I have argued in Chapter 4 that reproductive value is not a good measure of mate value. Another possible explanation is that if individuals typically combine information from multiple cues in real world mate choice, then it may be adaptive to prefer exaggerated signs of youth for some cues and exaggerated signs of maturity for other cues, depending on the rates at which different cues change over time. Another possibility is that "neotenous" traits are preferred not so much because they are neotenous as because they are feminine—they may be sex markers as much as age markers. Finally, it is misleading to suggest that a linear regression that predicts age as a function of facial proportions from early to young adulthood continues to predict age when linearly extrapolated backwards to more "neotenous" proportions, since trends in facial growth are not linear throughout the life span. The supernormal facial proportions produced by backward linear extrapolation of young adult to old adult trends may not characterize average human beings at *any* age. Some of the lines of research discussed below could help address these topics.

Perceived age. Berry (1985) shows that artificially generated faces with big eyes and reduced vertical dimensions are not only judged to be more attractive than faces with the opposite characteristics, but are also judged to be younger. One obvious next step is to obtain age estimates for photographic samples to discover how far *perceived* age correlates both with age-related proportion indices and with ratings of attractiveness.

Beyond age and sensory bias. There may be adaptive advantages to choosing mates with neotenous features over and above the advantages of choosing mates of a particular age and sex. Among older individuals, perceived age may actually be a more accurate indicator of health status than chronological age. In one study (Borkan 1980), physicians estimated the ages of more than 1000 elderly men, and researchers calculated the difference between perceived age and actual age, and carried out medical tests on the top 15% (those who looked youngest for their age) and the bottom 15% (those who looked oldest for their age). On 15 out of 24 tests of physical functioning (including lung, heart, kidney, hearing and eye functions), members of the younger *looking* group really were significantly "biologically" younger than age-matched members of the older looking group. Thus, in this study, perceived age was a reflection of "biological" age, which was not identical to chronological age.

By the same token, neotenous features might be correlated with components of mate value other than chronological age. A preliminary analysis of the present data set uncovered no evidence that indices of facial neoteny or ratings of facial attractiveness have any relationship to variables such as age at menarche, stature, or feminine body proportions (waist to hip ratio) which have arguably been relevant to fitness in our evolutionary past; thus there may be no adaptive advantage for males to preferring neotenous features over and above the advantages of choosing mates of a particular age and sex. But more research will be needed to settle how far biological age (as distinct from chronological age) is a meaningful construct, and whether it is correlated with craniofacial neoteny when chronological age is controlled.

Skin and Hair Color

Van den Berghe and Frost (1986) examine the Human Relations Area Files for information regarding preferred skin color. They find that "of the 51 societies for which any mention of native skin color preference (or of a cosmetic preference from which color preference can be directly inferred) is made, 47 state a preference *for the lighter end of the locally represented spectrum,* although not necessarily for the lightest possible skin color" (p. 92, italics in original). The four exceptions are ambiguous rather than showing a clear preference for dark skin. Skin color preferences show a consistent sex difference. "Of the 47 positive cases . . . 30 mention a preference for lighter skin only in women, compared to 3 for men. Fourteen accounts mention both sexes. The overall impression is that a light skin is a more consequential asset for women than for men in the vast majority of societies" (p. 94).

Van den Berghe and Frost establish that colonialism cannot account for the widespread preference for lighter than average skin, although it may accentuate that preference in particular cases. The preference is found even where contact with outsiders has been extremely limited, and many of the societies for which a preference for light skin color is reported are also reported to find European facial features and the extremely light skin of Europeans unattractive. By the same token, preference for light skin characterizes many technologically simple and unstratified societies in which it is unlikely that class differences in exposure to sunlight are involved. This leaves essentially two broad classes of likely explanation for species-typical skin color preferences in humans, one involving sensory/cognitive bias, and one involving fecundity markers.

Color Symbolism

Both the categorization of colors and their emotional connotations show considerable cross-cultural regularity. Berlin and Kay (1969) argue that color terms are added to languages in a predictable order. Someone who knows how many color terms a language has can predict fairly accurately what those terms are. Every language distinguishes at least two colors: the minimal color vocabulary includes white (and other light or warm colors) and black (and other dark or cool colors). Languages with three color terms distinguish white, black and red. Turner (1967:59ff) discusses the symbolism of white, black and red among the Ndembu of Zambia for whom white is the color of life, black the color of death, and red an ambivalent color, suggesting both vitality and bloodshed. Turner argues that the same symbolic associations are present in many other cultures (see also Strathern 1971). Gergen (1975) shows that in Western literature, white is associated with triumph, light, innocence, joy, divine power, purity, regeneration, happiness, gaiety, peace, chastity, truth, modesty, femininity, and delicacy, while black is associated with woe, gloom, darkness, dread, death, terror, wickedness, curses, mourning, mortification, defilement, error, annihilation, strength, and deep quiet. In the United States both African Americans and European Americans rate the color white as more positive but less powerful than black. Positive associations for white, and negative associations for black are extremely widespread cross-culturally, with a few exceptions (for instance, white is a funeral color in some cultures).

On one argument, then, preferences for light (but not necessarily "white") skin may be products of a sensory bias toward light colors deriving from universal experiences like the contrast between night and day and the association between lightness and cleanliness (see also Guthrie 1970).

Lightness, Femininity and Fecundity

However, van den Berghe and Frost suggest another explanation for skin color preferences. Skin color in humans is a marker of both sex and age. In any fairly homogeneous population, infants of both sexes are generally lighter than adults. Skin color slowly darkens throughout childhood. At puberty, males continue to darken, but females become lighter. After attaining a peak of lightness in adolescence, female skin color gradually darkens with increasing age.

These sex differences in skin color apparently result from a physiological link between estrogen production and melanin production. In fact, women experience slight changes in skin color over the course of their menstrual cycles, with skin color being lightest at ovulation. Skin color, in other words, is a marker of both lifelong and cyclical changes in female fecundity. Van den Berghe and Frost argue that the male attraction to a lighter than average (but not necessarily "white") skin color is the expression of an adaptation for assessing female fecundity, both age related and otherwise.

This hypothesis could be tested: if light skin color is in part a marker of nubility, then faces differing in skin color but otherwise similar should be judged to differ in age.

How Important Is Color?

I collected data on skin color for female and male US samples. I used a Photovolt reflectometer to measure reflectance at three different frequencies (blue, green, and amber) at two different sites: on the underside of the upper arm and on the forehead. Reflectance is the fraction of incident light reflected at a given frequency; a mirror, which reflects almost all incident light will have a reflectance close to 1.00; a black surface will have a reflectance close to 0.

All reflectances at both sites are highly correlated with each other (Spearman's *r*'s ranging from .7 to .9). But there is no significant correlation between measures of skin color and ratings of physical attractiveness by Brazilians, US Americans, Russians or Ache—although Ache females show an almost significant aversion to light skinned males. It may be that the photographs do not allow accurate estimates of skin color; a possible further line of research is to collect subjective ratings of photographic skin color and compare these with reflectometer measurements and with ratings of attractiveness. But for the time being, all we can say is that the effect of skin color on attractiveness does not appear to be very powerful within age classes within a broad ethnic category like "European." Sun-tanning is popular in both the United States and Brazil, and it may be that culture overrides more typical response to light skin in these populations. Ache men repeatedly stress the attractions of white skin, so it is surprising that they do not show any sign of preferring light skin when evaluating US females. It may be that the lightest skinned females in the US sample are too far outside the accustomed range of variation for the Ache to find them especially attractive.

There is stronger evidence in this study for a relationship between hair color and attractiveness. I asked US subjects to describe their hair color. The differences in attractiveness between women who described their hair color as blond (or dark blond) and other women, expressed in terms of standard deviations, are .16, .64**, .28+, and .02 for Brazilian, US, Russian and Ache raters (one-tailed t-test for US Americans and Russians). While blond women are considered more attractive, at least in the two populations with an appreciable frequency of blondness, blond men do not fare as well; differences in attractiveness between blond men and others are −.55*, −.79**, −.29, and .04 for Brazilian, US, Russian and Ache raters (two-tailed t-test for US Americans and Russians). Blond hair, like fair skin, is a neotenous trait; in some populations which favor sun-tanning, hair color may be more salient than skin color as an age and fecundity marker.

BODY SHAPE

The Waist to Hip Ratio

In a recent series of papers, Singh (1993a, b) summarizes a large body of physiological research demonstrating that the waist to hip ratio (WHR) stands out among a number of measures of body size and shape as a correlate of female age and fecundity. Before puberty, average female WHRs (ratios of minimum body circumference at the waist to body circumference at the point of maximum protrusion of the buttocks) are similar to average male WHRs, in the range of .85 to .95. At puberty, with the growth of the pelvis and the deposition of fat in the hips, buttocks and thighs, average female WHR declines rapidly to .67 to .80. Average female WHR increases slowly over the course of adulthood, in step with declining fecundity, and is once again in the male range among postmenopausal women.

Changes in female WHR track not only age-related changes in fecundity, but variation in ovarian function within age cohorts, as assessed by age at onset of puberty, regularity of menstrual cycles, levels of circulating estrogen, and probability of conception among sexually active noncontracepting women. WHR seems to be a stronger and more consistent signal of fecundity than other possible indicators such as breast size, body size and percent body fat.

Given the relationship between fecundity and mate value, a low WHR is a good candidate for a universal of female attractiveness, even in the face of cultural variation in ideal body weight and other aspects of body shape. Singh presents several data sets suggesting that males in the US find low WHRs attractive. In a series of line drawings depicting 12 women ranging from underweight to normal weight to overweight, and with WHRs of .7, .8, .9 and 1.0, men consistently rated low WHR women as more attractive than high WHR women within each weight category. Singh also shows that Miss America contestants since the 1920s and Playboy centerfolds since the 1950s maintain low WHRs, mostly in the range from .68 to .72. The near invariance in WHR over time in these samples is especially remarkable because body weight and the absolute values of waist and hip circumference change considerably.

Breasts, Buttocks, and Thighs

While a low waist to hip ratio may be universally attractive to men, ethnographies also suggest considerable variation in preferences regarding female secondary sexual characteristics such as hips, buttocks, thighs and breasts (Ford and Beach 1951). Below I will compare the United States and Brazil in this respect. Much of the treatment is descriptive, but I will also propose some avenues for further research.

Social psychological research confirms the conventional wisdom that US American men are particularly attracted to large breasts (Thompson 1992; Wildman et al. 1976). Nora Ephron (1975) writes about being a small-breasted woman in the United States:

> After I went into therapy, a process that made it possible for me to tell total strangers at cocktail parties that breasts were the hang-up of my life, I was often told that I was insane to have been bothered by my condition. I was also told, by close friends, that I was extremely boring on the subject. And my girl friends, the ones with nice big breasts, would go on endlessly about how their lives had been far more miserable than mine. Their bra straps were snapped in class. They couldn't sleep on their stomachs. They were stared at whenever the word "mountain" cropped up in geography. And *Evangeline,* good God what they went through every time someone had to stand up and recite the prologue to Longfellow's *Evangeline:* " . . . stand like druids of eld. . . / With beards that rest on their bosoms." It was

much worse for them, they tell me. They had a terrible time of it, they assure me. I don't know how lucky I was, they say.

I have thought about their remarks, tried to put myself in their place, considered their point of view. I think they are full of shit. [p. 12]

Ephron might have had an easier time of it in Brazil. There the US attraction to large breasts seems so odd that Brazilians familiar with US movies and television programs sometimes assume that all US women have large breasts, and have trouble understanding that US movie and TV producers make a point of selecting big-breasted actresses because US men find them attractive. "Anything more than will fit in the mouth is wasted," several Brazilian men have told me, and "Lemons are better than papayas." "Papayas" (*mamões*), a common Brazilian expression for large breasts, with its implication of elongation and irregularity, is far less flattering than the US "melons."

Brazilian men are especially attracted to women's buttocks. Parker's review of Brazilian sexuality discusses Brazilians' cult of the *"bunda"* (1991:116–19). (*Bunda* has approximately the force of "butt" or "ass" in English.) Brazilians sometimes refer to this attraction as "the national preference" (*a preferência nacional*). If US men, resorting to an economic metaphor, refer to a big-breasted woman as "well-endowed," Brazilian men call a shapely posterior a "savings account" (*poupança*). The typical female pose on the covers of US erotic magazines is full frontal; the typical pose on Brazilian magazine covers shows a woman presenting her backside to the camera, and looking over her shoulder.

Figure 5.3 presents the mean responses of Brazilian, US and Russian males and females who were presented with a silhouette of a side view of a woman's body and asked, "Would this woman be most attractive if her breasts were the same size, larger, or smaller?" The question was repeated for buttocks and thighs. "Smaller" was scored as 1, "the same size" as 2, and "larger" as 3. (I omit Ache responses, because Ache seemed to have problems interpreting the silhouette.)

Brazilian raters of both sexes prefer the smallest breasts and the largest buttocks and thighs; US American raters of both sexes prefer the largest breasts and the smallest buttocks. A Kruskal-Wallis one-way ANOVA shows that there is significant between-group variance in all three size preferences for both sexes (all $p < .01$). A Wilcoxon rank sum test shows all differences between US and Brazilian raters of both sexes significant at $p < .05$, as well as all differences between Russian and Brazilian males, and between Russian and US females.

It is entirely possible that differences between the United States and Brazil in male erotic focus (breasts versus buttocks and thighs) are a nonadaptive by-product of cultural "drift," or of cognitive biases connected to larger cultural themes that distinguish the two countries (e.g. Parker, 1991:116–19). Nonetheless, the differences do raise some interesting questions for evolutionary psychology.

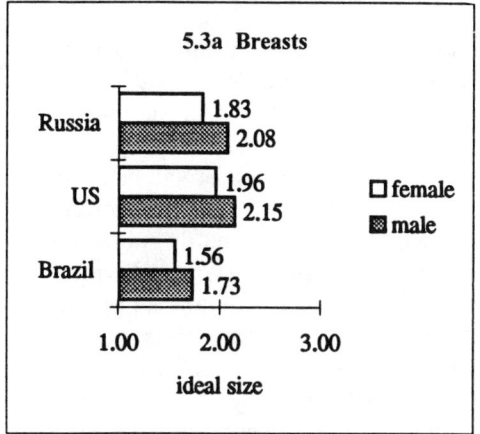

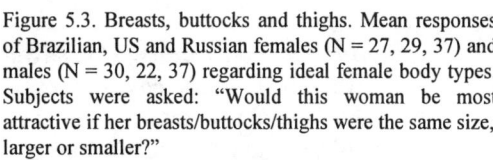

Figure 5.3. Breasts, buttocks and thighs. Mean responses of Brazilian, US and Russian females (N = 27, 29, 37) and males (N = 30, 22, 37) regarding ideal female body types. Subjects were asked: "Would this woman be most attractive if her breasts/buttocks/thighs were the same size, larger or smaller?"

    1 = smaller than silhouette is most attractive
    2 = same size as silhouette is most attractive
    3 = larger than silhouette is most attractive

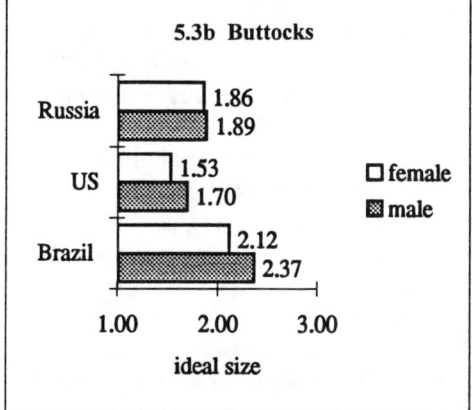

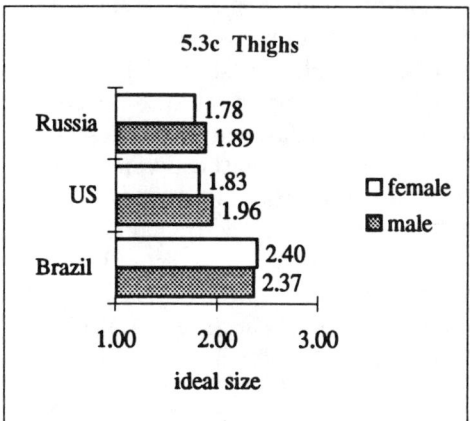

Kruskal-Wallis one-way nonparametric Anova shows significant ($p < .05$) between population variation in ideal female dimensions for all features for both sexes of raters.

Sensitive period learning. Sensitive period learning (or imprinting) will be adaptive in response to environmental factors that change little over the course of a lifetime, but greatly over evolutionary time. By contrast, short-term reversible learning will be more adaptive in response to factors that change considerably over the course of a lifetime, while hard-wired responses will be more effective for factors that change little over evolutionary time spans. The production and recognition of language sounds—phonemes—is apparently subject to sensitive period learning, rather than reversible learning or hard-wiring. Phonology changes slowly enough over the course of a single life span that the phonology-learning machinery can safely shut down around the beginning of puberty—people have a hard time learning to speak a new language without an accent after this point—but it changes rapidly enough on a longer time scale that any hard-wired system for producing and recognizing phonemes would be obsolete in a few thousand years.

The visual "sexual releasers" to which human beings are exposed are likely to change to some degree over the course of millennia, partly as a result of local microevolution, and even more as a result of changes in clothing and ornamentation. It may be that while human beings have a broad innate "template" of the physical appearance of a high-mate-value member of the other sex, imprinting during childhood or puberty "fine-tunes" this template to accommodate local variations in the shape, ornamentation and exposure of the body. One topic for further research, then, is how far the acquisition of population-specific standards of physical attractiveness is governed by sensitive-period learning. Do Brazilians who move to the United States as adults experience an "Americanization" of their standards of physical attractiveness, or is it just as difficult for an adult to lose a visual erotic focus acquired early in life as to lose a foreign accent?

Sex differences. Superimposed on cross-cultural variation in erotic focus is a consistent sex difference. In all but one case, males find exaggerated female secondary sexual characteristics more attractive than females do. Most of the individual differences are not significant at $p < .05$, but the pattern is too consistent to be the result of chance ($p < .01$, binomial test on sign differences for 9 cases). As discussed above and in Chapter 2, there is a conflict of interest between males and females over tradeoffs between survival and reproduction. Under any mating system except lifelong monogamy without remarriage, the tradeoffs that maximize mate value are not those that maximize fitness. This conflict of interest may be involved in the evolution of human female sex-specific fat distribution (Low and Alexander 1987), and may result in consistent male/female differences in attitudes toward fertility advertisements in the female figure.

CONCLUSION: SEXUAL SELECTION AND HUMAN PROPORTIONS

In presenting data regarding age cues from facial proportions, skin color, and figure, I considered each set of cues separately. But it is important to keep in mind that there may be more information in multiple cues when they are considered jointly. For example, suppose some index of facial proportions changes gradually with age, while the development of secondary sexual characteristics like breasts and buttocks occurs more rapidly and at an early age. If one were trying to select females of a particular age (x') using information from facial proportions alone, one would pick females with facial proportions corresponding to age x'. But if one combined information from facial proportions and body proportions, one would do better to pick females with more youthful facial proportions provided they had adult body proportions, because the expected age given particular facial proportions *and* an adult figure is higher than the expected age given particular facial proportions alone. In other words, in this particular example, one should be biased toward youthfulness regarding facial proportions and biased toward maturity regarding body proportions. This conclusion depends on how rapidly body and facial proportions change with age; it would be reversed if, for example, body proportions attained their maximum rate of change after, rather than before, age x'. In either case, the use of multiple cues to assess mate value means that the most attractive facial proportions will not necessarily be those associated with the age of maximum mate value.

Preferences regarding age cues in face and figure may have evolutionary consequences. Specifically, male preferences may have led to the evolution both of cues in the female figure that advertise sexual maturity and of cues in the face that advertise youth.

Consider first evolution below the neck. Primate females sometimes show signs of estrus well before the onset of full adult reproductive capacity. The early development of sexual signals may give females a chance to practice adult sexual behavior before they are physically ready to bear young. In species in which females transfer out of their natal groups on reaching maturity (e.g. chimpanzees) the early development of sexual signals may act as a "passport," allowing pre-reproductive females to investigate neighboring groups (Pusey 1990, Scott 1984).

The characteristic fat distribution of the adult human female may serve a similar signaling function. Females attaining puberty change in shape as well as size. The pelvis expands and widens and protrudes further to the rear in preparation for childbirth, while mammary tissue begins to develop in the breasts. These changes are accentuated by the accumulation of fat in the hips, buttocks, thighs and breasts. In other words, adult female fat distribution acts as a puberty amplifier, making females look as if they are in a more advanced stage of puberty than a hypothetical female with a more even fat distribution. Human females conceal ovulation, but advertise nubility.

There may be adaptive advantages for females in advertising, even exaggerating, the attainment of puberty. Hill's data for the Ache show that in early adolescence the mortality rates for females drop below those for males, as females begin to receive attention and food from interested males. Among the Ache and many other peoples, especially in very small scale societies with weak fraternal interest groups, puberty is advertised not only by physical changes but by ceremonies, often including beautification rituals (reviewed in Paige and Paige 1981).

Even after puberty there may be advantages to females in presenting exaggerated advertisements of fecundity. As noted in Chapter 2, unless males and females mate monogamously for life without remarriage, the allocation of effort between survival and reproduction that maximizes a female's mate value to any one male is probably not the same as the allocation that maximizes female fitness. Suppose there is some trait, F, that increases the survival chances of a female's current offspring by 10%, while reducing her own chances of survival by 1%, relative to non-F females. And suppose the father of a female's current offspring stands a good chance of not being the father of subsequent offspring. Then F females could have both higher mate value for the father of a female's current offspring, and lower fitness, than non-F females. Under these conditions, a female making a deceptive advertisement—who looked as if she were F but really wasn't—could gain through attracting above-average mates without losing through reduced viability. In the long run, natural selection will often eliminate deceptive advertisements, but what begins as a deceptive advertisement may turn into an evolutionarily stable honest advertisement as it becomes more frequent. (See discussion in Chapter 2 of piloerection and amplifiers.)

Low et al. (1987) argue that fat storage in the breasts and hips may be a deceptive fecundity advertisement, increasing the apparent size of the pelvis and volume of mammary tissue. This argument has been faulted on several grounds: the authors are not explicit about the conflicts of interest between females and their mates over female fertility/viability tradeoffs that make deceptive advertisements of fertility likelier than other deceptive advertisements (Donald Symons, pers. comm.). And they do not spell out how initially deceptive advertisements could be evolutionarily stable (Caro 1987). The arguments I present above are meant to suggest that none of these objections is grounds for dismissing the Low et al. hypothesis out of hand (cf. Caro 1987, for a review of the many hypotheses advanced to explain just the evolution of female breasts).

If cues from the figure provide reliable evidence about the attainment of puberty, then facial morphology may be adapted to advertise youth. Over the past 100,000 years a number of regional populations of modern *Homo sapiens* have shown trends toward increasing craniofacial neoteny, including reduced prognathism, increased brachycephaly and general gracilization (Weidenreich 1945; Newman 1962; Brace and Mahler 1971; Frayer 1981). Biological anthropologists who have considered these trends have generally attributed them to ecological adaptation, but sexual selection for neotenous features in females and correlated changes among males may also have played a part. Sexual selection for female facial neoteny is likely to have become especially important once increases in life expectancy resulted in a large proportion of the female population living past the age of menopause.[4]

NOTES

1. There is some confusion in the literature on the subject of cheekbones. Cunningham argues that men are attracted to women with large eyes, small noses, and small chins and jaws because these are juvenile traits. On the other hand, he argues that men are attracted to women with high cheekbones and narrow cheeks because these are mature traits. Cunningham gives no clear rationale why this particular combination of juvenile and mature traits is favored, rather than some other, or even the opposite combination. Thornhill and Gangestad (1993) argue that prominent cheekbones in women reflect high levels of testosterone. Since testosterone reduces immunocompetence, they argue that high cheekbones are a Zahavian handicap (see Chapter 2). Only someone whose immune system is in good shape will be able to afford compromising it with high testosterone levels, and developing the attendant adornments. This theory enjoys some support in the literature when it comes to the sexual adornments of the males of some bird species (Folstad and Karter 1992; Ligon et al. 1990), but it is unlikely to explain the attractiveness of high cheekbones in women. If high cheekbones in women are attractive because they are associated with high testosterone levels, then why are other masculine characteristics including prominent brows, heavy chins and jaws, large noses, and abundant face and body hair not equally attractive?

    As discussed in the quotation from Enlow above, "high" (not large) cheekbones are a feminine characteristic because they result from women's lesser facial protrusion. The reader can verify this by comparing women's and men's faces in 3/4 view (halfway between full frontal and profile views); the greater relative prominence of women's cheekbones is particularly evident in this view because they are not overshadowed by the protrusive midface and brows characteristic of men. For the same reason, "high" cheekbones are also characteristic of populations with relatively flat faces, for instance, East Asians, American Indians, and Southern African San. (There is no consensus among anthropologists on why relatively flat faces characterize these populations in particular—Brues 1977; Tobias 1978.)

    I will have little to say about cheekbones in the data analysis sections of this chapter. They do not end up being strongly correlated with age or sex in the full frontal photographs used in this analysis. Future analyses will incorporate landmark measurements from profile photographs (discussion in Chapter 3), and may reveal more about the role of cheekbones and facial flatness in attractiveness.

2. Results for Ache females are anomalous. For Westerners rating Ache females, a high EW/FH is *negatively*, although not significantly, correlated with attractiveness. Part of the reason for these results may be an interaction between eye size and shape. Many Ache have narrow eyes because they have epicanthic folds, and this appears to influence Western responses. Ache females with a

high EW/FH are also likely to have narrow eyes (a high ratio of Eye Width to Eye Height, EW/EH). The correlation between log EW/FH and log EW/EH for Ache females is .65**. All Westerners rating Ache females show a significant aversion to narrow eyes. The correlations between log EW/EH and attractiveness are $-.36**$, $-.31*$, and $-.44**$ for Brazilian, US American and Russian raters respectively. Russians may have an especially strong aversion to narrow eyes; findings reported in Chapter 7 show that Russian raters also give lower ratings than any other group of raters to Asian American faces when rating the US American sample. When EW/EH is partialed out, correlations between attractiveness and EW/FH for Western raters are positive (.11, .10, and .08 for Brazilian, US American and Russian raters).

The consideration of eye shape also raises an uncomfortable possibility. Both Ache and Hiwi raters give high ratings to US and Brazilian females with high values of EW/FH. Is this because male Indian raters are attracted to women with large eyes in relation to face height (the neoteny effect), or just because Brazilian and US females with especially high values of EW/FH also have especially low values of EH/EW, and thus resemble Ache (the averageness effect—see Chapter 5)? Controlling for log EW/EH reduces the correlation between log EW/FH and attractiveness only by a trivial amount for Ache raters (from .43** to .39**, and from .37** to .36** for ratings of US and Brazilian females respectively), and not at all for Hiwi raters. In other words, male Indian raters really are attracted to big eyes (in relation to face height) not just to narrow ones.

3. The null hypothesis in this case is that d_f (the probability that a neotenous female face, $k = .1$, will be rated more attractive than the original face, $k = 0$) is equal to d_m (the probability that a neotenous male face will be rated more attractive than the original face). But for all possible values of $d_f = d_m$, the probability of getting the observed results both for females and for males—that is, the product of the probability for males and the probability for females—is less than .01.

4. A more complete account of the morphological consequences of signal selection in *Homo sapiens* would consider regional variation, which would probably require allowing for imprinting and other forms of learning in conjunction with ecologically adaptive variation in body shape and cultural differences in clothing and adornment. It would also require allowing for signaling functions of morphology other than sexual attraction. For example, secondary sexual characters of the male face perceived as more "dominant," including beards and strong brow ridges, may be adapted not only to attract females but to intimidate potential rivals and mates (Guthrie 1970; Mazur et al. 1984, 1994).

CHAPTER 6

Symmetry, Averageness and Health

It is not news that obvious indicators of poor health like gross deformity and skin lesions generally contribute to physical unattractiveness. However, the inhabitants of the world's wealthiest nations may be unaware of just how common such conditions were and are in other times and places. To anyone whose perspective on the past is influenced by experience in the modern Third World, one of the anachronisms evident even in Hollywood's more meticulous historical reconstructions is the infrequency of missing teeth and fingers, stunted growth and premature aging, pipestem arms and legs, healed wounds and open sores.

I will be concerned in this chapter with more subtle outward signs that may be markers, not of any specific disease or injury, but of a general state of good or poor health. Some of these signs may actually be evolved *advertisements* of health status, along the lines discussed in Chapter 2.

FLUCTUATING ASYMMETRY

Organisms are adapted for "normal" conditions—where normal means both historically common and historically favorable to survival and reproduction. Suppose that genotype G_1 will make an organism 10% more successful in environment A and 10% less successful in environment B than genotype G_2. If an organism has a 90% chance of finding itself in environment A, and a 10% chance of finding itself in environment B, then, other things being equal, G_1 will increase the organism's fitness by 8% (= $0.1 \times 0.9 - 0.1 \times 0.1$) compared with G_2. In other words, given that adaptation involves tradeoffs, organisms will adapt to common conditions at the expense of being poorly adapted to uncommon conditions.

Or suppose that environment A is more conducive to survival than environment B, so that an organism with genotype G_1 has an expected reproductive success of 10 offspring in environment A and 1 in environment B, while the expected reproductive success of an organism with genotype G_2 is 10% greater in environment A (11 offspring) and 10% less in environment B (.9 offspring). In this case, assuming an organism is just as likely to find itself in environment A as in environment B ($p_A = p_B = 0.5$), genotype G_2 will increase the organism's reproductive success by 8.2%, or $1.082 = (11 \times 0.5 + 0.9 \times 0.5)/(10 \times 0.5 + 1 \times$

0.5). In other words, given tradeoffs in adaptation, it doesn't pay to put too much into adaptations for environments in which you are unlikely to survive and reproduce anyway. (Perhaps this is why so few people built fallout shelters during the Cold War.)

This line of reasoning suggests that there should be a *general* breakdown of adaptation in unusual or unfavorable circumstances. Readers familiar with evolutionary theory regarding the evolution of senescence will recognize the logic of this argument; there is a general breakdown in adaptation with increasing age because genes that cause kidney failure (or heart failure or whatever) in 90 year old humans are less strongly selected against than genes that cause kidney failure in 20-year-olds; most people die of other causes before the former set of genes has any chance to take effect.

Waddington (1957) argued that the development of adaptations is typically *canalized*—guided by negative feedback mechanisms adapted to keep development "on track" in the face of possible perturbing influences. According to the argument developed above, there should be a general breakdown in canalization, and a resultant increase in maladaptive variance, among organisms in unusual or unfavorable circumstances.

In bilaterally symmetrical organisms, the failure of developmental homeostasis adds random "noise" to the process of development, making opposite sides of the organism less similar—a phenomenon known as fluctuating asymmetry. Fluctuating asymmetry—defined as random deviations from perfect symmetry, or from biologically normal, directional asymmetry—should thus be a marker of developmental stress. A considerable literature in biology confirms the association of fluctuating asymmetry with unusual and unfavorable conditions. In nonhuman organisms, inbreeding, elevated homozygosity, parasite load, undernutrition and exposure to pollution are all associated with increased fluctuating asymmetry (Parsons 1990). In humans, correlates of fluctuating asymmetry include inbreeding, premature birth, psychosis and mental retardation (Livshits 1991).

Clearly fluctuating asymmetry is a likely indicator of mate value. In the last few years several researchers have demonstrated that asymmetry influences mate choice in nonhuman organisms. Thornhill (1992a) shows that male scorpionflies are more attractive to females if they are more symmetrical. They are also more likely to win fights with other males (Thornhill 1992b). Even when females cannot see males, but choose them on the basis of smell, they choose symmetrical males more often; apparently symmetry and odor give correlated cues about a male's mate value.

Bilaterally symmetrical traits are likely to be particularly vulnerable to developmental disruption when they are complex and/or exaggerated. Complex, exaggerated paired structures or patterns are thus particularly well suited to the "honest advertisement" of health status. The elongated plumes of many birds, the elaborate facial markings of many primates, the breasts of human females, and many other symmetrical traits of no obvious ecological utility are all obvious candidates for honest advertisements of resistance to developmental stress. Møller and Höglund (1990) and Møller (1991) demonstrate that not only do female swallows prefer males with especially symmetrical tails, but also that males' tails are more symmetrical the longer they are, and that tail size and tail symmetry are associated with low ectoparasite loads. Apparently tails are advertisements of health status, and healthier males can produce both larger and more symmetrical tails.

What of our own species? Before the current interest in fluctuating asymmetry, Judith Langlois (pers. comm.) investigated the relationship between symmetry and attractiveness. She used a computer graphics system to generate perfectly symmetrical faces, and found that symmetry did not increase attractiveness. However, Gangestad et al. (1994) and Grammer and Thornhill (1994) present data suggesting that fluctuating asymmetry (or rather its absence) *is* a component of human physical attractiveness. The first paper measures asymmetry in seven bilateral body traits in 35 females and 37 males, and finds a significant negative correlation between body asymmetry and facial attractiveness for males, and a negative but nonsignificant relationship for females. The second study finds significant negative correlations among 16 females and 16 males between facial asymmetries and facial attractiveness.

On the other hand, results from this study give little support to the hypothesis. I begin by summarizing some findings from Jones and Hill (1993), and present some new analyses.

There is more measurement error involved in the measurement of fluctuating asymmetry than in the measurement of averageness, since differences between the right and left side of one person's face are typically smaller than differences between two different faces. When I remeasured faces, measurement error was less than twenty percent for all of my 247 distance measurements, but over fifty percent for most measurements of right/left distance differences. I selected just six measurements (from inside and outside of corners of eye to outside corner of lip, bottom midpoint of nasal septum, and to chin) that seemed particularly reliable (measurement error less than thirty percent). I made a point of selecting measurements with a strong vertical component on the grounds that these would be less affected than more horizontal measurements by small side-to-side deviations in head position. For each measurement I subtracted left from right distances, divided by the mean of left and right, and subtracted the median left-right difference for that measurement and that sample (to correct for directional—nonfluctuating—asymmetry). The first index of fluctuating asymmetry (FA1) is the average of these six numbers for each photograph. Measurement error variance as a proportion of total variance for FA1 is .31.

Table 6.1 presents data on the relationship between log FA1 and facial attrac-

Table 6.1. Correlations between two measures of fluctuating asymmetry and ratings of physical attractiveness.

Photos of	Rated by	Photographs of			
		Females		Males	
		FA1	FA2	FA1	FA2
Brazilians	Brazilians(19,11)	-.15	.16	-.22	.21
N=51,23	US Americans(12,20)	-.08	-.06	-.27	.04
	Russians(11,14)	-.25 *	.05	.07	.13
	Ache Indians(11,13)	.14	.03	.08	.31
	Hiwi Indians(4,4)	-.03	.18	.26	.16
US Americans	Brazilians(20,23)	.07	.10	-.12	.07
N=51,31	US Americans(11,18)	-.01	.18	.07	.22
	Russians(12,14)	-.10	.03	-.23	.26
	Ache Indians(20,21)	-.07	-.22	-.03	-.07
	Hiwi Indians(0,0)	n.a.	n.a.	n.a.	n.a.
Ache Indians	Brazilians(17,16)	-.07	n.a.	-.04	n.a.
N=41,42	US Americans(12,15)	-.09	n.a.	-.10	n.a.
	Russians(12,12)	-.23 +	n.a.	.03	n.a.
	Ache Indians(15,15)	.03	n.a.	-.12	n.a.
	Hiwi Indians(7,4)	-.03	n.a	.05	n.a
Pooled samples	Brazilians(56,50)	-.05	.13	-.13	.14
N=143,96	US Americans(35,53)	-.06	.06	-.10	.13
	Russians(35,40)	-.20 *	.04	-.04	.19
	Ache Indians(46,49)	.03	-.10	-.02	.12
	Hiwi Indians(7,5)	-.03	.18	.16	.16

tiveness. The results are unimpressive. Among all samples of raters, only Russian women show a significant attraction to faces with low FA1. Even if measurement error reduced correlations to some extent, the effect of FA1 on attractiveness seems to be weak. It is worth mentioning that to get log FA1 for the US female sample to approximate a normal distribution it was necessary to remove one outlier, a woman whose right inner eye corner (endocanthion) was substantially lower than her left, whose FA1 (.026) was five times the sample mean, and who received below-average attractiveness ratings from all populations of raters. There is little reason to doubt that such an obvious deviation from bilateral symmetry will reduce physical attractiveness, but it is less clear how much fluctuating asymmetry reduces physical attractiveness when such outliers are excluded.

Since the publication of Jones and Hill 1993, I have constructed another index of fluctuating asymmetry using actual facial measurements rather than measurements from photographs. For Brazilian and US subjects of both sexes, but not for Ache, I have caliper measurements on both sides of the face of distances between the bridge of the nose and the outer corner of the eye (nasion to exocanthion), outer corner of the eye to upper notch of ear (exocanthion to porion) and upper notch of the ear to chin (porion to gonion, see Chapter 3 for further discussion). I constructed an index of fluctuating asymmetry (FA2) by averaging fluctuating asymmetries of these three pairs of measurements. (Since I took each distance measurement on each side of the head twice, I averaged the two measurements. I also looked at the correlations between FA2 calculated using only the first set of measurements and FA2 calculated only using the second set of measurements and calculated that measurement error variance as a fraction of total variance for FA2 is .17.) Table 6.1 presents data on the relationship between log FA2 and facial attractiveness. Once again the results are unimpressive.

In summary, Gangestad et al. (1994) find a significant negative correlation between fluctuating asymmetry in body measurements and facial attractiveness for males but not for females. Grammer and Thornhill (1994) report a significant correlation between facial fluctuating asymmetry and facial attractiveness for both sexes, but with small sample sizes ($N = 16$ males, 16 females). This study finds mostly insignificant trends mostly in the right direction for one measure of fluctuating asymmetry (FA1), and no discernible trend at all for another (FA2). All of these results are consistent with fluctuating asymmetry being a component of attractiveness, but not a very important one. It is possible that fluctuating asymmetry is more important as a component of attractiveness in populations under heavy stress from undernutrition and pathogens.

The Attractions of Averageness:
Health, Age and Information Processing

Between 1878 and 1881, Francis Galton, cousin to Charles Darwin, explorer, advocate of eugenics, and inventor of fingerprinting, correlation coefficients, and the ultrasonic dog whistle (still known as the Galton whistle) presented a series of reports on some experiments in composite photography. He carried out these experiments by briefly exposing a series of facial photographs in front of a camera to produce a new, multiply exposed photograph that blended the features of a number of individual faces—a kind of pictorial average. Galton was interested in the physiognomical theory that character is reflected in the face, and wanted to know if, for example, the composite of a number of criminals' faces would show the villainous distinguishing features of the criminal face in particularly clear form.

> I have made numerous composites of various groups of convicts, which are interesting negatively rather than positively. They produce faces . . . with no villainy written on them. The individual faces are villainous enough, but they are villainous in different ways, and when they are combined, the individual peculiarities disappear. [Galton 1907:224]

Not only were composites of "villainous" faces not especially villainous looking, but "the features of the composites are much better looking than those of the components." Galton found the same principle in operation when he made composites of noncriminals. "All composites are better looking than their components, because the averaged portrait of many persons is free of the irregularities that variously blemish the looks of each of them" (p. 224). Galton had discovered that average features are more attractive.

The idea that average features are especially attractive has a long history in Western civilization. Greek sculptors believed that the most attractive features would be those that struck a mean between two extremes. In the fifth century B.C., Polyclitus developed a set of mathematical formulas, "the canon of Polyclitus" (now lost), that were supposed to reflect an ideal Golden Mean in facial and bodily proportions, although he apparently based his system on intuition rather than on measurement of real people. Renaissance artists like da Vinci and Dürer also believed that intermediate proportions were ideal although they too relied on intuition and number mysticism more than on real measurement (Olds 1992). In fact, one recent investigation concludes that the "neoclassical proportion canon"—a set of ratios and angles relating different facial features developed by modern Western artists—does not describe *either* typical *or* ideal features among modern North American whites (Farkas et al. 1987).

Galton's researches are therefore perhaps the first real, albeit accidental test of the theory that average features are more attractive. However, they did little to stimulate further research and theory until the 1979 publication of *The Evolution of Human Sexuality* (Symons 1979). Symons cited Galton's results, and argued "if the ideal of facial beauty is largely the population average . . . individuals *must* possess an unconscious 'innate' mechanism that operates in a manner analogous to composite portraiture and derives a standard of facial attractiveness by averaging observed faces" (p. 195). He suggested that such a face-averaging esthetic mechanism might have been produced by natural selection if most metric physical traits were under stabilizing natural selection most of the time so that individuals with extreme values of traits had lower fitnesses and lower mate values.

Since then several studies have appeared suggesting that faces with proportions especially close to average proportions are more attractive than most faces. Langlois and Roggman (1990) rely on computer graphics to produce composite faces which blend the features of a number of faces. Computer technology makes it possible to overcome some of the problems that affected Galton's research; images can be expanded or shrunk to fit on top of each other, making the composite less blurry. Langlois and Roggman find that these composite faces are rated more attractive than most of the original faces going into the composite, and that there is a monotonic increase in the perceived attractiveness of a composite as the number of faces going into a composite increases (from 2 to 4 to 8 to 16 to 32). Benson and Perret (1992), using a more complex graphics system, show that the averageness effect results partly because the composite faces have smoother complexions, and partly because they have proportions close to average proportions.

Other studies relying on measurements of faces also find that attractive faces are more average. Farkas and Munro (1987) calculate 155 "proportion indices" (ratios between landmark distances) based on linear measurements from the faces of two hundred young adult North American women of European ancestry. They compare a group of 34 faces consistently rated above average in attractiveness by a large pool of raters, and 21 rated below. Only 11.6% of mean proportion indices differ significantly between the two groups. The authors report means and standard deviations for a subset (37) of indices. Inspection of their tables shows that less attractive females have higher standard deviations for 28 of these indices, more attractive females have higher standard deviations for just 8, and the standard deviations are the same for 1.

These findings do not contradict the arguments and evidence from Chapter 5 that attractive features may be supernormal features. Faces differ along many dimensions; people may be attracted to supernormal traits along age- and sex-loaded dimensions, while being attracted to average traits along other dimensions. In fact, composite faces, although above average in attractiveness, do not seem to be the most attractive possible faces. Alley (1991) notes that, although Langlois and Roggman's composite faces are more attractive than *most* of the faces going into the composite, there are some individual noncomposite faces rated more attractive than any of the composites. And while most of Farkas and Monro's proportion indices don't differ significantly between attractive and unattractive faces, they find nonetheless that the eyes of attractive women are relatively larger and their lips relatively fuller. They also present photographs of a woman from their sample rated highly attractive and another rated unattractive; my measurements of the photos show that the eyes of the two females are of equal size, but the one rated more attractive has a shorter face, shorter nose, and fuller lips, in line with the findings in Chapter 4.

What of the present data set? I use two different indices to measure how much each face in six population samples differs from the average face in that sample, a version of the Pattern Variability Index (PVI) of Garn et al. (1985), and the Euclidean Distance Matrix Index (EDMI) of Lele and Richtsmeier (1991).[1] Changing the size of a face without changing its shape will not change the value of either index. The EDMI is more sensitive than the PVI to a single unusually placed landmark.

Table 6.2 shows the correlations of log PVI and log EDMI with age-corrected attractiveness. (I take the logarithms of the indices to correct for significant right skewness, as measured by a Lilliefors test for normality. I get virtually identical results using the original values of the indices.) Negative correlations mean that more deviant faces are less attractive. Results differ somewhat from Table 3 in Jones and Hill (1993) because I have fixed an error in Ache female PVI and EDMI values.

Table 6.2. Correlations between two indices of non-average facial proportions and attractiveness ratings. Shading highlights three cases in which individuals are rating members of their own populations. The pooled ratings pool these cases.

Photos of	Rated by		Photographs of Females		Males	
			PVI	EDMI	PVI	EDMI
		avg=	.033	.29	.037	.30
		stdev=	.008	.10	.007	.10
Brazilians	Brazilians(19,11)		-.16	-.18	-.23	-.26
N=51,23	US Americans(12,20)		.01	-.02	-.31 +	-.19
	Russians(11,14)		-.19 +	-.15	.01	-.04
	Ache Indians(11,13)		-.10	.00	.08	-.04
	Hiwi Indians(4,4)		-.10	.04	.18	.11
		avg=	.034	.31	.034	.29
		stdev=	.008	.14	.008	.10
US Americans	Brazilians(20,23)		-.11 +	-.21 +	-.24	-.16
N=52,31	US Americans(11,18)		-.07	-.18	-.19	.06
	Russians(12,14)		-.12	-.25 *	-.28	.00
	Ache Indians(20,21)		-.04	-.06	-.31 *	-.45 *
	Hiwi Indians(0,0)		n.a.	n.a.	n.a.	n.a.
		avg=	.036	.30	.036	.32
		stdev=	.010	.10	.010	.13
Ache Indians	Brazilians(17,16)		-.29 *	-.34 *	-.19	-.17
N=41,42	US Americans(12,15)		-.22 +	-.20	-.25 *	-.28 *
	Russians(12,12)		-.25 +	-.23 +	-.33 *	-.39 **
	Ache Indians(15,15)		-.15	-.19	-.28 *	-.26 *
	Hiwi Indians(7,4)		-.48 **	-.33 **	.25	.14
Pooled ratings N=144,96	Braz+US+Ache(45,44)		-0.13 +	-0.19 *	-0.23 *	-0.15 +

According to the face averaging hypothesis, raters will be especially attracted to faces especially close to the average in their own populations. Boxes are placed to show cases where raters are rating members of their own population. For the pooled sample I pool data within these boxes only. Table 6.2 provides moderate support for the face averaging hypothesis. (Positive correlations for some of the ratings carried out by Hiwi women may reflect the very small number of raters.)

Why should the averageness effect be stronger for the Ache than for the other groups sampled? And why are even non-Indian raters sometimes attracted to Ache faces close to average Ache proportions? Part of the answer may be that departures from average proportions are correlated with age for the Ache (r =.22, .26, .39, .14 for PVI and EDMI for males—first two numbers—and females), so the estimate of the effect of non-average features on physical attractiveness is sensitive to assumptions about the effects of age on attractiveness. Also, while the variability of Ache faces is about the same as that for the other groups (judging by averages and standard deviations of PVI and EDMI), the causes of variability are probably different; the range of ages is much greater in the Ache sample than in the others, conditions of life have been much harder for the Ache, and the Ache are probably more genetically homogeneous than other populations sampled. It is possible that departures from average features resulting from aging and a hard life detract more from attractiveness than departures resulting from genetic heterogeneity in modern multiethnic societies. Correcting for age can remove some of these effects, but (if people age at different rates) not all of them.

Brazil may be something of a special case. In Table 6.2, where Brazilians are rating Brazilians, the correlations of attractiveness with PVI and EDMI for females—first two numbers—and males are –.16, –.18, –.23, and –.26. Suppose we recalculate the indices using measurements of US American rather than Brazilian faces as the standard. In other words, suppose we measure how much each Brazilian face differs from the average US American face, rather than from the average Brazilian face. The corresponding correlations with attractiveness in this case are consistently stronger (–.21+, –.26*, –.26, and –.33*). Brazilians seem to be evaluating Brazilian faces as much by how closely they match US American proportions as by how closely they match Brazilian proportions. This probably reflects both the influence of North American and European media, and a local class structure in which the rich are disproportionately European in ancestry and appearance, and the poor disproportionately African. I will have more to say about this in Chapter 7.

Evidence from other studies suggests that average faces are indeed more attractive. So why are correlations between averageness and attractiveness in this study not stronger? Part of the answer—at least for females—may lie in interference between neoteny effects and averageness effects. Several females in the samples get high attractiveness ratings, and have high values of EDMI only because they have particularly large eyes. A better test of the averageness effect might involve recalculating PVI and EDMI with a more restricted set of landmark distances, eliminating those distances most subject to change with age.

I have said little about *why* there should be any effect of averageness on attractiveness. Most evolution-minded treatments of the topic have argued that averageness, like symmetry, is likely to be associated with health and developmental stability, but there are several other possible explanations.

Average features as a health marker. Symons suggested that a preference for average features would be adaptive for features under stabilizing selection. It is not clear that subtle variations in facial morphology have strong direct fitness consequences. However, as noted above, even if variations in facial morphology do not have strong direct fitness consequences, they may be important as markers of developmental stress. Fluctuating asymmetry means that developmental stress has caused small random disruptions of developmental canalization, so that one side of an organism differs from the other. But the same small random variations that cause opposed sides of an organism to differ will also cause the organism to differ randomly from healthy members of the population—in other words averageness and symmetry should be correlated. Soulé (1982) presents theory and evidence that modal phenotypes typically have lower levels of fluctuating asymmetry (but see Livshits 1993 for a more critical review). Both fluctuating asymmetry *and* departures from average proportions may reflect a history of environmental insult and genetic load, and forecast a future of reduced viability and fecundity. Insofar as there are direct or indirect evolutionary advantages to choosing a healthy and fertile mate, selection will favor individuals who steer clear of potential mates that display either fluctuating asymmetry *or* departures from average proportions.

Pediatricians sometimes include the notation FLK ("funny looking kid") in their charts in recognition of the fact that unusual proportions are often a sign of medical problems (Garn et al. 1985; B. Holly Smith, pers. comm.). Garn et al. (1985) and Deutsch (1987) review evidence that a number of psychiatric and other health-related syndromes are associated with minor dysmorphology. Waldrop et al. (1978) show that minor physical anomalies (abnormally large head, low set ears, eyes unusually far apart) among newborns predict short attention span, peer aggression, and impulsiveness at age three. In nonhuman organisms, extreme values of traits are often associated with elevated levels of homozygosity, and diminished resistance to environmental insult (Lerner 1954). Koeslag (1990) reviews evidence that attraction to average features ("koinophilia") is widespread among nonhuman organisms, and that koinophilic sexual selection has important macroevolutionary consequences.

One can make a plausible case, then, that departures from average proportions are markers of the breakdown of developmental canalization. But of course there are other sources of physical variation, and other possible explanations of the association of averageness and attractiveness.

Runaway sexual selection. Fisher's theory of runaway sexual selection (see Chapter 2) has frequently been criticized because the theory seems to make it entirely a matter of historical accident whether one trait or another is favored by sexual selection. However, recent mathematical work by Pomiankowski et al. (1991) suggests that we can make some predictions about what traits will be enduringly favored by runaway sexual selection. They argue that as long as there are costs to mate choice, runaway sexual selection will lead only to transient episodes of trait exaggeration, *except for traits subject to biased mutation.* For example, given costs to mate choice, runaway sexual selection will favor an equilibrium combination of exaggerated pigmentation and preference for exaggerated pigmentation as long as mutations are more likely to reduce the intensity of pigmentation than to increase it.

Mutation is biased with regard to averageness. Whether a mutation makes a structure larger or smaller, wider or narrower, brighter or duller, it is very likely to make it less average. Lande (1975) presents evidence that for polygenic morphological characters mutation commonly adds from 10^{-2} to 10^{-1} to trait variance per generation. In other words, averageness is subject to precisely the sort of mutational erosion required in Pomiankowski's version of runaway sexual selection to produce enduring exaggeration of traits and trait preferences. Finding out whether runaway sexual selection makes a contribution to the attraction to averageness would involve finding out how much mutation contributes to the variance of sexually selected traits, presumably in controlled breeding experiments.

Average features and aging. Faces may grow more variable as they grow older. In this case a preference for average features might simply be an adaptation to age-related changes in mate value, and the discussion of face averaging would belong in the previous chapter. The indices of non-average features, the EDMI and the PVI, increase with age among the Ache (see above). But it is only fair to mention that when EDMI and PVI are included as possible age predictors in a stepwise multiple regression—see Chapter 5—both drop out of the final predictor equation.

Several people, upon seeing copies of some of Langlois and Roggman's composite and noncomposite photos, have remarked that the faces in the composite photos look younger than non-composite faces. Researchers in possession of a large sample of composite photographs might want to investigate their perceived ages.

Averageness and information processing. Langlois and Roggman (1990) suggest another explanation for the attraction to average features: it may be more difficult to get socially and reproductively important information from an unusually proportioned face than from one with more familiar proportions. I argued in Chapter 5 that individuals may have an innate template of neotenous

Table 6.3. Correlations between two measures of neoteny, two measures of fluctuating asymmetry, and two measures of non-average facial proportions, pooled across all female samples, with two-tailed significance tests.

	PredictedAge1	PredictedAge2	FA1	FA2	EDMI
PredictedAge2	0.475 **				
FA1	-0.128	0.06			
FA2	-0.029	0.099	-0.043		
EDMI	0.235 **	0.201 *	0.108	-0.056	
PVI	0.179 *	0.139 +	0.241 **	-0.122	0.809 **

Table 6.4. Comparison of the effects of seven indices of facial proportions on ratings of facial attractiveness. The first column of numbers gives the correlation of each index with ratings of attractiveness, averaged over populations of raters. The second column gives the strength of the effect in terms of "years worth" of attractiveness per standard deviation—thus the change in facial attractiveness associated with a one standard deviation decrease in "Neoteny1" is equal to the change associated with 5.0 years of aging (based on male assesments of female aging). Indices of neoteny from Chapter 5, other indices from Chapter 6.

Indices of		Correlation	Strength of effect (yrs)
Neoteny	Neoteny1(females)	.26 **	-5.0
	Neoteny2(females)	.23 *	-4.4
	Neoteny3(males)	.03	-0.6
Fluctuating asymmetry	FA1	-.04	0.9
	FA2	.11	-2.0
Non-average proportions	PVI	-.18 **	3.5
	EDMI	-.17 **	3.3

facial features. But this template is likely to work more effectively if it is calibrated to local, non-age related variation in facial proportions. In other words, the process of constructing an image of average facial features, *a lá* Symons and Langlois and Roggman, may be a way of fine tuning what would otherwise be a rather cartoonish innate template, to allow for more accurate "reading" of ages (and other relevant features) of faces.

Suppose you want to guess the ages of individuals based on their facial proportions. If nose size increases with age you can use nose size as an age estimator. But how accurately will you estimate the age of an individual with an unusually narrow and long nose, given that one cue (nose width) suggests youth, while another (nose height) suggests age? Some of my own experiences during fieldwork with the Ache suggest that unfamiliar facial proportions may in fact make age and sex assessments more difficult. I commonly made major mistakes in estimating the ages of adult Ache. And Ache sometimes had difficulty distinguishing the sex of US Americans and Brazilians in photographs of individuals whom no American or Brazilian would have had any difficulty identifying as male or female. This subject deserves more systematic treatment; it may be that differences in the rate of aging, or cues from hair styles were more important in producing these confusions than anything to do with facial proportions *per se*. But it could be that unusually proportioned faces are unattractive because they are *unreliable* indicators of mate value, not because they are reliable indicators of *low* mate value. I noted in Chapter 5 that I plan to collect age estimates for faces in my photographic samples; it will be interesting to see whether unusual facial proportions affect either the average or the variance in age estimates.

SUMMING UP: NEOTENY, ASYMMETRY, AVERAGENESS

Table 6.3 shows correlations for all female photographic subjects between two measures of neoteny (PredictedAge1 and PredictedAge2), two measures of averageness (log EDMI and log PVI) and two measures of fluctuating asymmetry (log FA1 and log FA2). As in previous tables, I used Fisher's z to pool results for different populations; results for individual populations are similar to pooled results.

Not surprisingly, the two measures of neoteny are strongly correlated with each other, as are the two measures of averageness. Log FA1 and log FA2 however, are nearly uncorrelated. (Several other studies, including Livshits 1993 and van Valen 1962, have found little or no correlation between fluctuating asymmetries at different sites.) There are some moderate correlations across categories as well: between PredictedAge1 and PredictedAge2 and log EDMI and log PVI, for example, and between log PVI and log FA1. A series of regression analyses of facial proportions and female attractiveness, presented at length in Jones 1994, demonstrates that one or another index of neoteny appears in most regressions, while indices of averageness and symmetry appear intermittently.

Finally, a summary of the results of Chapters 5 and 6 regarding facial proportions is given in Table 6.4. For each of seven indices of facial proportions the first column of the table presents a mean correlation with ratings of physical attractiveness. For indices of female facial neoteny (Neoteny1 and Neoteny2), correlations are averaged over the shaded areas in Table 5.3; for other indices, correlations are averaged over pooled correlations at the bottoms of tables (Tables 5.3, 6.1 and 6.2). Indices of fluctuating asymmetry and non-average proportions are averaged over both sexes. All averages are carried out by converting correlations to Fisher's z's, taking their mean, and taking the inverse of Fisher's z. Significance tests are one-tailed.

The second column in Table 6.4 shows how many "years' worth" of physical attractiveness are associated with a one standard deviation change in each index. In Chapter 4, the average decline in attractiveness associated with one year of aging was .052 standard deviations for females, and .03 for males. This implies that the .26 standard deviation decrease in attractiveness associated with a 1 standard deviation decline in Neoteny1 is equal to the decline in attractiveness associated with 5.0 years of female age.

NOTE

1. To calculate the PVI, I begin by calculating the median of each of 247 log-transformed distances between facial landmarks for each of six samples. Then, for each log distance for each face in each sample, I calculate the difference from the sample median. Finally, for each face I calculate the standard deviation of the 247 differences. The higher the PVI, the more the face differs from the proportions of the median face in the sample. Thus, if all the measurements of a face are 10% bigger than the median measurements in the relevant population (1.1, 1.1, 1.1, ...), the standard deviation of the logarithms of these measurements will be zero; the face is bigger than average, but its *proportions* are those of the average face. But if one of the measurements of a face is 10% bigger than the median, one 20% bigger, one 10% smaller, and so on (1.1, 1.2, .9, ...), then the standard deviation of the logarithms of those measurements will be greater than zero, reflecting the difference in proportions between this face and the average face.

The Euclidean Distance Matrix Index for each face is the logarithm of the ratio of the largest to the smallest differences from the sample median (Lele and Richtsmeier 1991). Again, if all the measurements of a face are ten percent larger than the median, then the logarithm of the ratio of the largest to the smallest of these differences will be $\log(1.1/1.1) = \log(1) = 0$, while any landmark distance in a face that differs from its median by a different percentage than any other will result in an EDMI greater than zero.

CHAPTER 7

Race, Social Status, and Attractiveness

Scholars of race and ethnicity often neglect the topic of physical attractiveness in favor of more "practical" topics like class and status differences (cf. Hoetink 1967; Franklin 1968; Isaacs 1975; Stember 1976; and Russell et al. 1992). This relative neglect partly reflects a reluctance to approach an uncomfortable topic. Physical attractiveness is a sensitive topic, ethnicity is a sensitive topic, and the combination of the two is doubly sensitive. But it also reflects the lack of a theory of physical attractiveness in the social sciences, a theory to which behavioral ecologists and evolutionary psychologists may be able to contribute.

Judgments of physical attractiveness may well play an important role in relations between ethnic groups. Somatic prejudice seems to be a recurring feature of racist theorizing; in eighteenth and nineteenth century Europe, "all racists held to a certain conception of beauty—white and classical—and thought that . . . middle class virtues of work, of moderation and honor . . . were exemplified through outward appearance" (Mosse 1985:xxvi). The very persistence of ethnic groups over time depends on the maintenance of social boundaries (Barth 1969), including boundaries to mating, and will be influenced by standards of physical attractiveness. The aim of this chapter is to show the mutual relevance of the theory of the psychology of attractiveness outlined in previous chapters and culturally situated studies of physical attractiveness and ethnicity—to show the interplay of human nature and history. I begin by considering how some of the general principles of physical attractiveness discussed in previous chapters may influence cross-ethnic judgments of attractiveness, and end by presenting relevant results from fieldwork in Brazil.

PSYCHOLOGICAL MECHANISMS, SOCIAL CONSEQUENCES

Esthetic responses to members of other ethnic groups may reflect the social status of those groups and stereotypes about them. But responses may also be side effects of criteria of physical attractiveness developed independently of their ethnic associations. Age, sex, and health cues, including averageness, symmetry, craniofacial neoteny, skin color, stature, fatness and fat distribution are all criteria of physical attractiveness that may spill over to affect cross-ethnic esthetic responses. I will consider three principles of physical attraction that may be especially relevant in interethnic situations—attraction to "average" features, attraction to supernormal stimuli (specifically color and stature), and attraction to markers of high social status.

Average Features, Somatic Distance and the Somatic Norm Image

Hoetink's (1967) discussion of physical attraction in multiracial societies introduces two useful concepts: the *somatic norm image* and *somatic distance*. The somatic norm image is a shared image of the ideal physical type; somatic distance is the degree of difference from the somatic norm image. Hoetink's ideas derive from the comparative sociological study of race relations in what he calls the "Greater Caribbean": the Caribbean itself, the US American South, and the Brazilian Northeast. These ideas dovetail with evidence reviewed in Chapter 5 that standards of facial beauty result in part from the operation of a Face Averaging Device. If evaluating a face is partly a matter of quantifying the difference between that face and a prototypical face of average proportions, then the usual esthetic response to unusual—"somatically distant"—features should be unfavorable. Below I briefly review evidence that somatically distant features have commonly been regarded as unattractive in situations of interethnic contact, and present some relevant data from this study.

Non-European responses to European features. Although it was common for eighteenth and nineteenth century Europeans to assume that European faces (especially those represented in classical Greek and Roman sculpture) represented the height of beauty (Mosse 1985), scholars who were familiar with even the limited ethnographic material available at the time were able to show that native populations not much exposed to European influences commonly found Europeans unattractive. Midfacial prognathism—the projection of the middle region of the face, including the nose—a distinctive characteristic of European and Middle Eastern faces—seems to have come in for especially unfavorable comment in the rest of the world.

Darwin (1981[1872]) cited sources who reported that "the Chinese of the interior think Europeans hideous with their white skin and prominent noses" (p. 345), while in Africa "the negroes rallied Mungo Park on the whiteness of his skin and the prominence of his nose, both of which they considered as 'unsightly and unnatural conformations' " (p. 346; see pp. 343–50 for many similar instances).

Westermarck (1971) noted that "the Australian natives 'laugh at the sharp noses of Europeans, and call them in their own language "tomahawk noses" much preferring their own style of flat broad noses' " (p. 8) and recorded the comments of a Tahitian to a European missionary: "What a pity it is that English mothers pull their children's noses so much, and make them so frightfully long" (p. 8).

In 1860, just after the opening of Japan to the outside world, a delegation of 83 *samurai* arrived in Washington DC and met with President Buchanan. Their reactions to American women, recorded in their diaries, included the following: "The women's skin was white, and they were charming in their gala dresses decorated with gold and silver but their hair was red and their eyes looked like dog eyes, which was quite disheartening," and "Occasionally I saw women with black hair and black eyes. They must have been of some Asian race. Naturally they looked more attractive and beautiful" (Wagatsuma 1968:136).

In this century, Malinowski (1987[1927]) noted that Trobriand Islanders commonly told him that they considered Europeans physically unattractive, although they sometimes politely added that Malinowski was good-looking for a white man. Hogbin (1946), working in New Guinea, wrote:

> Europeans are most emphatically not envied for their blonde coloring, which is regarded as far too reminiscent of albinos. Condolences were offered to me on two occasions on account of my pallor, and Jaua [one of Hogbin's informants] was probably expressing the opinion of the majority when he said that if he were white he supposed that he, too, would be ashamed and cover his body with as many clothes as possible. [p. 198]

European responses to non-European features. Jordan (1968) has documented the early history of English and American attitudes to Africans and African Americans. Negative reactions to the black skin, "horrid Curles," and "disfigured" lips of West Africans are apparent from the time of the earliest English voyages to sub-Saharan Africa (from 1550), well before large-scale English involvement in the slave trade, although some early explorers were sophisticated enough to recognize that Africans had different ideals of beauty (pp. 8–10). Of course the development of slavery and colonialism (discussed below) played a major role in the later evolution of European (and world) standards of beauty, but it is clear that responses to somatic distance, as well as the idealization of white-skinned femininity also played a role (see below for Roman and Arab idealization of light skin and light hair in women).

Ache and others: results from this study. In previous chapters I presented attractiveness ratings for University of Michigan students of European ancestry only. In addition to 52 females and 35 males of European ancestry, my University of Michigan sample includes 5 females and 3 males of East Asian ancestry, and 3 females and 1 male of African ancestry. Table 7.1 shows the average attractiveness ratings given by Russians, US Americans, Brazilians and Ache to photographs of University of Michigan students of both sexes of European, East Asian and African ancestry.

This sample was not designed to look for racial differences in attractiveness ratings, and includes only small numbers of Asian and African Americans. Even so, all four populations of raters give different average attractiveness ratings to faces belonging to different racial/ethnic categories. For all populations of raters there is significant variation in facial attractiveness scores between the three

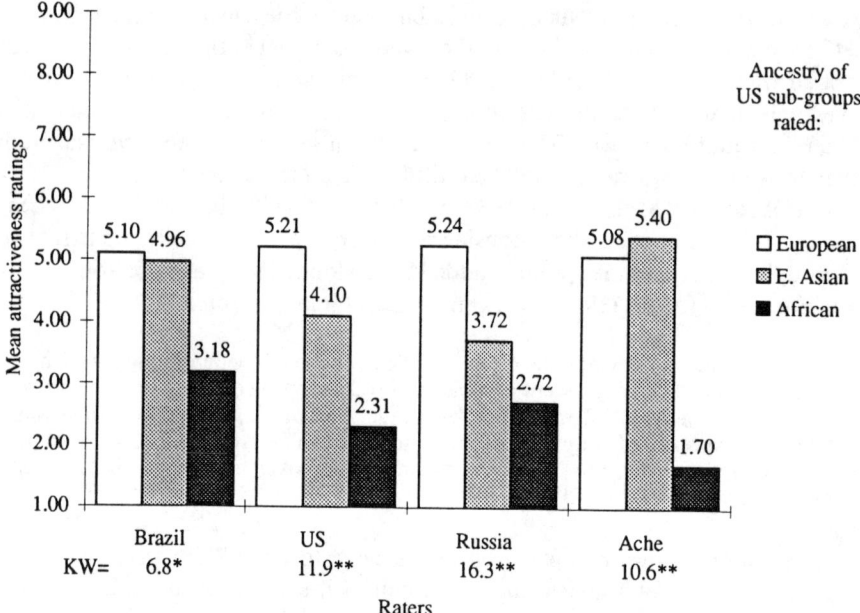

Figure 7.1 Race and attractiveness, US sample. Mean ratings of attractiveness given to three ethnic subdivisions of the US photographic samples (female and male combined) by raters from four populations. The numbers at the bottom of the graph ("KW=") are test statistics from Kruskal-Wallis one-way nonparametric analysis of variance. They measure the extent to which each sample of raters gives different attractiveness ratings to different ethnic subdivisions. (N = 81, 8, 4 for European, East Asian and African subgroups.)

racial categories, as measured by a Kruskal-Wallis one-way analysis of variance. The Kruskal-Wallis test statistics reported in Figure 7.1 measure the magnitude of the between-race variation. Brazilian raters show the smallest differences in the ratings of attractiveness that they give to different racial categories. Russians show the largest, mostly because they give low attractiveness ratings to Asian Americans as well as to African Americans.

For Western (Brazilian, US, and Russian) raters racial differences in attractiveness could reflect in part their current and historical relations with the groups being rated. For example, the especially low ratings given to Asian Americans by Russian raters may reflect the troubled history of Russian relations with Central Asians and East Asians. And the low ratings given to African American faces even by Brazilian raters, who live in a city with a black majority, is surely influenced by the disadvantaged position of blacks both locally and in the world system (see below).

But it is unlikely that the Ache prejudice in favor of Asian American faces, and against African American faces, reflects stereotypes about Asians or Africans. Most Ache have never in their lives met anyone of Asian or African ancestry, and know little or nothing about the social position of the two groups in the larger world. Racial somatic prejudice among the Ache seems to have far more to do with "somatic distance." The Ache have an ethnocentric standard of beauty. They are light-skinned and physically robust, and look down on their darker, slighter Indian and mestizo neighbors. They are also not particularly attracted to the white anthropologists and missionaries who have lived among them. Kim Hill (pers. comm.) writes: "The Ache have frequently commented on how ugly Europeans are particularly because of their long noses (they call us *pyta puku*—long nose—behind our backs) and because they are so hairy." One white anthropologist's nose earned him the nickname "Anteater." Although the Ache have had virtually no contact with Asians or Asian Americans, they are curious about East Asian faces, generally attracted to them, and aware of the similarity between these faces and their own. On the other hand, the Ache frequently made negative remarks about the dark skin of blacks, their hair texture and the shape of their faces in the process of rating them. Such racial somatic prejudice is expected even in the absence of racial stereotypes as long as attractiveness is partly a function of averageness or prototypicality.

Supernormal Features

As I argued in Chapter 5, human beings prefer extreme (or supernormal) values of some traits over average values. Population differences in such traits may have consequences for interethnic perceptions of attractiveness.

Color. I noted in Chapter 5 that a male preference for lighter than average skin color in female partners is a cultural universal or near universal. This preference may depend on the emotional symbolism of white and black, or it may reflect an attraction to feminine/neotenous traits. It is not simply a recent result of colonial expansion. Female preferences regarding male skin color are less consistent. It should be stressed that male skin color preferences are relative, not absolute. Men brought up in dark-skinned populations may be attracted to skin somewhat lighter than the local average, but, as the quotes above make clear, they are commonly not attracted to "white" (or pink) skin.

The positive value attached to light coloring, especially for women, has affected relations between classes and ethnic groups across a wide range of stratified societies. Jordan (1968:9) writes: "It was important, if incalculably so, that the English discovery of black Africa came at a time when the accepted standard of ideal beauty was a fair complexion of rose and white. Negroes not only failed to fit this ideal but seemed the very picture of its perverse negation."

The Indian caste system has been the subject of innumerable scholarly works, and is standard fare in introductory anthropology and sociology courses. But many non-Indians who have read about the system are unaware that it is, in theory and in practice, a hierarchy of color. Caste in India involves a hierarchy of *jati*—endogamous occupational groups. Over the whole of traditional India these *jati* number in the thousands. The *jati* in turn are grouped into four ranked *varna* (Brahmans at the top, followed by Kshatriya, Vaishya, and Sudra) plus the untouchables. The Sanskrit word *varna* means color, and each of the four *varna* has its associated color—white for the Brahmans, red or bronze for the Kshatriya, yellow for the Vaishya, and black for the Sudra (Isaacs 1975). These colors are related to Hindu beliefs about the impure and polluting character of the lower castes. The color values are not just symbolic; members of higher castes are in fact generally lighter skinned than members of lower castes. The difference is an average difference; there is some overlap in skin color between castes, and a Southern Indian Brahman is likely to be darker than a Northern Indian Sudra (Isaacs 1975). Alongside these caste differences runs an idealization of light skinned women.

> In many Indian languages the words for *fair* and *beautiful* are often used synonymously. The folk literature places a high value on fair skin color. The ideal bride, whose beauty and virtue are praised in the songs sung at marriages, almost always has a light complexion. A dark girl is often a liability to her family because of the difficulty of arranging a marriage for her. [Beteille 1975:173]

The Indian caste system may have its origins in the Aryan invasions of the second millennium B.C. Although the Aryans were certainly not the blond blue-eyed Nordics of European racist mythology, they were probably lighter in skin color than the people they conquered. Caste differences in skin color may have their origins in this ancient stratification between invaders and natives.

Other societies, however, present social stratification in skin color even without any historical background of conquest by light-skinned groups. In Japan, whiteness has been associated with feminine beauty from the earliest recorded times, and white face powder has been part of women's cosmetics for over a millennium. In Japan, members of the upper classes are traditionally said to be lighter skinned. Hulse (1967) confirms the class differences in skin color using skin reflectance measurements and presents evidence suggesting that these differences have a genetic basis, presumably as a result of hypergamy (marrying up) by lighter skinned women.

Finally, both classical Roman and Islamic history present cases in which dark skinned groups have conquered or otherwise dominated peoples with lighter skins.

> [In Roman society] before the first century B.C., a . . . *femineus pallor* was . . . regarded in polite society as an essential mark of the feminine ideal of beauty, even if dark-complexioned women . . . could also be seen as beautiful. [Thompson 1989:131]

From the first century B.C. onward, Northern European slaves entered the Roman market in large numbers.

> The importation of blond northern slave girls . . . introduced a change in the feminine ideal. . . . Roman society's experience of "nordic" feminine whiteness established the model of the blond, "milk-white," and rosy cheeked beauty in upper-class circles. . . . Smart Roman women whose natural complexions exemplified the feminine norm anyway emphasized their *femineus pallor* by the use of cosmetics, while the darker sort of woman (if she was fashionable) took pains to acquire a lighter complexion by creaming and bleaching. [Thompson 1989:131–32]

As blond hair came into fashion, some women resorted to dyeing to lighten their hair and "blond wigs were an essential fashion item in ancient Rome" (Gunn 1973:42). Roman hair dyes evidently left something to be desired; Ovid wrote of a woman whose hair fell out when she tried to dye it blond: "Now Germany will send you some slave-girl's hair; a vanquished nation shall furnish thy adornments" (cited in Gunn 1973:43).

The Roman response to *men* with light skin and light hair was different. A Roman man wearing a blond wig was probably a comic actor playing the part of a buffoonish northerner. Fair coloring in men was attractive only to other men seeking "Ganymedes"—feminine, passive homosexual partners (Thompson 1989:132).

Black Africans (*Aethiopes*), by contrast, usually evoked a negative esthetic response. Individual Romans might be attracted to dark-skinned beauties, or enjoy sampling a range of skin colors for the sake of variety, but attractive dark-skinned women and men were more likely to be described as beautiful *although* black than as beautiful *because* black.

Roman society developed nothing comparable to the elaborate pseudoscientific theories of racial superiority characteristic of modern Europe during its Age of Expansion. Broad stereotypes about North Europeans and *Aethiopes* did exist—Northerners ferocious, brave, and not too bright; *Aethiopes* quick-witted, lazy and lascivious—but these were not an overwhelming barrier to upward mobility for a savvy outsider with the right patrons. Romans' different esthetic responses to Northern Europeans and *Aethiopes* seem to have been more a product of pre-existing biases regarding color and somatic distance than of different "racial" stereotypes about the relative character and moral worth of the two groups.

Esthetic reactions to skin color affected ethnic group relations in the Islamic world, as well (Lewis 1990). Whiteness is a traditional criterion of female beauty in Arab society. Although Islamic theology rejects racism, abundant literary evidence demonstrates that negative esthetic reactions to black Africans were common in the Islamic Middle East. Light-skinned slaves, mostly originating in Slavic Europe and the Caucasus, commanded higher prices than dark skinned slaves, mostly originating in Africa. The price differential was greatest in the case of female slaves, who were commonly purchased for sexual use. Fair Circassian slave women from the Caucasus were particularly famed for their beauty, and particularly likely to end up in the harems of the rich and powerful.

Stature. Color is such a salient marker of racial differences that it is sometimes used as a synonym for race. However, there are many other somatic traits that are both racially variable and esthetically relevant. Consider stature. Abundant research shows that short men are at a disadvantage in mate competition. Martel and Biller (1987) summarize relevant research for the US, while Gregor (1979) shows that the stigmatization of short men is a cultural near-universal.

Arkoff and Weaver (1966) show that both Japanese-American and European-American men generally want to be taller and more robust than they are, but body dissatisfaction is more pronounced among Japanese-Americans. Ogawa (1973) notes that Japanese-Hawaiians traveling to the American mainland commonly experience increased body dissatisfaction, partly on account of their stature, as they move from an environment in which East Asians are a majority to one in which they are a minority. Kelsky (1992) discusses the phenomenon of Japanese women who are attracted to European American and African American men and who take vacations in Hawaii with the aim of picking up *gaijin* (non-Japanese) boyfriends. The allegedly more romantic and considerate behavior of these men is part of what makes them attractive as boyfriends, but their body size is also important to some women. The reverse phenomenon—Japanese men picking up *gaijin* women—is less common, at least partly because many Japanese men find *gaijin* women physically intimidating. "Generally . . . , Japanese men . . . seem rather overwhelmed and discouraged by the large physique of a white woman" (Wagatsuma 1968).

Social Status

I have argued throughout this study that human beings probably have an innate "template" of what a physically attractive face and body look like, but that this template is "fine tuned" by experience to accommodate special features of the local population. I reviewed various lines of evidence suggesting that human beings have a Face Averaging Device which constructs imaginary composite faces out of perceived faces. This composite face may be involved both in face recognition and in facial attraction.

But if attractive features are, at least in part, average features, the average in question may be a *weighted* average. The features of high status people may be given more weight than others in the construction of the ideal composite. The history of fashion in the West is in part a history of the diffusion of esthetic standards from high status and culturally central groups to the rest of society (Bell 1976), and such groups are also likely to be disproportionately influential in the formation of standards of beauty of face and body.

Physical Attractiveness and the Theory of Sexual Selection

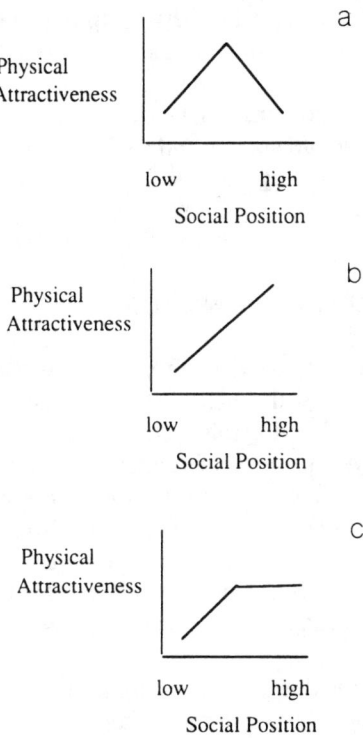

Figure 7.2. Race, averageness and social status. In a racially mixed society, the most attractive type may be the mean type (upper figure), or the type associated with the highest social status (middle figure) or some combination (lower figure).

Suppose we look at a stratified society in which, for historical reasons, there are differences in physical appearance between high status groups and low status groups. (To keep things simple, let us assume that medium status groups are intermediate in physical appearance.) Figure 7.2 compares how averageness effects and social status effects might influence standards of attractiveness under these conditions. If standards of attractiveness were established purely by averaging, with no individual contributing more than any other to the "somatic norm image," then the relationship between physical features and attractiveness might look something like 7.2a, with the attraction to average features producing a preference for intermediate types. (The actual outcome could be more complicated if the distribution of physical types were multimodal.)

If standards of attractiveness were strongly affected by differences in social status, with high status individuals making a disproportionate contribution to the somatic norm image, the relationship between physical features and attractiveness would look more like 7.2b. In fact, if status effects were strong enough, the somatic norm image might even be a supernormal version of the high status type, one that presented the distinguishing features of high status individuals in an exaggerated form. (This would correspond to the features of low status individuals receiving not just a low weight in the formation of standards of attractiveness, but a *negative* weight.)

BEAUTY IN THE WORLD SYSTEM

All human beings increasingly participate in a single "world system." This world system is sometimes called the *capitalist* world system, but capitalism is only one of the forces at work in tying this system together. The world system is also a world *geopolitical* system, in which some states (Habsburg Spain, the Soviet Union) have played military and political roles out of all proportion to their economic strength. Finally, the world system is also a world *cultural* system. Along with the expansion of Western economic and military power has come an expansion of Western high culture and popular culture. One consequence has been the worldwide spread of Western ideals of physical attractiveness.

Wagatsuma (1968) discusses this process in Japan. I have already noted that the Japanese traditionally idealized feminine whiteness, and from the beginning of Western contact, Japanese found the fair skin of European and European American women attractive. However, responses to other European features, including skin texture, shape of facial features, and hair color and texture, were generally negative. This began to change in the twentieth century. "The subtle, not fully conscious, trend toward an idealization of Western physical features by the Japanese apparently became of increasing importance by the twenties" (p. 139). After the Second World War, Japanese standards of feminine beauty underwent substantial Westernization. Wavy hair and permanents became fashionable, along with hair lightening via dyes, while actresses often resorted to surgery to reduce their epicanthic folds, and build up the bridges of their noses (p. 139). By 1954, this process had gone far enough for novelist Shusaku Endo to write:

> I do not know why and how only the white people's skin became the standard of beauty. I do not know why and how the standard of human beauty in sculpture and paintings all stemmed from the white body of the Greeks, and has been so maintained until today. But what I am sure of is that in regard to the body, those like myself and Negroes can never forget miserable inferiority feelings in front of people possessing white skin, however vexing it might be to admit it. [Cited in Wagatsuma, 1968:140.]

Spanish and US American domination has had similar consequences in the Philippines. Isaacs writes:

> Among Filipinos I found an almost obsessive pre-occupation with color and physical characteristics. It turned up in the way individuals referred to almost every aspect of everyday life, in connection with mating and dating, the raising of children, and it seemed to be a matter of note and mention at almost every point of contact between people of varying groups and kinds in the population.

The somatic norm image in the Philippines is light-brown-skinned and Caucasian, although most of the population is "Malay" in appearance. Chinese features are considered particularly unattractive. In recent years, however, Filipino intellectuals have attacked their country's "yearning for whiteness," and the somatic norm image may be shifting in a "Malayan" direction with the political rise of a new postcolonial elite.

Members of West Indian societies generally show a similar attraction to European features, and a rejection of African ones, even where a majority of the population is of African descent. It was research in the West Indies that led Hoetink (1967) to the idea of the "somatic norm image," and to the proposal that in racially stratified societies this image is disproportionately weighted toward the appearance of the dominant group. Not only Hoetink, but Lowenthal (1971, especially Chapter 7), Henriques (1968), and Wagley (1958) provide abundant documentation of this racial somatic prejudice. The attraction to European physical features is expressed in cosmetic practices like skin bleaching, hair dyeing and hair straightening. It expresses itself within families in favoritism toward light skinned children with "better" hair and facial features. In the workplace, lighter, more European-looking women are more likely to gain employment that puts them in the public eye. And in relations between the sexes, men are more likely to marry light-skinned women, while women who have children out of wedlock are more likely to have them with lighter skinned men.

In the United States, many African Americans are aware of prejudice against dark skins and African features within their community. The evidence has recently been summarized at book length (Russell et al. 1992). Favoritism by slave owners toward mulattos (who were in some cases their own offspring) is well documented. Mulattos maintained a distinct identity, including separate social clubs, churches, and private educational facilities up to the 1920s, even in the face of white insistence that any individual with detectable African ancestry was "colored" (Williamson 1984). The result was the establishment within the black community of a stratification based on skin color, hair type and physiognomy that persists right up to the present. Herskovits (1968:61), comparing samples of well-to-do and poor blacks in Harlem in the 1960s, showed that the more successful had lighter skins, narrower noses, and thinner lips. A more recent study (Hughes 1990) found a gap in income and socioeconomic status between dark and light skinned blacks as great as that between the latter and whites.

The result of somatic stratification within the African American community and of exposure to a more numerous and materially successful white community is an attraction to blacks with relatively light skin and European features. This attraction is more marked in the case of men's evaluations of women than in the case of women's evaluations of men (Russell et al. 1992:107). "Whitening" of appearance via hair straightening, skin bleaching, colored contact lenses, and cosmetic surgery is one consequence. Another is the tendency of successful-black men to marry light skinned black women (Herskovits 1968).

It is not only African Americans who are affected by the US American somatic norm image. Philip Roth's Portnoy declares:

> O America! America! it may have been gold in the streets to my grandparents, it may have been a chicken in the pot to my father and mother, but to me, a child whose earliest memories are of Anne Rutherford and Alice Faye, America is a *shikse* nestling under your arm whispering love love love love love.... I want Jane Powell too, God damn it! and Corliss and Veronica. I want to be the boyfriend of Debbie Reynolds—it's the Eddie Fisher in me coming out, that's all, the longing... for those bland blond exotics called *shikses*. [Roth 1967:146–52]

My University of Michigan photographic subjects included a Jewish woman who told me that she felt rejected by both Jewish and Gentile men in the United States owing to her strong Jewish features, but who experienced a dramatic increase in her perceived physical attractiveness when she traveled to Israel, where her face and color were closer to local norms.

There is no reason to think that Europeans and their overseas descendants will maintain a dominant position in the world system forever. However, it seems likely that future societies will typically feature both social stratification and somatic differences between social strata. In societies in which physical features covary with social status, individuals' and groups' social positions—especially their bargaining power in the mating and marriage market—may depend not just on their economic and political assets but on their somatic distance from dominant groups.

BELEZA TROPICAL: RACE AND SOMATIC PREJUDICE IN BRAZIL

Race in Brazil

For nearly a century Brazil and the United States have been a magnet for comparative historical studies, because of the very different paths taken by the two countries in the development of slavery and race relations. When racial theories were in full flower in the nineteenth and early twentieth centuries, some Brazilian scholars developed the theory of "whitening" (*embranqueamento*) as an alternative to North American theories of the perils of racial mixture. According to the theorists of *embranqueamento,* Brazil's black population was getting whiter with each passing generation. The triumph of the white race in Brazil would be assured by the humane process of asymmetrical miscegenation, rather than by United States–style segregation (Skidmore 1974).

A later generation of social scientists rejected such frank racism but maintained the belief that race relations were more humane in Brazil than in the United States. Gilberto Freyre's monumental multivolume cultural history of Brazil (1963, 1964, 1970) did not deny the violence and suffering involved in slavery, but argued that the white Brazilian's tolerance of miscegenation had led over the long run to a "racial democracy" in Brazil.

At first, many blacks and white liberals in the United States welcomed this idealized picture of a nonracist Brazil, which made a happy contrast with an avowedly racist United States in which white supremacy was upheld by law and by extra-legal violence. Pierson's 1942 book *Negroes in Brazil* declared that "Brazil has no race problem. . . . [Brazilians] have, somehow, regained that paradisiac innocence with respect to differences of race, which the people of the United States have somehow lost" (p. xvi). Tannenbaum (1947) argued that differences between the two countries in the legal and religious status of slaves made slavery less dehumanizing in Brazil than in the United States.

But subsequent research, both ethnographic and historical, soon demonstrated that this initial perception of Brazilian racial equality was seriously flawed. Wagley and coworkers (Wagley 1952) demonstrated a considerable fund of prejudice against blacks in Brazil, expressed both in folk sayings and in personal behavior. Of particular relevance to this work, Hutchinson's study (1952:32–37) of race relations in a rural community of the Bahian coastal zone and Harris's study (1952:57–58) of a community in central Brazil documented esthetic prejudice against African features, particularly hair texture and facial proportions. Another generation of United States and Brazilian scholars have provided abundant documentation of racial inequality and anti-black prejudice in Brazil (see, for example, Fernandes 1969; Wagley 1958; Wagley 1971; Turner 1985; Fontaine 1985).

Although Brazilians are a long way from any "paradisiac innocence with respect to differences of race," there is a real and important difference between United States and Brazilian race relations. The difference lies not so much in the social position of slaves and persons of African descent as in the position of persons of mixed race.

> The key that unlocks the puzzle of the differences in race relations in Brazil and the United States is the mulatto escape hatch. Complex and varied as the race relations

in the two countries have been and are today, the presence of a separate place for the mulatto in Brazil and its absence in the United States nevertheless define remarkably well the heart of the difference. [Degler 1971:224]

Pierre van den Berghe's distinction between "paternalistic" and "competitive" modes of interethnic relations points in the same direction (van den Berghe 1967). Under the paternalistic mode of race relations, strong patron-client relations between upper and lower racial strata forestall the development of overt racial hostility and segregationism on the part of the upper strata and/or solidarity on the part of the lower which is characteristic of the competitive mode. Brazil and most of Latin America fit the paternalistic mode; the United States and South Africa fit the competitive mode (see also Harris 1964). In a more recent treatment of the paternalistic/competitive distinction, van den Berghe (1981) stresses that the "paternalism" of the paternalistic mode of inter-ethnic relations is often not just a sentimental ideological smokescreen but a biological fact. At the heart of paternalism, he suggests, are sexual and reproductive liaisons—and *de facto* polygyny—involving males from dominant groups and females from subordinate ones. Van den Berghe's discussion points to the same conclusion as Degler's: the key difference between Brazilian and United States race relations is the attitude toward miscegenation and the position of the mulatto.

Why do miscegenation and the mulatto receive such different treatment in Brazil and the United States? From the beginning there have probably been differences between the two countries in the sheer level of miscegenation, resulting in part from differences in the sex ratio during the colonial period: Portuguese colonists were likely to be single men seeking their fortunes; English and other colonists in the early United States were more likely to arrive in families. But at least as important as differences in the *number* of individuals of mixed race were differences in their social position. Ironically, the radically democratic character of US society and the high status of women in American life blocked the ascent of the mulatto.

> Most poor southern whites concentrated upon opposing the competition of blacks, whether they were free or slave.... Their economic interests and their social status were more threatened by Negroes than were those of the upper classes.... The poor white man on the make had much to gain in status as well as in material goods if he and his fellows could single out Negroes as inferiors. As they gained political power they used it to enhance their own position by legally and otherwise reducing the status of Negroes. [Degler 1971:257–60]

From the beginning of the nineteenth century to the middle of the twentieth poor whites in the southern United States were powerful enough to write into law and put into practice the political and economic disenfranchisement of virtually *all* individuals with detectable African ancestry. If Brazilian society was founded on an alliance between rich whites and mulattos, US society was founded on an alliance of rich and poor whites that left little place for the mulatto.

White women, too, were more powerful and less sequestered in the United States than in Brazil, and in a better position to prevent their husbands from putting time and material resources into interracial polygyny (Degler 1971). Alexander (1979) and Betzig (1986) argue that there is a connection between the imposition of monogamy (including the decline of the sexual double standard) and the rise of democracy. In polygynous societies, they argue, solidarity between rich and poor is weak because the harems and love affairs of rich men are perceived as a threat to the sexual and marital opportunities of poor men. But, supposing that there is something to this argument, the comparative history of Brazil and the United States—one country relatively polygynous and hierarchical, and one relatively monogamous and egalitarian—suggests that monogamy and social solidarity have a darker side. In a multiethnic society they may be associated as much with nationalism, segregation and racial polarization—the competitive mode of interethnic relations—as with democracy (see also Mosse 1985, which traces the connections between nationalism and sexual ideologies).

Of course both Brazil and the United States display considerable variation between regions and over time. Williamson (1984:15–24) shows that in some parts of the US South, particularly Louisiana and South Carolina before 1850, there was something close to a Brazilian-style "mulatto escape hatch." And within Brazil, race relations are more competitive in São Paulo and other centers of industry and immigration than in the more traditional *nordeste*. Ironically, however, the civil rights revolution in the United States in many ways simply reaffirmed the contrast between the two countries. In Brazil the same special place for the mulatto that blocked the emergence of US-style white supremacy now blocks the consolidation of a US-style black nationalist movement or affirmative action agenda. The 1970s did see the rise of a Brazilian black power movement, culminating in 1978 in the foundation of the *Movimento Negro Unificado* (Unified Black Movement) (Bacelar 1989, Gonzalez 1985). The MNU is a radical left antiracist movement organized to struggle against what it sees as an oppressive white capitalist system. But while the MNU has succeeded in provoking furious denunciations from Brazil's largely white elite, it has so far not gained wide popular support among the working class and unemployed who constitute the majority of Brazil's black population (Bacelar 1989:89). Efforts to organize blacks as a voting bloc have been generally unsuccessful: "Blacks don't vote for blacks" (*Negro não vota em negro*) say many Brazilians, both black and white (Fontaine 1985:69). The country's tradition of paternalism and clientelism, and the possibility of identities intermediate between black and white, today undermine black solidarity just as they earlier undermined white solidarity.

While black political mobilization is weakly developed in Brazil, at least in comparison with the United States, black cultural groups have flourished since the 1970s. In Salvador the *blocos afros*—black musical and cultural groups that sponsor processions during Carnival—are especially prominent (Bacelar 1989). Several *blocos afros* have held black beauty contests aimed at promoting an African ideal of beauty among Bahians. Julio Braga (pers. comm.), a professor at UFBA, described efforts to change the standards of beauty of Brazilian blacks as part of a larger program of consciousness raising (*conscientização*) on the part of black cultural groups. To date, however, such consciousness raising has done little to inhibit the open expression of racial somatic prejudice in lower class communities like Campo Alto and Arembepe.

Racial Classification and Perceptions of Attractiveness

Multidimensional scaling and racial classification. Brazilian Portuguese has a large vocabulary to express subtle differences in racial/somatic features. In this vocabulary, terms that clearly refer to race—*indio, negro* (Indian, Negro)—overlap with what US Americans would consider nonracial categories—*loiro, moreno* (blond, brown/dark-skinned). Because colloquial Brazilian racial categorization focuses on physical appearance rather than descent, full siblings may be assigned to different racial categories.

In the mid-1960s Conrad Kottak asked 100 Arembepeiros to give the race (*qualidade*) of drawings of nine somatically contrasting individuals and discovered that villagers used more than forty racial terms. However, "Arembepeiros were inconsistent in their use of the terms. For one drawing, villagers offered nineteen different racial terms, and the least number of terms for any drawing was nine" (Kottak 1992:75).

During my fieldwork in Arembepe in 1992, I carried out further research on racial categorization for Kottak. This research was a follow-up to a major multi-community analysis of television and culture in Brazil (Kottak 1990). Since television programs typically use only a handful of racial categories, Kottak was interested in finding out whether the introduction of television to Arembepe had simplified the villagers' racial vocabulary. I used thirty photographs of Salvadoran females that I had collected during my 1989 pilot study (see Chapter 3). I asked 40 males and 40 females to give the *qualidade* of each photograph. My interview subjects gave me 50 racial/somatic categories, although just ten categories accounted for 94% of categorizations. Analysis showed no significant correlation between number of racial categories used and daily hours of television viewing or years of television exposure.

I have since made use of these data in my own research. In addition to racial categorizations of the photographs, I also collected ratings of physical attractiveness from another 20 raters, using the 3 × 3 row sort/column sort procedure described in Chapter 3.

Racial categorization data are more useful in assessing racial somatic prejudice if they can be put on some kind of scale—one showing, for example, that *morena* (brown/ dark-skinned) is intermediate between *preta* (black) and *branca* (white), and *morena clara* (light brown) is intermediate between *morena* and *branca*. For this purpose I used monotonic Kruskal multidimensional scaling (MDS), a nonparametric statistical procedure that puts categorical variables on a continuous scale of one or more dimensions on the basis of their similarity to one another. I used the MDS package available on Systat. Laura Klem of the University of Michigan's Institue for Social Research provided invaluable technical advice.

The first step in MDS is the production of a similarity matrix in which element $\{i, j\}$ is some measure of the similarity between item i and item j. For this analysis I created a matrix of Spearman correlation coefficients between racial categories. Element $\{i, j\}$ was the correlation over all photographs between the number of times that each photograph was classified as belonging to racial category i and the number of times that it was classified in category j. For example, there was a strong positive correlation ($r = .91**$) between the number of times different photographs were classified as *branca* (white) and the number of times they were classified as *clara* (light), and a strong negative correlation ($-.74**$) between *branca* and *escura* (dark).

Table 7.1 and Figure 7.3 present the result of a two-dimensional scaling of 50 racial categories. (I use two dimensions because three added little to the variance explained.) The two dimensions together account for 56% of variation in racial classification.

Dimension 1 (the x axis) might be called the *negra/branca* axis (*negra* = -1.40 on Dimension 1, *branca* = 1.51). Dimension 1 alone accounts for 51% of variation in racial classification. In other words, Arembepeiro racial classification, insofar as it is not simply idiosyncratic or inconsistent, seems to be largely concerned with placing individuals on a scale with African features at one end and European features at the other.

Dimension 2 (the y axis) might be called the *morena/sarará* axis (*morena* = $-.98$ on Dimension 2, *sarará* = $.87$). *Sarará* refers to individuals who combine light skin and light, even blond, hair with pronounced African hair texture and facial features. *Morena* means "brown" or "dark-skinned." It is the most commonly used category. *Morena* itself accounts for 39% of categorizations; variants of *morena* (e.g. *morena clara* = light brown, *morena escura* = dark brown) account for another 15%. Apart from being dark skinned, individuals classified as *morena* vary enormously. Some could pass for dark skinned Europeans, others have pronounced African features. Two less commonly used terms, *cabo*

Table 7.1. Brazilian racial categories used by informants, with literal English translation, total number of times used, percentage of times used and position on first and second MDS axis

BRAZILIAN TERM	ENGLISH TRANSLATION	FREQUENCY NO.	%	MULTI-DIM. SCALING DIM1	DIM2
amarela	yellow	13	*	1.16	0.08
branca	white	492	21	1.51	0.09
branca escura	dark white	1		0.74	-0.05
branca parda	brown white	1		0.35	0.69
clara	light	141	6	1.36	0.17
cabocla	Indian/mixed	15		-0.46	-1.15
cafusa	Indian/mixed	1		-0.42	-0.09
canela	cinnamon	8		-0.81	-0.76
cor de formiga	ant color	2		-0.66	-0.59
crioulo	creole	1		-0.31	0.41
cravo	clove	2		-0.15	0.6
cabo verde	(see text)	6		0.79	-0.56
escura	dark	75	3	-1.3	0.55
galega	Galician	3		0.48	0.7
india	Indian	3		-0.4	-0.05
jambo		1		0.08	-0.58
loira	blond	7		0.45	0.94
lima	lime	1		-0.04	0.51
morena	brown	922	39	-0.94	-0.98
morena clara	light brown	261	11	1.36	-0.4
morena escura	dark brown	87	4	-1.4	-0.2
morena legitima	true brown	3		0.04	1.08

Physical Attractiveness and the Theory of Sexual Selection

mestica	mixed	2	0.84	-0.32
mulata	mulatto	76	-1.17	-0.34
mulata clara	light mulatto	7	0.93	-1.04
mulata escura	dark mulatto	8	-0.73	-0.24
negra	Negro	58	-1.4	0.26
negra clara	light Negro	3	-1.4	0.26
nega	Negro	3	-0.98	0.53
neguinha	little Negro	4	-1.13	0.49
preta	black	56	-0.88	0.74
parda	brown	13	0.74	0.78
preta escura	dark black	1	-0.66	0.65
pele vermelha	red skin	1	-0.42	-0.09
rosa	pink	5	0.64	-0.68
ruiva	red head	7	0.98	0.45
russa	Russian	1	0.61	0.28
sarara	(see text)	51	0.8	0.8
saruaba	sarara	5	0.6	0.87
vermelha	red	5	1.02	-0.77
morena cravo	clove brown	1	-0.63	0.26
morena especial		1	0.08	-0.58
morena recriativa		1	-0.62	-0.39
morena cor parda		1	0.05	-0.32
morena castanha		1	0.39	-0.33
branquela		1	0.4	0.15
morena cor de jabuticaba		1	-0.11	-0.86
morena normal		1	0.35	-0.8
morena bronzeada		1	-0.11	-0.86
morena gaza		1	0.35	0.69
TOTAL		2362		

*empty FREQUENCY % cells mean frequency <1%

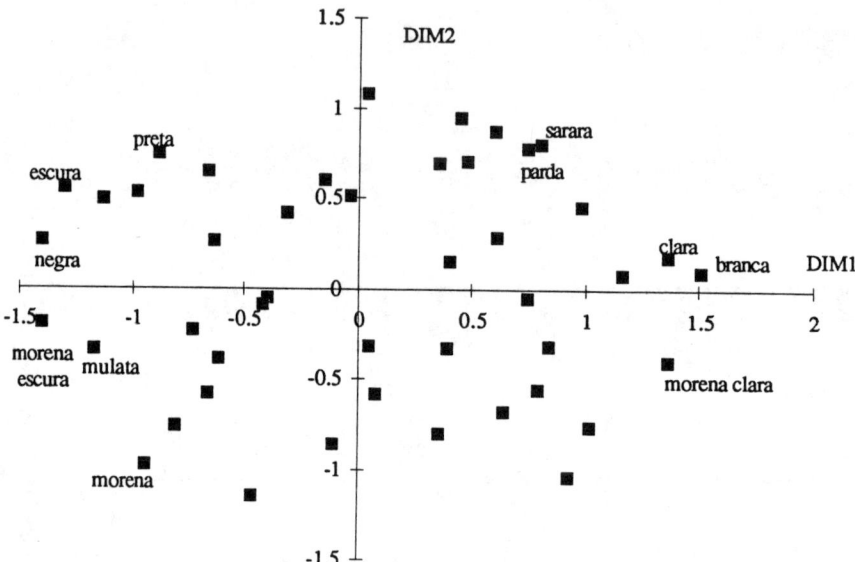

Figure 7.3. Brazilian racial categories and multidimensional scaling. Each point represents one category. The closer points are to one another, the more often the corresponding categories were applied to the same photographs. The ten most frequently used categories are labeled.

verde, referring specifically to the combination of dark skin and European features, and *cabocla*, referring to American Indian features, also score low on Dimension 2.

Averageness, social status and attractiveness. In a discussion earlier in this chapter of the effects of social status on standards of physical attractiveness, I proposed two extreme scenarios. Under a pure averaging effect, faces with average or intermediate characteristics will be perceived as most attractive; under a pure social status effect, faces with characteristics associated with high status groups will be perceived as most attractive (see Figure 7.2). These hypotheses can be tested with the multidimensional scaling results of the previous section. Each female in the photographic sample can be assigned a position on Dimensions 1 and 2 by averaging her scores on each dimension over all 80 categorizations given to her.

The correlation between physical attractiveness and scores on Dimension 2 is negative—suggesting that *sarará* is less attractive than *morena*—but not significant (Spearman's $r = .29$). (I use a nonparametric test because scores on Dimension 2 are bimodally distributed, with peaks around -0.5 and -0.1.)

Results for Dimension 1 (the *negra/branca* axis) are particularly interesting. Figure 7.3 shows the relationship between each female's attractiveness rating and

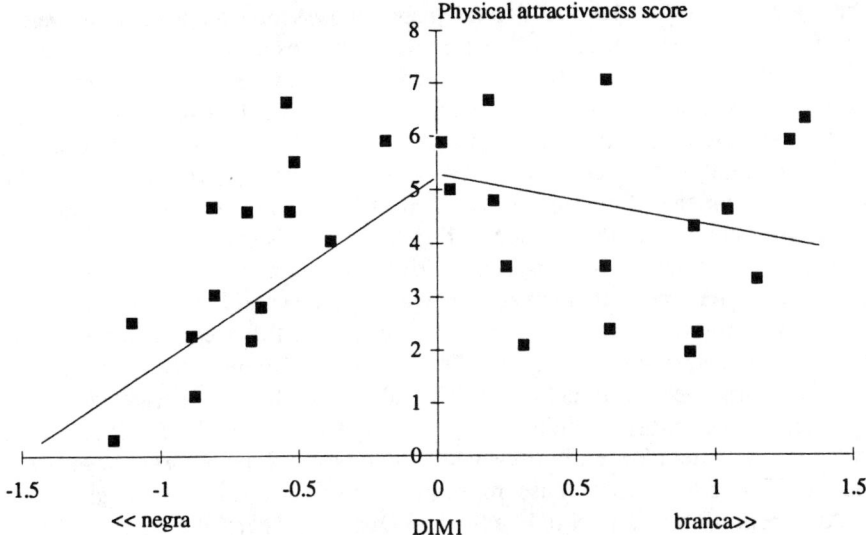

Figure 7.4. Attractiveness and the negra/branca axis. Scattergram of ratings of physical attractiveness of Brazilian females and position along the negra/branca axis (DIM1 from Figure 7.3) shows a nonlinear effect. Each point represents one photograph.

her score on Dimension 1. I have tested the social status hypothesis by calculating the correlation between attractiveness and Dimension 1 (DIM1); I have tested the averaging hypothesis by calculating the correlation between attractiveness and the *absolute value* of Dimension 1 (|DIM1|) (see Figure 7.1a, b). Both tests yield results in the expected direction; but results are insignificant for DIM1 and only marginally significant for |DIM1| (Pearson's r's = .29, −.32+). More interesting results turn up when the social status effect and the averageness effect are tested simultaneously. When *both* DIM1 and |DIM1| are fed into a stepwise linear regression, the two together turn out to be significant predictors (R^2 = .23 *).

$$\text{Attractiveness} = .840 \cdot \text{DIM1} - 1.881 \cdot |\text{DIM1}| - 3.753 \qquad (7.1)$$

The two variables contribute about equally to the regression; the regression coefficient is smaller for DIM1 than for |DIM1| only because DIM1 is more variable. The resulting regression line is shown in Figure 7.4. This analysis seems to show a combination of averaging effects and social status effects—at one end of the scale a strong esthetic bias against *negra*, at the other end of the scale no strong bias in favor of *branca*. On the left half of the scale, the half closest to *negra*, there is a powerful association between attractiveness and position along the *negra/branca* axis. Among fifteen females whose scores on this axis fall below the median, the Pearson's correlation between Dimension 1 and attractiveness is .77**. On the right half of the scale, the half closest to *branca*, the correlation disappears (Pearson's r = .02). Another analysis of the data supports this conclusion: the number of times that a woman is classified as *negra* shows a strong and significant negative correlation with attractiveness (Spearman's $r = -.52**$), while the number of times she is classified as *branca* shows a weaker and only marginally significant positive correlation (Spearman's $r = .34+$).

Another data set is also consistent with the proposition that Brazilians perceive little difference in attractiveness between *morena* and *branca*. My Brazilian university sample is skewed toward individuals with European features, partly because it is disproportionately middle class in a predominantly working class city, and partly because it includes individuals from other, less Africanized parts of Bahia. It probably includes many individuals who would be classified as black in the United States, but few who would be classified as *preta* or *negra* in Brazil. (That is why I did not use this sample in my study of racial categorization in Arembepe.) This sample, unlike the previous one, is carefully posed and suitable for the measurement of facial landmarks. In ratings of attractiveness collected from residents of the Campo Alto *favela,* there is no correlation between nasal index (nose width divided by nose height) and attractiveness (Pearson's r = .08), and a marginally significant *positive* correlation between lip height and attractiveness (Pearson's r = .24+). In other words, moderate expression of African features does not reduce perceived attractiveness among this group of raters. (For white US and Russian raters, by contrast, nasal index is negatively, but not significantly, correlated with attractiveness ($r = -.12, -.10$), and lip height is uncorrelated ($r = -.08, .10$).

Earlier in this chapter, I made a comparison between the expected effects of *averageness* and *social status* on physical attractiveness in ethnically stratified societies (see Figure 7.2). The results of the analyses in this section suggest that both effects are in operation in Arembepe and Campo Alto. Social status effects and averageness effects combine to produce somatic prejudice against pronounced African features; social status effects and averageness effects cancel out to ensure that pronounced European features are not favored over intermediate features.

Discussions of race in Brazil are often reminiscent of the old saw that the optimist sees the glass as half full, while the pessimist sees it as half empty. This analysis is no exception. On the one hand, lower class Bahian standards of beauty are not merely copied from the local white elite or from overseas. The "beautiful *morena*" (*morena bonita*), product of a long history of miscegenation, is part of the "somatic norm image" for much of the population, celebrated in story and song. Jorge Amado's novel *Gabriela, clove and cinnamon* (Amado 1962) and Caetano Veloso's song *Beleza pura* (Veloso 1979) are just two examples. Bahians often take as much pride in this distinctive local product as they do in their local cuisine and their popular music. But somatic prejudice against pronounced African features is no less evident. Straight hair is "good hair" or "soft hair" (*cabelo bom, cabelo liso*), tightly curled hair is "bad" or "hard" (*ruim, duro*). Wide noses and lips are not just wide or full but gross (*grosso*). Brazilians are generally franker than US Americans about their somatic prejudices, and my notebooks record a stream of negative remarks in response to photographs of women with strong African features. Thus the results of this analysis suggest that the earlier generation of researchers who saw Brazilian miscegenation as leading to a distinctively Brazilian standard of beauty, and the later generation who documented the ubiquity of Brazilian racial prejudice, including somatic racial prejudice, were each partly correct.

While the review and analysis presented in this chapter are discouraging, they should not lead to fatalism. Racial somatic prejudice is widespread, but it is variable in its expression, and sensitive to social context. Better understanding of this variability is likely to come from the study of individual variation in standards of attractiveness and from a more refined analysis of the meaning of social status.

Individual variation. One of my informants in Campo Alto gave exceptionally high ratings to Asian American females when rating photographs from the US female sample. When I asked him about this, he told me that as a young man he had worked on a farm in the interior of Bahia owned by a Japanese-Brazilian man; he had carried on a clandestine affair with the owner's daughter until he was drafted into the army. Nearly 40 years later he was still nostalgic about this romance, and it still influenced his standard of beauty. I have known other Brazilians, both black and white, who have told me they are especially attracted to African features; some of them had similar stories about their early experiences.

I have had little to say about individual variability in standards of physical attractiveness in this study, but the analysis in Chapter 3 suggests that it is an important factor. The topic is little studied, although some work suggests that both behavior genetic differences (Chiarelli 1985) and sensitive-period learning (Wilson 1987) may play a role. Individual differences deserve more study in their own right. Bringing evolutionary theory into the social sciences should mean, among other things, understanding how psychological processes produce differences as well as similarities between individuals. It should mean understanding how individuals emerge as more than just uniform products of a particular class or ethnic group.

The meaning of social status. The concept of social status may have multiple dimensions, and may differ among subcultures within a larger culture, and this may affect the development of standards of attractiveness. Consider an analogy from sociolinguistics: the evolution of language may involve more than the imitation of upper class speech by lower classes; subcultures may mark themselves off with divergent dialects, and upper class speech may incorporate lower class idioms.

Some of the potential complexity of the relationship between social status and judgments of attractiveness is suggested by Brazilian attitudes toward suntanning (*bronzeamento*). Tanning at the beach is a popular activity among Salvadorans of all shades and both sexes. A tan is not a mark of upper-class status because the upper classes are lighter skinned than the lower, and the beach is as accessible to the poor as to the rich. The "status" advertised by a tan is not membership in the elite, but participation in a locally esteemed style of leisure. Brazilians often advised me to work on my tan, not so as to look more upper class, but so as to look less like a work-obsessed *norte americano*.

The relationship between race, status and attractiveness is thus a complicated topic, which this chapter only begins to explore. Human nature—the evolved psychological mechanisms constituting the human mind—enters this study not simply as a hard-wired hierarchy of esthetic values, but as a set of mechanisms for generating esthetic standards as a function of individual experience and surrounding cultural values.

Chapter 8

Conclusion

This study has produced a number of findings:

Cross cultural agreement. The five populations in the study show significant agreement in their assessments of facial attractiveness.

Age and attractiveness. Attractiveness declines with age among adult females and males, at a rate of approximately .05 standard deviations per year among females, and .03 among males.

Age markers and facial proportions. Research in the United States and Europe suggests that female faces with "neotenous" (youthful) proportions are considered especially attractive. Such proportions include skeletal features—large eyes in relation to the vertical dimensions of the face—and soft tissue features—small noses and full lips. The present study shows that men in each society studied show an attraction to neotenous female faces, those which present markers of youthfulness in an exaggerated or "supernormal" form. Women do not show an attraction to males with neotenous faces.

Age and fecundity markers, color and figure. Ethnographic and historical evidence document a widespread pattern of attraction to females with lighter than average skin color, but the evidence from this study does not suggest a strong role for skin color in attractiveness. It does, however, demonstrate an attraction to blond hair in females among US Americans and Russians. This study also confirms and quantifies differences in erotic focus between Brazilian and US American men, with Brazilians most attracted to women with prominent buttocks and small breasts, and US Americans showing the reverse preferences. Russian preferences are intermediate. In each population, males choosing the ideal female figure prefer more exaggerated secondary sexual characteristics than females choosing ideal female figures.

Averageness. Earlier research shows that when individual photographs of faces are combined by computer to make a composite face, the composite face is typically rated more attractive than most of the individual faces composing it; the more faces go into the composite, the more attractive the resulting face. There are also anthropometric data suggesting that especially attractive faces cluster especially closely around the mean for most—but not all—traits. Results from this study show some tendency for individuals to rate members of the other sex from their own populations as more attractive when the proportions of their faces, measured on photographs, are closer to the population average.

Symmetry. Stress on an organism during the course of development often results in random departures from bilateral symmetry, a phenomenon called "fluctuating asymmetry" (FA). In humans, inbreeding, premature birth, and a variety of prenatal stresses (maternal smoking, alcohol consumption, or diabetes) are all associated with elevated FA. Recent work by Gangestad and Thornhill (1994) and Thornhill and Grammer (1994) suggests that FA may be negatively associated with attractiveness in humans. But facial symmetry is not significantly correlated with attractiveness in this study.

Race and somatic prejudice. In a multiracial population, the perceived attractiveness of somatic features that vary between ethnic groups may depend both on the relative population sizes of different groups, and on their respective social positions. In Bahia, Brazil, individuals of African ancestry are in the majority, but whites and light-skinned *mestiços* have more money and political power and higher social status. My research in Brazil shows that there is a nonlinear relationship between ratings of attractiveness and "racial" features. Individuals with pronounced African features are rated significantly less attractive than individuals with intermediate features, while individuals with intermediate features are not rated significantly more or less attractive than individuals with pronounced European features.

The application of the theory of sexual selection to human mate choice and the cross-cultural study of physical attractiveness are very new areas of inquiry. Far more research will be needed in many more populations before the major findings of this study can be accepted as firm conclusions. But even the provisional evidence available to date goes a long way toward vindicating Darwin's faith in the mutual relevance of the study of human physical attractiveness and the theory of sexual selection.

Bibliography

Alexander, R. D. (1979). *Darwinism and Human Affairs.* Seattle: University of Washington Press.

Alley, T. R., and M. R. Cunningham (1991). Averaged faces are attractive, but very attractive faces are not average. *Psychological Science* 2:123–25.

Amado, J. (1962). *Gabriela, clove and cinnamon.* New York: Knopf.

Anderson, C. M. (1986). Female age: male preference and reproductive success in primates. *International Journal of Primatology* 7:305–26.

Andersson, M. (1994). *Sexual selection.* Princeton, New Jersey: Princeton University Press.

Arkoff, A., and B. Weaver (1966). Body image and body dissatisfaction in Japanese-Americans. *Journal of Social Psychology* 68:323–30.

Atran, S. (1990). *Cognitive Foundations of Natural History: Towards an Anthropology of Science.* Cambridge, UK: Cambridge University Press.

Bacelar, J. (1989). *Etnicidade: ser negro em Salvador.* Salvador, Brazil, Ianama: Programa de Estudos do Negro na Bahia (PENBA).

Balmford, A., and A. F. Read (1991). Testing alternative models of sexual selection through female choice. *Trends in Ecology and Evolution* 6: 274–76.

Baron-Cohen, S. (1995). *Mindblindness: An Essay on Autism and Theory of Mind.* Cambridge, MA: MIT Press.

Barth, F. (1969). *Ethnic Groups and Boundaries: The Social Organization of Culture Difference.* Boston: Little, Brown.

Bateman, A. J. (1948). Intra-sexual selection in *Drosophila. Heredity* 2:349–68.

Behrents, R. G. (1985a). *Growth in the Aging Craniofacial Skeleton.* Ann Arbor, MI, Center for Human Growth and Development, The University of Michigan.

Behrents, R. G. (1985b). *An Atlas of Growth in the Aging Craniofacial Skeleton.* Ann Arbor, MI, Center for Human Growth and Development, The University of Michigan.

Bell, Q. (1976). *On Human Finery.* London: Hogarth Press.

Benson, P., and D. Perrett (1992). Face to face with the perfect image. *New Scientist* 133:32–35.

Berlin, B., and P. Kay (1969). *Basic Color Terms: Their Universality and Evolution.* Berkeley: University of California Press.

Berndt, R. M., and C. M. Berndt (1951). *Sexual Behavior in Western Arnhem Land.* New York, Viking Fund.

Berry, D. S., and S. Brownlow (1989). Were the physiognomists right? personality correlates of facial babyishness. *Personality and Social Psychology Bulletin* 15:266–79.

Berry, D. S., and L. Z. McArthur (1985). Some components and consequences of a babyface. *Journal of Personality and Social Psychology* 48:312–23.

Berry, D. S., and L. Z. McArthur (1986). Perceiving character in faces: the impact of age-related craniofacial changes on social perception. *Psychological Bulletin* 100:3–18.

Berry, D. S., and L. Z. McArthur (1988). The impact of age-related craniofacial changes on social perception. *Social and Applied Aspects of Perceiving Faces.* T. R. Alley, ed. Hillsdale, NJ: Lawrence Erlbaum Associates.

Berscheid, E. (1981). An overview of the psychological effects of physical attractiveness and some comments upon the psychological effects of knowledge of the effects of physical attractiveness. *Psychological Aspects of Facial Form.* Ann Arbor, MI, Center for Human Growth and Development. The University of Michigan.

Berscheid, E., K. Dion, E. Walster and G. W. Walster (1971). Physical attractiveness and dating: a test of the matching hypothesis. *Journal of Experimental Social Psychology* 7:173–89.

Berscheid, E., and E. Walster (1974). Physical attractiveness. *Advances in Experimental Social Psychology* 7: 157–215.

Beteille, A. (1975). Race and descent as social categories in India. *Color and Race.* J. H. Franklin, ed. Boston: Houghton Mifflin. 166–185.

Betzig, L. (1986). *Despotism and Differential Reproduction.* New York: Aldine de Gruyter.

Bikchandani, S., D. Hirshleifer, and I. Welch (1992). A theory of fads, fashion, custom, and cultural change as informational cascades. *Journal of Political Economy* 100:992–1026.

Binford, L. R. (1980). Willow smoke and dog's tails: hunter-gatherer settlement systems and archeological site formation. *American Antiquity* 45:1–17.

Boone, S. A. (1986). *Radiance from the Waters: Ideals of Feminine Beauty in Mende Art and Culture.* New Haven: Yale University Press.

Borgia, G. (1979). Sexual selection and the evolution of insect mating systems. *Sexual Selection and Reproductive Competition in Insects.* New York: Academic Press.

Borgia, G. (1986). Sexual selection in bower birds. *Scientific American* 254:92–100.

Borkan, G. A., and A. H. Norris (1980). Assessment of biologic age using a profile of physical parameters. *Journal of Gerontology* 35:177–84.

Boyd, R., and P. Richerson (1985). *Culture and the Evolutionary Process.* Chicago: University of Chicago Press.

Brace, C. L., and P. E. Mahler (1971). Post-Pleistocene changes in the human dentition. *American Journal of Physical Anthropology* 34:191–203.

Bradbury, J. W., and M. B. Andersson, eds. (1987). *Sexual Selection: Testing the Alternatives.* Chichester, England: Wiley.

Bradbury, J. W., and R. M. Gibson (1983). Leks and mate choice. *Mate Choice.* P. Bateson, ed. Cambridge, England: Cambridge University Press.

Braitenberg, V. (1984). *Vehicles: Experiments in Synthetic Psychology.* Cambridge, MA: MIT Press.

Brigham, J. C. (1986). The influence of race on face recognition. *Aspects of Face Processing.* H. Ellis, ed. Dordrecht, Netherlands: Martinus Nijhoff.

Brislin, R., and S. Lewis (1968). Dating and physical attractiveness: replication. *Psychological Reports* 22:976.

Broude, G. J. (1983). Male-female relationships in cross-cultural perspective: a study of sex and intimacy. *Behavior Science Research* 18:151–81.

Brown, W. L. (1957). Centrifugal speciation. *Quarterly Review of Biology* 32:247–77.

Brownmiller, S. (1984). *Femininity.* New York: Linden Press.

Bruce, V. (1988). *Recognizing Faces.* London: Lawrence Erlbaum Associates.

Brues, A. M. (1977). *People and Races.* Prospect Heights, IL: Waveland Press.

Bull, R., and N. Rumsey, eds. (1988). *The Social Psychology of Facial Appearance.* New York: Springer-Verlag.

Burley, N. (1986). Comparison of the band color preferences of two species of estrildid finch. *Animal Behaviour* 34:1732–41.

Burley, N. (1986). Sexual selection for aesthetic traits in species with biparental care. *American Naturalist* 127: 415–45.

Buss, D. M. (1989). Sex differences in human mate preferences: evolutionary hypotheses tested in 37 cultures. *Behavioral and Brain Sciences* 12:1–49.

Campbell, B., ed. (1972). *Sexual Selection and the Descent of Man.* London: Heineman.

Carey, S. (1979). A case study: face recognition. *Explorations in the Biology of Language.* E. Walker, ed. Cambridge, MA: MIT Press.

Caro, T. (1987). Human breasts: unsupported hypotheses reviewed. *Human Evolution* 2: 271–82.

Cavalli-Sforza, L. L., and M. W. Feldman (1981). *Cultural Transmission and Evolution: A Quantitative Approach.* Princeton, NJ: Princeton University Press.

Cavalli-Sforza, L. L., A. Piazza, P. Menozzi and J. Mountain (1988). Reconstruction of human evolution: bringing together genetic, archeological, and linguistic data. *Proceedings of the National Academy of Science* 85:6002–6.

Cavior, N., and L. R. Howard (1973). Facial attractiveness and juvenile delinquency among black and white offenders. *Journal of Abnormal Child Psychology* 1: 202–13.

Chagnon, N. (1988). Male Yanomamö manipulations of kinship classifications of female kin for reproductive advantage. *Human Reproductive Behavior: A Darwinian Perspective,* L. Betzig, M. Borgerhoff Mulder and P. Turke, eds. Cambridge, England: Cambridge University Press.

Chiarelli, B. and E. R. Massa (1985). The hereditary basis of mating preference: an investigation carried out on MZ and DZ twins. *Journal of Human Evolution* 14: 379–84.

Chomsky, N. (1980). *Rules and Representations.* Oxford: Blackwell.

Clutton-Brock, T. H., and G. A. Parker (1992). Potential reproductive rates and the operation of sexual selection. *The Quarterly Review of Biology* 67:437–56.

Coale, A. J. and P. Demeny (1983). *Regional Model Life Tables and Stable Populations.* New York: Academic Press.

Collier, J., and S. Yanagisako, eds. (1987). *Gender and Kinship: Essays Toward a Unified Analysis.* Stanford, CA: Stanford University Press.

Cosmides, L., J. Tooby and J. Barkow, eds. (1992). *The Adapted Mind: Evolutionary Psychology and the Generation of Culture.* New York: Oxford University Press.

Cronin, H. (1991). *The Ant and the Peacock: Altruism and Sexual Selection from Darwin to Today.* New York: Cambridge University Press.

Cross, J. F., and J. Cross (1971). Age, sex, race, and the perception of facial beauty. *Developmental Psychology* 5: 433–99.

Cunningham, M. R. (1986). Measuring the physical in physical attractiveness: quasi-experiments in the sociobiology of female facial beauty. *Journal of Personality and Social Psychology* 50: 925–35.

Daly, M., and M. Wilson (1988). *Homicide.* New York: Aldine de Gruyter.

Daly, M., and M. Wilson (1978). *Sex, Evolution and Behavior: Adaptations for Reproduction.* North Scituate, MA: Duxbury Press.

DaMatta, R. (1990). *Carnavais, Malandros e Heróis: Para uma Sociologia do Dilema Brasileiro.* Rio de Janeiro: Editora Guanabara Koogan S.A.

Darwin, C. R. (1956[1887]). Recollections of the development of my mind and character. *The Darwin Reader.* Bates, M. and P. Humphrey, eds. New York: Charles Scribner's sons.

Darwin, C. R. (1981[1871]). *The Descent of Man, and Selection in Relation to Sex.* Princeton, NJ: Princeton University Press.

Darwin, C. R. (1967[1869]). *On the Origin of Species.* New York: Atheneum.

Davis, G. W. F., and P. O'Donald (1976). Sexual selection for a handicap: a critical analysis of Zahavi's model. *Journal of Theoretical Biology* 57: 345–54.

Dawkins, R. (1976). *The Selfish Gene.* Oxford: Oxford University Press.

Degler, C. (1971). *Neither Black nor White: Slavery and Race Relations in the United States and Brazil.* Madison, WI: University of Wisconsin Press.

Degler, C. (1991). *In Search of Human Nature: The Decline and Revival of Darwinism in American Social Thought.* New York: Oxford University Press.

Deutsch, C. K. (1987). Disproportion in psychiatric syndromes. *Anthropometric Facial Proportions in Medicine.* L. G. Farkas and I. R. Munro, eds. Springfield, IL: Charles C. Thomas.

do Valle Silva, N. (1985). Updating the cost of not being white in Brazil. *Race, Class and Power in Brazil*. P. M. Fontaine, ed. Los Angeles, Center for African American Studies, University of California.

Dobzhansky, T. (1937). *Genetics and the Origin of Species*. New York: Columbia University Press.

Dugatkin, L. A. (1992). Sexual selection and imitation: females copy the mate choice of others. *American Naturalist* 139: 1384–89.

Durham, W. H. (1991). *Coevolution: Genes, Culture, and Human Diversity*. Stanford, CA: Stanford University Press.

Ekman, P. (1982). *Emotion in the Human Face*. Cambridge, UK: Cambridge University Press.

Elder, G. (1969). Appearance and education in marriage mobility. *American Sociological Review* 34: 519–33.

Ellis, H. (1926). *Studies in the Psychology of Sex, volume IV*. Philadelphia: F.A. Davis.

Ellul, R. and A. Schlegel (1988). Marriage transactions: labor, property, status. *American Anthropologist* 90: 291–309.

Ember, M. and C. Ember (1983). *Marriage, Family, and Kinship*. New Haven, CT: HRAF Press.

Emlen, S. T., and L. W. Oring (1977). Ecology, sexual selection, and the evolution of mating systems. *Science* 197: 215–23.

Endler, J. A. (1986). *Natural Selection in the Wild*. Princeton, NJ: Princeton University Press.

Enlow, D. H. (1990). *Facial Growth*. Philadelphia: Harcourt Brace Jovanovich.

Enquist, M., and A. Arak (1993). Selection of exaggerated male traits by female aesthetic senses. *Nature* 361: 446–48.

Ephron, N. (1975). *Crazy Salad: Some Things about Women*. New York: Alfred A. Knopf.

Euba, T. (1986). The human image: some aspects of Yoruba canons of art and beauty. *Nigeria Magazine* 54:9–21.

Farkas, L. G., and I. Munro (1987a). Linear proportions in above and below average women's faces. *Anthropometric Facial Proportions in Medicine*. L. G. Farkas and I. Munro, eds. Springfield IL: Charles C. Thomas.

Farkas, L. G., and I. Munro (1987b). The validity of neoclassical facial proportion canons. *Anthropometric Facial Proportions in Medicine*. L. G. Farkas and I. Munro, eds. Springfield, IL: Charles C. Thomas.

Farkas, L. G. (1981). *Anthropometry of the Head and Face in Medicine*. New York: Elsevier.

Farkas, L. G., and I. R. Munro, eds. (1987). *Anthropometric Facial Proportions in Medicine*. Springfield, IL: Charles C. Thomas.

Fauss, R. (1988). Zur Bedeutung des Gesichts für die Partnerwahl. *Homo* 37: 188–201.

Fernandes, F. (1969). *The Negro in Brazilian Society*. New York: Columbia University Press.

Fisher, H. E. (1989). Evolution of human serial pairbonding. *American Journal of Physical Anthropology* 78: 331–54.

Fisher, R. A. (1958). *The Genetical Theory of Natural Selection.* New York: Dover.

Fitzpatrick, J. W. (1988). Why so many passerine birds? A response to Raikow. *Systematic Zoology* 37: 71–76.

Fodor, J. (1983). *The Modularity of Mind.* Cambridge, MA: Bradford Books.

Folkes, V. (1982). Forming relationships and the matching hypothesis. *Personality and Social Psychology Bulletin* 8:631–36.

Folstad, I., and A. J. Karter (1992). Parasites, bright males and the immunocompetence handicap. *American Naturalist* 139:603–22.

Fontaine, P. M., ed. (1985). *Race, Class and Power in Brazil.* Center for African American Studies, University of California, Los Angeles.

Fontaine, P. M. (1985). Blacks and the search for power in Brazil. *Race, Class and Power in Brazil.* P. M. Fontaine, ed. Center for African American Studies, University of California.

Ford, C. S. and F. Beach (1951). *Patterns of Sexual Behavior.* New York: Harper.

Franklin, J. H., ed. (1968). *Color and Race.* Boston: Houghton Mifflin.

Frayer, D. W. (1981). Body size, weapon use, and natural selection in the European Upper Paleolithic. *American Anthropologist* 83:57–73.

Frayser, S. (1985). *Varieties of Sexual Experience: A Perspective on Human Sexuality.* New Haven, CT: HRAF Press.

Freyre, G. (1963). *The Mansions and the Shanties: The Making of Modern Brazil.* New York: Knopf.

Freyre, G. (1964). *The Masters and the Slaves: A Study in the Development of Brazilian Civilization.* New York: Knopf.

Freyre, G. (1970). *Order and Progress: Brazil from Monarchy to Republic.* New York: Knopf.

Frisancho, A. R. (1990). *Anthropometric Standards for the Assessment of Growth and Nutritional Status.* Ann Arbor: University of Michigan Press.

Fry, P. (1982). *Para Inglês Ver: Identidade e Politica na Cultura Brasileira.* Rio de Janeiro: Zahar Editores.

Galton, F. (1907). *Inquiries into Human Faculty and Its Development.* London: J. M. Dent.

Gangestad, S. W., and D. M. Buss (1993). Pathogen prevalence and human mate preferences. *Ethology and Sociobiology* 14: 89–96.

Gangestad, S. W., R. Thornhill, and R. A. Yeo (1994). Facial attractiveness, developmental stability, and fluctuating asymmetry. *Ethology and Sociobiology* 15:73–85.

Garber, P. M. (1989). Tulipmania. *Journal of Political Economy* 97:535–50.

Garn, S. M., M. LaVelle, and H. Smith (1985). Quantification of dysmorphogenesis: pattern variability index, s_z. *American Journal of Roentgenology* 144: 365–69.

Geist, V. (1978). *Life Histories, Human Evolution, Environmental Design.* New York: Springer.

Gergen, K. J. (1975). The significance of skin color in human relations. *Color and Race.* J. H. Franklin, ed. Boston: Houghton Mifflin.

Gibson, R. M., and J. Höglund (1992). Copying and sexual selection. *Trends in Ecology and Evolution* 7:229–32.

Goldman, N., and M. Montgomery (1989). Fecundability and husband's age. *Social Biology* 36:146–66.

Gonzalez, L. (1985). The unified black movement: a new stage in black political mobilization. *Race, Class and Power in Brazil.* P. M. Fontaine, ed. Center for African American Studies, University of California, Los Angeles.

Goody, J. (1976). *Production and Reproduction: A Comparative Study of the Domestic Domain.* New York: Cambridge University Press.

Goren, C. C., M. Sarty, and P. Y. Wu (1975). Visual following and pattern discrimination of face-like stimuli by newborn infants. *Pediatrics* 56:544–49.

Gould, S. J. (1977). *Ontogeny and Phylogeny.* Cambridge, MA: Belknap Press of Harvard University Press.

Gould, S. J., and R. C. Lewontin (1979). The spandrels of San Marco and the panglossian paradigm: a critique of the adaptationist programme. *Proceedings of the Royal Society of London, Series B* 205:581–98.

Gould, S. J., and E. Vrba (1982). Exaptation—a missing term in the science of form. *Paleobiology* 8:4–15.

Gowaty, P. A. (1992). Evolutionary biology and feminism. *Human Nature* 3: 217–49.

Grafen, A. (1990a). Sexual selection unhandicapped by the Fisher process. *Journal of Theoretical Biology* 144:473–516.

Grafen, A. (1990b). Biological signals as handicaps. *Journal of Theoretical Biology* 144:517–46.

Graham, J., and A. M. Kligman (1985). Physical attractiveness, cosmetic use and self-perception in the elderly. *International Journal of Cosmetic Science* 7:85–97.

Grammer, K., and R. Thornhill (1994). Human (*Homo sapiens*) facial attractiveness and sexual selection: the role of symmetry and averageness. *Journal of Comparative Psychology* 108:233–42.

Gregor, T. (1979). Short people. *Natural History* 88:14–23.

Gregor, T. (1985). *Anxious Pleasures: The Sexual Lives of an Amazonian People.* Chicago: University of Chicago Press.

Griffiths, P. E. (1990). Modularity, and the psychoevolutionary theory of emotion. *Biology and Philosophy* 5:175–96.

Grinker, R. R. (1990). Images of denigration: structuring inequality between foragers and farmers in the Ituri forest, Zaire. *American Ethnologist* 17:111–30.

Groves, C. P. (1989). *A Theory of Human and Primate Evolution.* Oxford, England: Clarendon Press.

Gunn, F. (1973). *The Artificial Face: A History of Cosmetics.* Worcester, England: Trinity Press.

Guthrie, R. D. (1970). Evolution of human threat display organs. *Evolutionary Biology* 1:257–302.

Hamilton, W. D., R. Axelrod, and R. Tanese (1990). Sexual selection as an adaptation to resist parasites (a review). *Proceedings of the National Academy of Sciences* 87:3566–73.

Hamilton, W. D., and M. Zuk (1982). Heritable true fitness and bright birds: a role for parasites? *Science* 218:384–87.

Harris, M. (1952). Race relations in Minas Velhas, a community in the mountain region of central Brazil. *Race and Class in Rural Brazil.* C. Wagley, ed. New York: Russell and Russell.

Harris, M. (1964). *Patterns of Race in the Americas.* New York: W. W. Norton and Co.

Harrison, G. A., J. M. Tanner, D. R. Pilbeam and P. T. Baker (1988). *Human Biology: An Introduction to Human Evolution, Variation, Growth, and Adaptability.* Oxford: Oxford University Press.

Hart, C., and A. Pilling (1960). *The Tiwi of North Australia.* New York: Holt.

Hartshorne, C. (1956). The monotony threshold in singing birds. *Auk* 95:758–60.

Harvey, P. H., and T. Clutton-Brock (1985). Life history variation in primates. *Evolution* 39:559–81.

Hatfield, E., and S. Sprecher (1986). *Mirror, Mirror: The Importance of Looks in Everyday Life.* Albany, NY: State University of New York Press.

Hedrick, R. J., and R. P. Flood (1990). On testing for speculative bubbles. *Journal of Economic Perspectives* 4:85–101.

Heimel, C. (1993). *Get Your Tongue Out of My Mouth, I'm Kissing You Goodbye.* New York: Atlantic Monthly Press.

Henriques, F. (1968). *Family and Colour in Jamaica.* London: MacGibbon and Kee.

Henry, L. (1961). Some data on natural fertility. *Eugenics Quarterly* 8:81–91.

Herskovits, M. (1968). *The American Negro.* Bloomington IN: Indiana University Press.

Hiatt, L. R. (1965). *Kinship and Conflict: The Study of an Anthropological Community in Northern Arnhem Land.* Sydney, Australia: Halsted Press Pty Ltd.

Hill, C., Z. Rubin, and L. A. Peplau (1976). Beakups before marriage: the end of 103 affairs. *Journal of Social Issues* 32:147–68

Hill, G. E. (1990). Female house finches prefer colorful males: sexual selection for a condition dependent trait. *Animal Behaviour* 40:563–72.

Hill, G. E. (1991). Plumage coloration is a sexually selected indicator of male quality. *Nature* 350:337–39.

Hill, K., and M. Hurtado (1991). The evolution of premature reproductive senescence in human females: an evaluation of the grandmother hypothesis. *Human Nature* 2:313–50.

Hirschfeld, L. (1993). Is the acquisition of social categories based on domain-specific competence or on knowledge transfer? *Mapping the Mind: Domain Specificity in Cognition and Culture.* L. Hirschfeld and S. Gelman, eds. Cambridge, England: Cambridge University Press.

Hoetink, H. (1967). *The Two Variants in Caribbean Race Relations: A Contribution to the Sociology of Segmented Societies.* London: Oxford University Press.

Hogbin, H. I. (1946). Puberty to marriage: a study of the sexual life of the natives of Wogeo, New Guinea. *Oceania* 16:185–209.

Holmes, S., and C. Hatch (1938). Personal appearance as related to scholastic records and marriage selection in college women. *Human Biology* 10:65–76.

Houle, D., D. K. Hoffmaster, S. Assimacopoulos and B. Charlesworth (1992). The genomic mutation rate for fitness in *Drosophila. Nature* 359:58–60.

Howell, D. C. (1987). *Statistical Methods for Psychology.* Boston: Duxbury Press.

Howell, N. (1979). *Demography of the Dobe !Kung.* New York: Academic Press.

Howells, W. W. (1989). *Skull Shapes and the Map.* Cambridge, MA: Harvard University Press.

Hughes, M. G., and B. Mertel (1990). The significance of color remains: a study of life chances, mate selection and ethnic consciousness among black Americans. *Social Forces* 68:1–16.

Hulse, F. S. (1967). Selection for skin color among Japanese. *American Journal of Physical Anthropology* 27:143–59.

Hutchinson, H. W. (1952). Race relations in a rural community of the Brazilian *recôncavo. Race and Class in Rural Brazil.* C. Wagley, ed. New York: Russell and Russell.

Huxley, J. (1938). Darwin's theory of sexual selection and the data subsumed by it, in the light of recent theory. *American Naturalist* 72:416–33.

Iliffe, A. (1960). A study of preferences in feminine beauty. *British Journal of Psychology* 51:267–73.

Immelman, K. (1972). Sexual and other long-term aspects of imprinting in birds and other species. *Advances in the Study of Behavior.* New York: Academic Press.

Isaacs, H. R. (1975). *Idols of the Tribe: Group Identity and Political Change.* New York: Harper and Row.

Isaacs, H. R. (1975). Group identity and political change: the role of color and physical characteristics. *Color and Race.* J. H. Franklin, ed. Boston: Houghton Mifflin.

Iwasa, Y., and A. Pomiankowski (1991). The evolution of costly mate preferences, II. The handicap principle. *Evolution* 45:1431–42.

Jackendoff, R. S., and F. Lehrdahl (1983). *A Generative Theory of Tonal Music.* Cambridge, MA: Cambridge University Press.

Jackson, L. A. (1992). *Physical Appearance and Gender: Sociobiological and Sociocultural Perspectives.* Albany, New York: State University of New York Press.

James, W. (1980[1890]). *Principles of Psychology, Vol II.* New York: Dover.

James, W. H. (1979). The causes of the decline in fecundability with age. *Social Biology* 26:330–34.

Jankowiak, W. (1993). *Sex, Death and Hierarchy in a Chinese City: An Anthropological Account.* New York: Columbia University Press.

Jankowiak, W. R., E. M. Hill and J. M. Donovan (1992). The effects of sex and sexual orientation on attractiveness judgements: an evolutionary interpretation. *Ethology and Sociobiology* 13:73–85.

Johnston, T. D. (1982). Selective costs and benefits in the evolution of learning. *Advances in the Study of Behavior.* New York: Academic Press.

Johnston, V. S., and M. Franklin (1993). Is beauty in the eye of the beholder? *Ethology and Sociobiology* 14:183–99.

Jones, D. (1994). The Evolutionary Psychology of Human Physical Attractiveness. PhD dissertation, University of Michigan.

Jones, D. (1995). Sexual selection, physical attractiveness and facial neoteny: cross-cultural evidence and implications. *Current Anthropology* 36:723–48.

Jones, D., and K. Hill (1993). Criteria of physical attractiveness in five populations. *Human Nature* 4:271–96.

Jones, I. L., and F. M. Hunter (1993). Mutual sexual selection in a monogamous seabird. *Nature* 362:238–39.

Jordan, W. (1968). *White Over Black: American Attitudes Toward the Negro, 1550–1812.* Kingsport, TN: University of North Carolina Press.

Keating, C. F. (1985). Gender and the physiognomy of dominance and attractiveness. *Social Psychology Quarterly* 48:61–70.

Kelsky, K. L. (1992). *Sex and the Gaijin Male: Contending Discourses of Race and Gender in Contemporary Japan.* Annual Meeting of the American Anthropological Association, San Francisco.

Kenrick, D. T. and R. Hogan (1991). Cognitive psychology. *The Sociobiological Imagination.* Albany, New York: State University of New York Press.

Kenrick, D. T., S. E. Gutierres, and L. L. Goldberg (1989). Influence of popular erotica on judgements of strangers and mates. *Journal of Experimental Social Psychology* 25:159–67.

Kenrick, D. (1994). Evolutionary social psychology: from sexual selection to social cognition. *Advances in Experimental Social Psychology.* New York: Academic Press.

Kingdon, J. (1980). The role of visual signals and face patterns in African forest monkeys (guenons) of the genus *Cercopithecus. Transactions of the Zoological Society of London* 35:431–75.

Kirkpatrick, M., T. Price and S. Arnold (1990). The Darwin-Fisher theory of sexual selection in monogamous birds. *Evolution* 44:180–93.

Kligman, A. M. (1993). Psychologic aspects of skin disorders in the elderly. *Aging Skin: Properties and Functional Changes.* New York: Marcel Dekker.

Kodrick-Brown, A., and J. H. Brown (1984). Truth in advertising: the kinds of traits favored by sexual selection. *American Naturalist* 124:309–23.

Koeslag, J. (1990). Koinophilia groups sexual creatures into species, promotes stasis, and stabilizes social behavior. *Journal of Theoretical Biology* 144:15–35.

Kondrashov, A. S. (1988). Deleterious mutations and the evolution of sexual reproduction. *Nature* 336:435–40.

Kosslyn, S. M. (1980). *Image and Mind.* Cambridge, MA: Harvard University Press.

Kottak, C. P. (1967). Race relations in a Brazilian fishing village. *Luso-Brazilian Review* 4:35–52.

Kottak, C. P. (1990). *Prime-Time Society: An Anthropological Analysis of Television and Culture.* Belmont, CA: Wadsworth Publishing.

Kottak, C. P. (1992). *Assault on Paradise: Social Change in a Brazilian Village.* New York: McGraw-Hill, Inc.

Krebs, D., and A. Adinolfi (1975). Physical attractiveness, social relations, and personality style. *Journal of Personality and Social Psychology* 31:245–53.

Lakoff, G., and M. Johnson (1980). *Metaphors We Live By.* Chicago: University of Chicago Press.

Laland, K. N. (1994). Sexual selection with a culturally transmitted mating preference. *Theoretical Population Biology* 45:1–15.

Lande, R. (1975). The maintenance of genetic variability by mutation in a polygenic character with linked loci. *Genetical Research* 26:221–35.

Lande, R. (1981). Models of speciation by sexual selection of polygenic traits. *Proceedings of the National Academy of Sciences (USA)* 78:3721–25.

Langlois, J. H., L. A. Roggman, R. J. Casey, J. M. Ritter, L. A. Rieser-Danner and V. Y. Jenkins (1987). Infant preferences for attractive faces: rudiments of a stereotype? *Developmental Psychology* 23:363–69.

Langlois, J. H., and L. A. Roggman (1990). Attractive faces are only average. *Psychological Science* 1:115–21.

Larrabee Jr., W. F., and K. H. Makielski (1993). *Surgical Anatomy of the Face.* New York: Raven Press.

Lee, G. R., and L. H. Stone (1980). Mate selection systems and criteria: variation according to family structure. *Journal of Marriage and the Family* 42:319–26.

Lee, R., and I. Devore, eds. (1966). *Man the Hunter.* Chicago: Aldine.

Lele, S., and J. T. Richtsmeier (1991). Euclidean distance matrix analysis: a coordinate-free approach for comparing biological shapes using landmark data. *American Journal of Physical Anthropology* 86:415–27.

Lerner, I. M. (1954). *Genetic Homeostasis.* London, England: Oliver and Boyd.

Lewis, B. (1990). *Race and Slavery in the Middle East: An Historical Inquiry.* New York: Oxford University Press.

Light, L. L., S. Hollander, and F. Kayra-Stuart (1981). Why attractive people are harder to remember. *Personality and Social Psychology Bulletin* 7:269–76.

Ligon, D., R. Thornhill, M. Zuk and K. Johnson (1990). Male-male competition, ornamentation and the role of testosterone in sexual selection in red jungle fowl. *Animal Behaviour* 40:367–73.

Livshits, G., and E. Kobylianski (1991). Fluctuating asymmetry as a possible measure of developmental homeostasis in humans: a review. *Human Biology* 63:441–66.

Livshits, G., and P. E. Smouse (1993). Multivariate fluctuating asymmetry in Israeli adults. *Human Biology* 65:547–78.

Lorenz, K. (1970). *Studies in Animal and Human Behavior.* Cambridge, MA: Harvard University Press.

Low, B. S. (1990). Marriage systems and pathogen stress in human societies. *American Zoologist* 30:325–39.

Low, B. S., R. D. Alexander, and K. M. Noonan (1987). Human hips, breasts, and buttocks: is fat deceptive? *Ethology and Sociobiology* 8:249–57.

Lowe, J. W. G., and E. D. Lowe (1982). Cultural pattern and process: a study of stylistic change in women's dress. *American Anthropologist* 84:521–44.

Lowenthal, D. (1971). *West Indian Societies.* New York: Oxford University Press.

Lumsden, C. J., and E. O. Wilson (1981). *Genes, Mind and Culture: The Coevolutionary Process.* Cambridge, MA: Harvard University Press.

Malinowski, B. (1987[1929]). *The Sexual Life of Savages in North-Western Melanesia: An Ethnographic Account of Courtship, Marriage and Family Life among the Natives of the Trobriand Islands, British New Guinea.* Boston: Beacon Press.

Marchetti, K. (1993). Dark habitats and bright birds illustrate the role of the environment in species divergence. *Nature* 362:149–52.

Mark, L. S., R. E. Shaw, and J. B. Pittenger (1988). Natural constraints, scales of analysis, and information for the perception of growing faces. *Social and Applied Aspects of Perceiving Faces.* Hillsdale, NJ: Lawrence Erlbaum Associates.

Markow, T. A., and K. Wandler (1986). Fluctuating dermatoglyphic asymmetry in normal and retarded males. *Psychiatric Research* 19:323–28.

Martel, L. F., and H. B. Biller (1987). *Stature and Stigma: The Biopsychological Development of Short Males.* Lexington, MA: D. C. Heath and Company.

Martinez-Alier, V. (1974). *Marriage, Class and Color in Nineteenth Century Cuba.* Cambridge: Cambridge University Press.

Maynard Smith, J. (1976). Sexual selection and the handicap principal. *Journal of Theoretical Biology* 57:239–42.

Maynard Smith, J. (1982). *Evolution and the Theory of Games.* Cambridge, England: Cambridge University Press.

Mayr, E. (1963). *Animal Species and Evolution.* Cambridge, MA: Harvard University Press.

Mazur, A., J. Mazur, and J. Keating (1984). Military rank attainment of a West Point class: effects of cadets' physical characteristics. *American Journal of Sociology* 90:125–50.

Mazur, A., C. Halpern and J. R. Udry (1994). Dominant looking male teenagers copulate earlier. *Ethology and Sociobiology* 15:87–94.

McArthur, L. Z., and D. S. Berry (1983). Impressions of baby-faced adults. *Social Cognition* 2:315–42.

McCabe, J. (1983). FBD marriage: further support for the Westermarck hypothesis of the incest taboo? *American Anthropologist* 85:50–69.

McCabe, V. (1988). Facial proportions, perceived age, and caregiving. *Social and Applied Aspects of Perceiving Faces.* T. R. Alley, ed. Hillsdale, NJ: Lawrence Erlbaum Associates.

McCall, R. B., and C. B. Kennedy (1980). Attention of 4-month old infants to discrepancy and babyishness. *Journal of Experimental Child Psychology* 29:189–201.

McKillip, J., and S. Riedel (1983). External validity of matching on physical attractiveness for same and opposite sex couples. *Journal of Applied Social Psychology* 13:328–37.

Meillassoux, C. (1964). *Maidens, Meal, and Money.* Cambridge, England: Cambridge University Press.

Mellor, C. S. (1992). Dermatoglyphic evidence of fluctuating asymmetry in schizophrenia. *British Journal of Psychiatry* 160: 467–72.

Menken, J., J. Trussell, and U. Larsen (1986). Age and infertility. *Science* 233:1389–94.

Miller, H., and W. Rivenbark (1970). Sexual differences in physical attractiveness as a determinant of heterosexual liking. *Psychological Reports* 27:701–2.

Møller, A. P. (1990). Fluctuating asymmetry in male ornaments may reliably reveal male quality. *Animal Behaviour* 40: 1185–87.

Møller, A. P., and J. Höglund (1991). Patterns of fluctuating asymmetry in avian feather ornaments: implications for models of sexual selection. *Proceedings of the Royal Society, Series B* 245:1–5.

Montagu, A. (1957). *The Reproductive Development of the Female.* New York: Julian Press.

Mosse, G. L. (1985). *Nationalism and Sexuality: Respectability and Abnormal Sexuality in Modern Europe.* New York: H. Fertig.

Mosse, G. L. (1985). *Toward the Final Solution: A History of European Racism.* Madison, WI: University of Wisconsin Press.

Mullins, E., and P. Sites (1984). The origins of contemporary eminent black Americans: a three generation analysis of social origins. *American Sociological Review:*672–85.

Munn, N. D. (1986). *The Fame of Gawa: A Symbolic Study of Value Transformation in a Massim (Papua New Guinea) Society.* New York: Cambridge University Press.

Murdock, G. P. (1967). *Ethnographic Atlas.* New Haven, CT: HRAF Press.

Murstein, B., and P. Christy (1976). Physical attractiveness and marriage adjustment in middle-aged couples. *Journal of Personality and Social Psychology* 34:537–42.

Needham, R. (1962). *Structure and Sentiment.* Chicago: University of Chicago Press.

Nei, M., and A. K. Roychoudhury (1982). Genetic relationship and evolution of human races. *Evolutionary Biology.*

O'Donald, P. (1980). *Genetic Models of Sexual Selection.* Cambridge, England: Cambridge University Press.

Ogawa, D. (1973). *Jan Ken Po: The World of Hawaii's Japanese-Americans.* Honolulu: University Press of Hawaii.

Olds, C. (1992). *The Good, the Bad and the Ugly: Theories of Facial Beauty in Western Art.* Doris Sloan Lecture, University of Michigan.

Orians, G. H. (1992). Evolved responses to landscapes. *The Adapted Mind.* L. Cosmides, J. Tooby and J. Barkow, eds. Oxford: Oxford University Press.

Ortner, S. B., and H. Whitehead (1981). Introduction: accounting for sexual meanings. *Sexual Meanings: The Cultural Construction of Gender and Sexuality.* S. B. Ortner, and H. Whitehead, eds. Cambridge, England: Cambridge University Press.

Paige, K. E., and J. Paige (1981). *The Politics of Reproductive Ritual.* Berkeley, CA: University of California Press.

Parker, G. A., and J. Maynard Smith (1990). Optimality theory in evolutionary biology. *Nature* 348:27–33.

Parker, R. G. (1991). *Bodies, Pleasures and Passions: Sexual Culture in Contemporary Brazil.* Boston: Beacon Press.

Parsons, P. A. (1990). Fluctuating asymmetry: an epigenetic measure of stress. *Biological Review* 65:131–45.

Partridge, L., and N. H. Barton (1993). Optimality, mutation and the evolution of ageing. *Nature* 362:305–11.

Patai, D. (1988). *Brazilian Women Speak.* New Brunswick, NJ: Rutgers University Press.

Patzer, G. (1985). *The Physical Attractiveness Phenomena.* New York: Plenum.

Perrett, D. I., K. A. May and S. Yoshikawa (1994). Facial shape and judgements of female attractiveness. *Nature* 368:239–42.

Pheterson, M., and J. Horai (1976). The effects of sensation seeking, physical attractiveness of stimuli, and exposure frequency on liking. *Social Behavior and Personality* 4:241–47.

Pierson, D. (1942). *Negroes in Brazil: A Study of Race Contact at Bahia.*

Pinker, S. (1994). *The Language Instinct: How the Mind Creates Language.* New York: William Morrow.

Polhemus, T. (1988). *Body Styles.* Luton, Bedfordshire: Lennard Publishing.

Pomiankowski, A. (1987a). The costs of choice in sexual selection. *Journal of Theoretical Biology* 128:195–218.

Pomiankowski, A. (1987b). Sexual selection: the handicap principle does work—sometimes. *Proceedings of the Royal Society of London, Series B* 231:123–45.

Pomiankowski, A., Y. Iwasa and S. Nee (1991). The evolution of costly mate preferences I. Fisher and biased mutation. *Evolution* 45:1422–30.

Pomiankowski, A., and L. Sheridan (1994). Linked sexiness and choosiness. *Trends in Ecology and Evolution* 9:242–44.

Price, R., and S. Vandenberg (1979). Matching for physical atractiveness in married couples. *Personality and Social Psychology Bulletin* 5:398–400.

Pruett-Jones, S. (1992). Independent versus nonindependent mate choice: do females copy each other? *The American Naturalist* 140:1000–1009.

Pulliam, H. R., and C. Dunford (1980). *Programmed to Learn: An Essay on the Evolution of Culture.* New York: Columbia University Press.

Pusey, A. E. (1990). Behavioural changes at adolescence in chimpanzees. *Behaviour* 115:203–46.

Raikow, R. J. (1986). Why are there so many kinds of passerine birds? *Systematic Zoology* 35:255–99.

Read, A. F. (1987). Comparative evidence supports the Hamilton and Zuk hypothesis on parasites and sexual selection. *Nature* 328:68–70.

Rees, J. A., and P. H. Harvey (1991). The evolution of animal mating systems. *Mating and Marriage.* V. Reynolds and J. Kellett, eds. Oxford, England: Oxford University Press.

Reeve, R., E. Smith, and B. Wallace (1990). Components of fitness become effectively neutral in equilibrium populations. *Proceedings of the National Academy of Sciences* 87:2018–20.

Richardson, J., and A. L. Kroeber (1940). Three centuries of women's dress fashions: a quantitative analysis. *Anthropological Records* 5:111–53.

Ridley, M. (1986). The number of males in a primate troop. *Animal Behaviour* 28:1848–58.

Ridley, M. (1993). *The Red Queen: Sex and the Evolution of Human Nature.* New York: MacMillan.

Riedl, B. I. M. (1990). Morphologisch-metrische Merkmale des männlichen und weiblichen Partnerleitbildes in ihrer Bedeutung für die Wahl des Ehegatten. *Homo* 41:72–85.

Riggio, R., and S. Woll (1984). The role of nonverbal cues and physical attractiveness in the selection of dating partners. *Journal of Social and Personal Relationships* 1:347–57.

Robertson, A. F. (1991). *Beyond the Family: The Social Organization of Human Reproduction.* Berkeley: University of California Press.

Rogers, A. R. (1993). Why menopause? *Evolutionary Ecology* 7:406–20.

Rogers, A. R. (1988). Does biology constrain culture? *American Anthropologist* 90:819–29.

Rosenblatt, P. C. (1974). Cross-cultural perspective on attraction. *Foundations of Interpersonal Attraction.* T. L. Huston, ed. New York: Academic Press.

Rosenblatt, P. C., and R. Anderson (1981). Human sexuality in cross-cultural perspective. *The Bases of Human Sexual Attraction.* M. Cook, ed. London: Academic Press.

Rosenblatt, P. C., and P. C. Cozby (1972). Courtship patterns associated with freedom of choice of spouse. *Journal of Marriage and the Family* 34:689–95.

Roth, P. (1967). *Portnoy's Complaint.* New York: Random House.

Rozin, P., and A. E. Fallon (1987). A perspective on disgust. *Psychological Review* 94:23–41.

Ruff, C. B. (1991). Climate and body shape in hominid evolution. *Journal of Human Evolution* 21:81–105.

Russell, K., M. Wilson and R. Hall (1992). *The Color Complex: The Politics of Skin Color among African-Americans.* New York: Harcourt Brace Jovanovich.

Ryan, M. J. (1986). Neuroanatomy influences speciation rates among anurans. *Proceedings of the National Academy of Sciences* 83:1379–82.

Ryan, M. J. (1990). Sexual selection, sensory systems and sensory exploitation. *Oxford Surveys in Evolutionary Biology.* Oxford: Oxford University Press.

Ryan, M. J., J. H. Fox, W. Wilczynski and A. S. Rand (1990). Sexual selection for sensory exploitation in the frog *Physalaemus pustulosus. Nature* 343:66–67.

Sacks, O. (1985). *The Man Who Mistook His Wife for a Hat.* New York: Summit Books.

Scheper-Hughes, N. (1992). *Death Without Weeping: The Violence of Everyday Life in Brazil.* Berkeley, CA: University of California Press.

Schopenhauer, A. (1911[1844]). *Die Welt als Wille und Vorstellung, Vol 2.* Munich: R. Piper.

Scott, L. M. (1984). Reproductive behavior of adolescent female baboons (*Papio anubis*) in Kenya. *Female Primates: Studies by Women Primatologists.* M. F. Small, ed. New York: Alan R. Liss.

Seiger, M. B. (1967). A computer simulation study of the influence of imprinting on population structure. *The American Naturalist* 101:47–57.

Seligman, M. E. P. (1970). On the generality of the laws of learning. *Psychological Review* 77:406–18.

Sheldon, B. C. (1994). Male phenotype, fertility, and the pursuit of extra-pair copulations by female birds. *Proceedings of the Royal Society of London, Series B* 257:25–30.

Sheperd, J., and H. Ellis (1972). Physical attractiveness and selection of marriage partners. *Psychological Reports* 30:1004.

Simpson, J. A., and S. W. Gangestad (1992). Sociosexuality and romantic partner choice. *Journal of Personality* 60:31–51.

Singh, D. (1993a). Adaptive significance of female physical attractiveness: role of waist-to-hip ratio. *Journal of Personality and Social Psychology* 65:293–307.

Singh, D. (1993b). Body shape and women's attractiveness: the critical role of waist-to-hip ratio. *Human Nature* 4:297–321.

Skidmore, T. E. (1974). *Black into White: Race and Nationality in Brazilian Thought.* New York: Oxford University Press.

Smith, V. L., G. L. Suchanek and A. W. Williams (1988). Bubbles, crashes and endogenous expectations in experimental spot asset markets. *Econometrica* 56: 1119–51.

Smuts, B. B., and R. W. Smuts (1993). Male agression and sexual coercion of females in non-human primates and other mammals: evidence and implications. *Advances in the Study of Behavior.* New York: Academic Press.

Soulé, M. E. (1982). Allomeric variation, I. The theory and some consequences. *American Naturalist* 120:765–86.

Squier, C. A., and N. W. Johnson (1976). *Human Oral Mucosa: Development, Structure and Function.* Oxford: Blackwell Scientific Publications.

Staddon, J. E. R. (1975). A note on the evolutionary significance of supernormal stimuli. *American Naturalist* 109:541–45.

Stember, C. H. (1976). *Sexual Racism: The Emotional Barrier to an Integrated Society.* New York: Harper Colophon.

Stiglitz, J. E. (1990). Symposium on bubbles. *Journal of Economic Perspectives* 4:13–18.

Strathern, A., and M. Strathern (1971). *Self-Decoration in Mount Hagen.* Toronto: University of Toronto Press.

Sulloway, F. J. (1979). *Freud, Biologist of the Mind: Beyond the Psychoanalytic Legend.* New York: Basic Books.

Susanne, C. (1977). Individual age changes of the morphological characteristics. *Journal of Human Evolution* 6:181–89.

Symons, D. (1979). *The Evolution of Human Sexuality.* Oxford: Oxford University Press.

Tannenbaum, F. (1947). *Slave and Citizen: The Negro in the Americas.* New York: Alfred A. Knopf.

Taylor, P., and N. Glenn (1976). The utility of education and attractiveness for females' status. *American Sociological Review* 41:484–98.

Taylor, P. D., and G. C. Williams (1982). The lek paradox is not resolved. *Theoretical Population Biology* 22:392–409.

ten Cate, C., and P. Bateson (1989). Sexual imprinting and a preference for supernormal partners in Japanese quail. *Animal Behaviour* 38:356–58.

Thakerar, J. N., and S. Iwawaki (1979). Cross-cultural comparisons in interpersonal attraction of females toward males. *Journal of Social Psychology* 108:121–22.

Thompson, J. K., and S. Tantleff (1992). Female and male ratings of upper torso. *Journal of Social Behavior and Personality* 7: 345–54.

Thompson, L. A. (1989). *Romans and Blacks*. Norman, OK: University of Oklahoma Press.

Thornhill, R. (1992a). Fluctuating asymmetry and the mating system of the Japanese scorpionfly, *Panorpa japonica*. *Animal Behaviour* 44:867–79.

Thornhill, R. (1992b). Fluctuating asymmetry, interspecific aggression and male mating tactics in two species of Japanese scorpionflies. *Behavioral Ecology and Sociobiology* 17:357–63.

Thornhill, R., and S. W. Gangestad (1993). Human facial beauty: averageness, symmetry, and parasite resistance. *Human Nature* 4:237–70.

Thornhill, R., and N. W. Thornhill (1983). Human rape: an evolutionary analysis. *Ethology and Sociobiology* 4:63–99.

Tobias, P. (1978). *The Bushmen: San Hunters and Herders of Southern Africa*. Capetown: Human and Rousseau.

Trivers, R. (1972). Parental investment and sexual selection. *Sexual Selection and the Descent of Man*. B. Campbell, ed. London: Heinemann.

Turelli, M., and A. S. Kondrashov (1992). Deleterious mutations, apparent stabilizing selection and the maintenance of quantitative variation. *Genetics* 132:603–18.

Turner, C. G. (1986). Dentochronological separation estimates for Pacific Rim populations. *Science* 232:1140–42.

Turner, J. M. (1985). Brown into black: changing racial attitudes of Afro-Brazilian university students. *Race, Class and Power in Brazil*. P. M. Fontaine, ed. Center for African American Studies, University of California, Los Angeles.

Turner, V. W. (1967). *The Forest of Symbols: Aspects of Ndembu Ritual*. Ithaca, NY: Cornell Univesity Press.

Udry, J. R. (1965). Structural correlates of feminine beauty preferences in Britain and the U.S.: a comparison. *Sociology and Social Research* 49:330–42.

Udry, J. R. (1977). The importance of being beautiful. *American Journal of Sociology* 83:154–60.

Udry, J. R., and B. K. Eckland (1984). Benefits of being attractive: differential payoffs for men and women. *Psychological Reports* 54:47–56.

van den Berghe, P. L. (1967). *Race and Racism: A Comparative Perspective*. New York: Wiley.

van den Berghe, P. L. (1970). *Race and Ethnicity: Essays in Comparative Sociology*. New York: Basic Books.

van den Berghe, P. L. (1981). *The Ethnic Phenomenon.* New York: Elsevier.

van den Berghe, P. L., and P. Frost (1986). Skin color preference, sexual dimorphism and sexual selection: a case of gene culture co-evolution? *Ethnic and Racial Studies* 9:87–113.

van Valen, L. (1962). A study of fluctuating asymmetry. *Evolution* 16:125–42.

Veloso, C. (1979). *Beleza pura* (recording). GAPA/SATURNO 60917270.

Waddington, C. H. (1957). *The Strategy of the Genes: A Discussion of Some Aspects of Theoretical Biology.* London: Allen and Unwin.

Wade, M. J., and S. G. Pruett-Jones (1990). Female copying increases the variance in male mating success. *Proceedings of the National Academy of Sciences* 87: 5749–53.

Wagatsuma, E., and C. L. Kleinke (1979). Ratings of facial beauty by Asian-American and Caucasian females. *Journal of Social Psychology* 109:299–300.

Wagatsuma, H. (1968). The social perception of skin color in Japan. *Color and Race.* J. H. Franklin, ed. Boston: Houghton Mifflin.

Wagley, C., ed. (1952). *Race and Class in Rural Brazil.* New York: Russell and Russell.

Wagley, C. (1958). *Minorities in the New World: Six Case Studies.* New York: Columbia University Press.

Wagley, C. (1971). *An Introduction to Brazil.* New York: Columbia University Press.

Waldrop, M. F., R. Q. Bell, B. McLaughlin and C. F. Halverson (1978). Newborn minor physical anomalies predict short attention span, peer aggression, and impulsivity at age 3. *Science* 199:563–64.

Walster, E., V. Aronson and D. Abrahams (1966). The importance of physical attractiveness in dating behavior. *Journal of Personality and Social Psychology* 4:508–16.

Weatherhead, P. J., and R. J. Robertson (1979). Offspring quality and the polygyny threshold: the sexy son hypothesis. *American Naturalist* 113:349–56.

Weidenreich, F. (1945). The brachycephalization of recent mankind. *Southwestern Journal of Anthropology* 1:1–54.

Weiner, A. B. (1976). *Women of Value, Men of Renown: New Perspectives in Trobriand Exchange.* Austin, TX: University of Texas Press.

Weiner, J. S. (1954). Nose shape and climate. *American Journal of Physical Anthropology* 12:1–4.

Weinstein, M., J. Wood, M. A. Stoto and D. Greenfield (1990). Components of age-specific fecundability. *Population Studies* 44:447–67.

West-Eberhard, M. J. (1983). Sexual selection, social competition, and speciation. *The Quarterly Review of Biology* 58:155–83.

West-Eberhard, M. J. (1991). Sexual selection and social behavior. *Man and Beast Revisited.* Washington D.C., Smithsonian Institute.

Westermarck, E. (1921). *The History of Human Marriage, Volume I.* London: MacMillan.

White, G. (1960). Physical attractiveness and courtship progress. *Journal of Personality and Social Psychology* 39:660–68.

White, R. (1989). Toward a contextual understanding of the earliest body adornments. *The Emergence of Modern Humans: Biocultural Adaptations in the later Pleistocene.* E. Trinkaus, ed. Cambridge, England: Cambridge University Press.

Wildman, R. W., R. W. Wildman II, A. Brown and C. Trice (1976). Notes on males' and females' preferences for opposite-sex body parts, bust sizes and bust-revealing clothing. *Psychological Reports* 38: 485–86.

Williams, G. C. (1957). Pleiotropy, natural selection, and the evolution of senescence. *Evolution* 11:398–411

Williams, G. C. (1966). *Adaptation and Natural Selection: A Critique of Some Current Evolutionary Thought.* Princeton, N.J.: Princeton University Press.

Williams, G. C. (1992). *Natural Selection: Domains, Levels, and Challenges.* New York: Oxford University Press.

Williams, G. C., and R. M. Nesse (1991). The dawn of Darwinian medicine. *The Quarterly Review of Biology* 66:1–22.

Williamson, J. (1984). *New People: Miscegenation and Mulattoes in the United States.* New York: New York University Press.

Wilson, E. O. (1975). *Sociobiology: The New Synthesis.* Cambridge, MA: The Belknap Press of Harvard University Press.

Wilson, G. D. (1987). An ethological approach to sexual deviation. *Variant Sexuality: Research and Theory.* G. D. Wilson, ed. London: Croom Helm.

Wolf, N. (1992). *The Beauty Myth: How Images of Beauty Are Used Against Women.* New York: Anchor Books.

Zahavi, A. (1975). Mate selection—a selection for a handicap. *Journal of Theoretical Biology* 53:205–14.

Zahavi, A. (1991). On the definition of sexual selection, Fisher's model, and the evolution of waste and of signals in general. *Animal Behaviour* 42:501–3.

Zuckerman, M., M. S. Buchsbaum, and D. L. Murphy (1980). Sensation seeking and its biological correlates. *Psychological Bulletin* 88:187–214.

Zuk, M. (1991). Parasites and bright birds: new data and a new prediction. *Bird-Parasite Interactions: Ecology, Evolution and Behavior.* J. E. Loye and M. Zuk, eds. Oxford: Oxford University Press.

Zuk, M. (1992). The role of parasites in sexual selection: current evidence and future directions. *Advances in the Study of Behavior.* New York: Academic Press.

Plates

Physical Attractiveness and the Theory of Sexual Selection 169

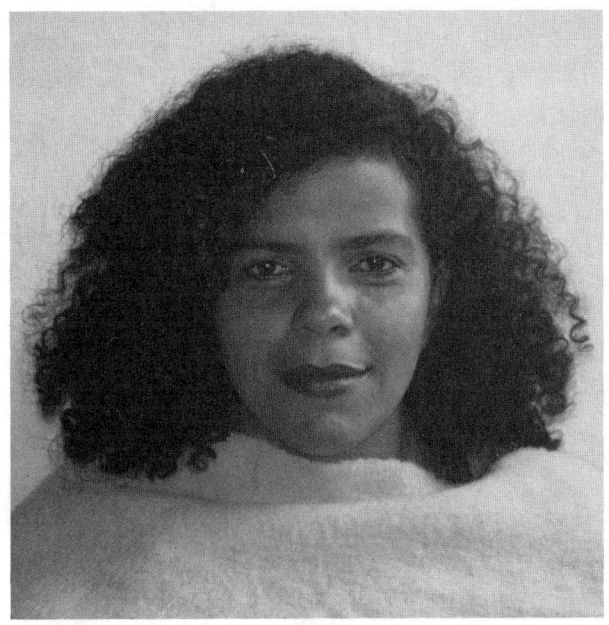

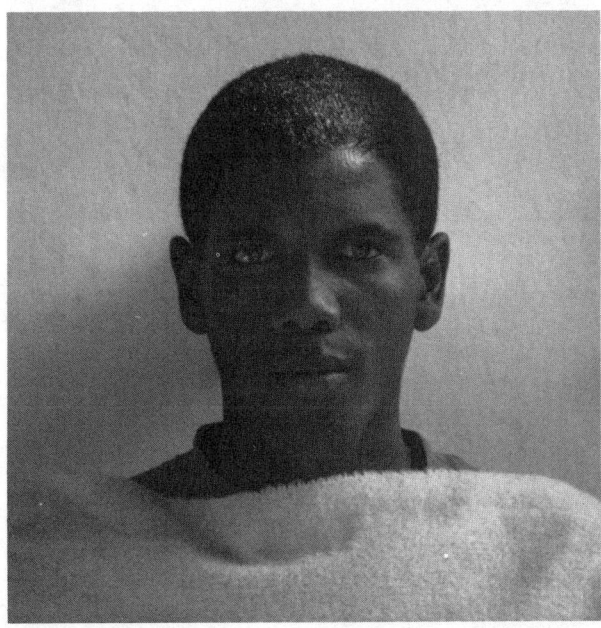

Sample of facial photographs used in this study: Brazilians.

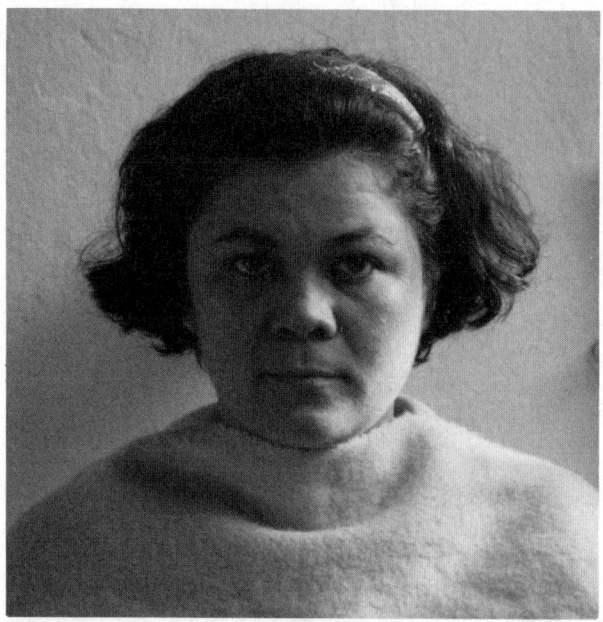

Sample of facial photographs used in this study: Brazilians.

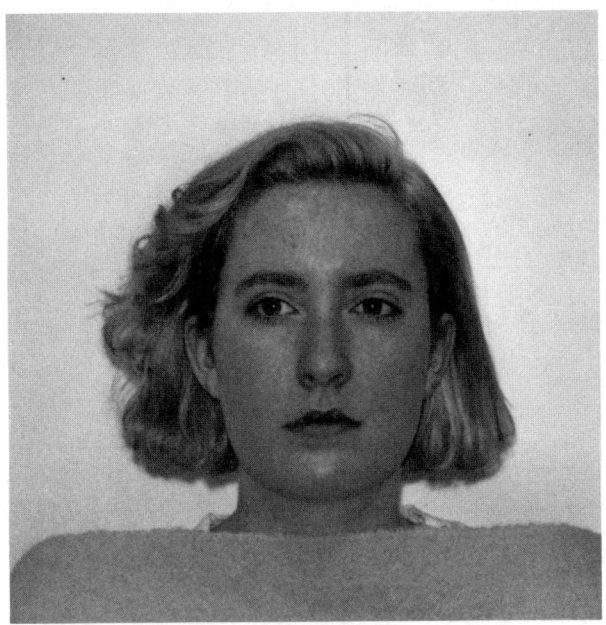
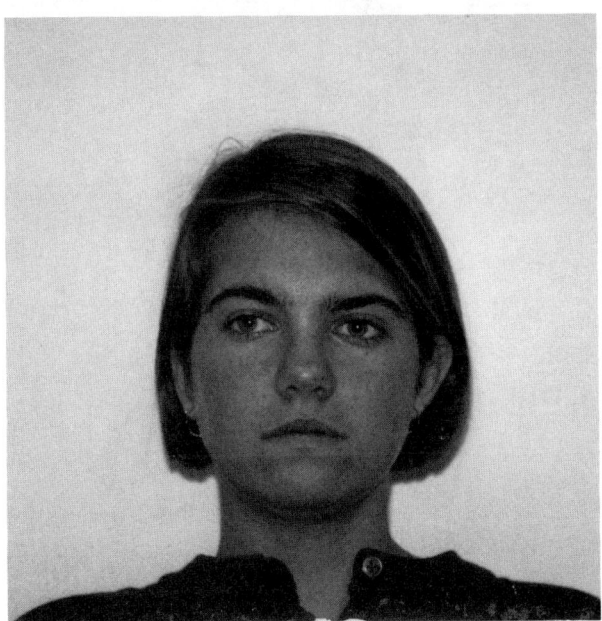

Sample of facial photographs used in this study: US Americans.

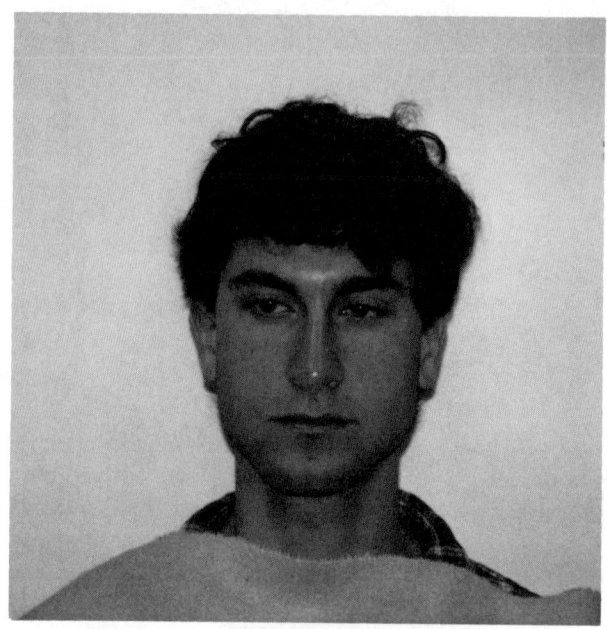

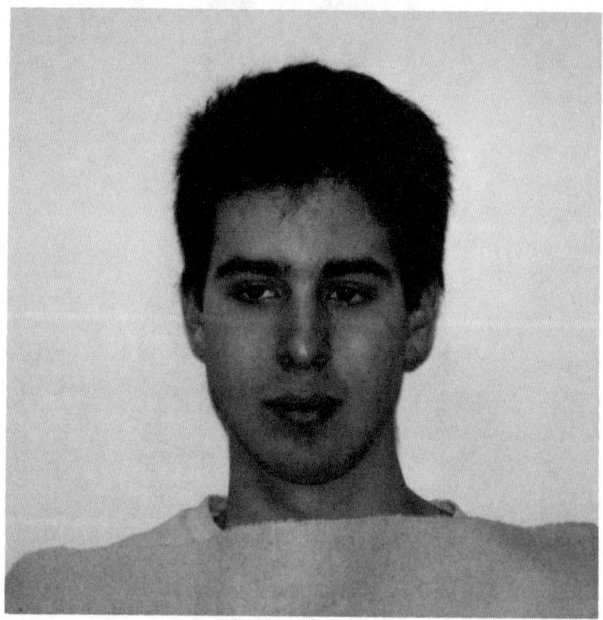

Sample of facial photographs used in this study: US Americans.

Physical Attractiveness and the Theory of Sexual Selection

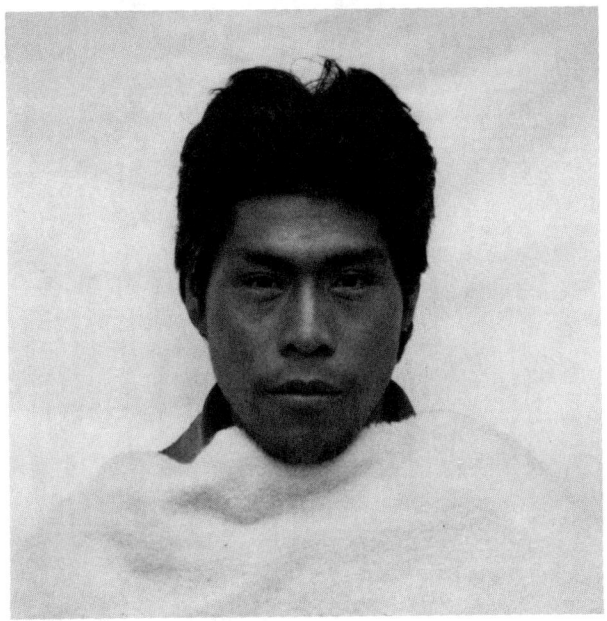

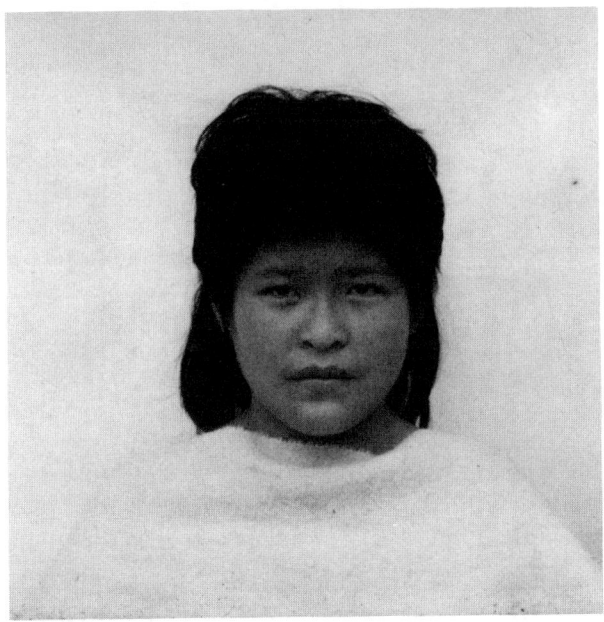

Sample of facial photographs used in this study: Ache.

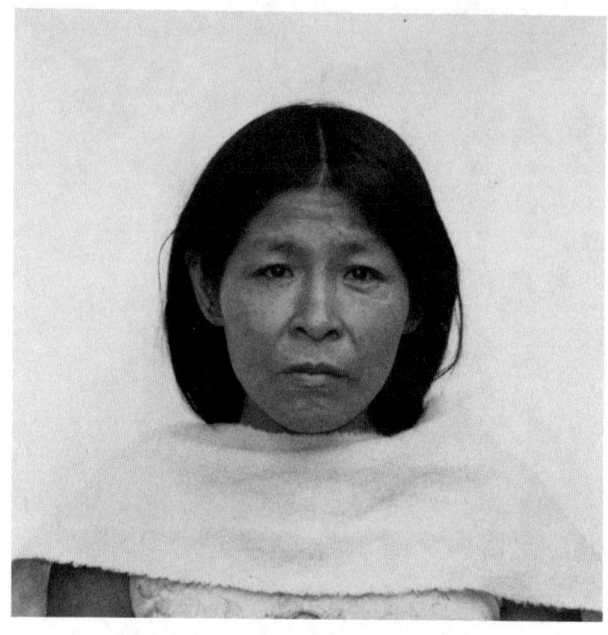

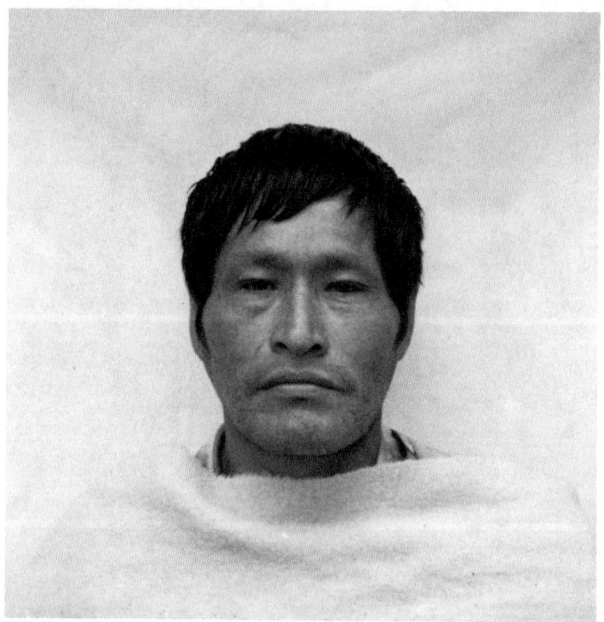

Sample of facial photographs used in this study: Ache.